AGE AND STRUCTURAL LAG

AGE AND STRUCTURAL LAG

Society's Failure to Provide Meaningful Opportunities in Work, Family, and Leisure

Edited by

Matilda White Riley
Robert L. Kahn
Anne Foner

Editorial Associate
Karin A. Mack

A Wiley-Interscience Publication
John Wiley & Sons, Inc.
New York • Chichester • Brisbane • Toronto • Singapore

This publication stems from
Program on Age and Structural Change (PASC)
Sponsored by the National Institute on Aging

This text is printed on acid-free paper.

This publication is designed to provide accurate and
authoritative information in regard to the subject
matter covered. It is sold with the understanding that
the publisher is not engaged in rendering legal, accounting,
or other professional services. If legal advice or other
expert assistance is required, the services of a competent
professional person should be sought.

Library of Congress Cataloging-in-Publication Data:

Age and structural lag / editors Matilda White Riley, Robert L. Kahn,
 Anne Foner : editorial associate Karin A. Mack.
      p. cm.
   "A Wiley-Interscience Publication."
   Includes bibliographical references and index.
   ISBN 0-471-01678-0 (alk. paper)
    1. Social change—United States. 2. Social structure—United
 States. 3. Aging—Social aspects—United States. 4. Age and
 employment—United States. I. Riley, Matilda White. 1911–   .
 II. Kahn, Robert Louis, 1918–   . III. Foner, Anne. IV. Title:
 Structural lag.
 HN59.2.A34 1994
 303.4'0973—dc20   93-46344

Printed in the United States of America

10 9 8 7 6 5 4 3 2 1

Contributors

Richard V. Burkhauser, economist. Professor, Syracuse University, and senior fellow in the All-University Gerontology Center there. He has published widely on the behavioral and income-distribution effects of government policy toward the aged and persons with disabilities. His most recent book is *Pensions in a Changing Economy*.

Anne Foner, sociologist. Professor Emerita, Rutgers University. Widely known for her major collaboration on the multidisciplinary and cross-national *Aging and Society* series, she has published extensively on such topics as retirement, age and politics, the family, age inequality, age and social change, and intergenerational justice. She is currently a leading member of the Program on Age and Structural Change (PASC) Network of the National Institute on Aging (NIA).

Tamara K. Hareven, social historian. Professor of Family Studies and History, University of Delaware and Adjunct Professor of Population Sciences, Harvard University. Founding editor, *Journal of Family History*. She is noted for her cross-cultural work on the history of the family, life transitions, and generational relations in the later years of life. The best known of her several books is: *Family Time and Industrial Time*. A work in process is: *Generation in Historical Time*.

John C. Henretta, sociologist. Professor at the University of Florida and collaborator on AHEAD: a United States national panel survey of assets, health, and family transfers in the over-70 population. He is well known for his age-related research on housing, income, long-term care, family, and retirement. He is currently working on cohort variations in work exit patterns.

Robert L. Kahn, social psychologist. Professor and Research Scientist, Institute for Social Research at the University of Michigan. Widely known for his book *The Social Psychology of Organizations* and the field that it represents, he is in demand as a consultant both in Europe and the United States. He is currently working with the MacArthur Foundation Program on Mental Health and Human Development, and with the National Institute on Aging on the Program on Age and Structural Change (PASC).

Jennie Keith, anthropologist. Centennial Professor of Anthropology and Provost at Swarthmore College. She is coeditor (with David Kertzer) of *Age and*

Anthropological Theory (Ithaca, NY, Cornell, 1984) and Codirector of Project AGE, a comparative study of social and cultural influences on aging based on industrial as well as preliterate societies.

Martin Kohli, sociologist. Professor at the Free University of Berlin, and former member of the Institute for Advanced Study at Princeton. He is well known for his broadly comparative studies on the life course, aging, family, work, and social policy. His most recent and widely quoted book is a collaborative volume, *Time for Retirement.*

Karin A. Mack, sociologist. Technical Information Specialist at the National Institute on Aging, and active in leadership of PASC. She is a member of the Retirement Research Committee of the American Sociological Association and teaches at the University of Maryland, where she is a PhD candidate.

William McNaught, economist. He is continuing work on the Commonwealth Fund's "Americans over 55 at Work Program," of which he served as Director of Research. In addition to his studies of employment policies for older workers, he has made major contributions in such areas as Social Security reform, defense budgeting, secondary mortgage markets, and child support enforcement.

Phyllis Moen, sociologist. Professor of Life Course Studies and Sociology and Director of the Life Course Institute at Cornell University. Formerly Director of the Sociology Program at the National Science Foundation, she has written extensively on women's roles and the well-being of families. Her most recent books are *Working Parents* and *Women's Two Roles.*

Andrejs Plakans, historian. Professor of European History at Iowa State University, and Associate Editor of the *Journal of Family History.* He is best known for his research and writings on European family and kinship structures. He is the author of *Kinship in the Past* and coeditor (with Tamara Hareven) of *Family History at the Crossroads.*

Joseph F. Quinn, economist. Professor of Economics and Department Chair, Boston College. His research focuses on the economics of aging, with emphasis on the importance of part-time work, patterns of labor force withdrawal, and determinants of the individual retirement decision. He is coauthor with Richard V. Burkhauser and Daniel A. Myers of *Passing the Torch: The Influence of Economic Incentives on Work and Retirement.*

John W. Riley, Jr. Consulting sociologist. Following three careers—academic, corporate, and military—he is currently collaborating with Matilda White Riley in national and international research on age and aging. Among his books in that area are *Aging and Society* (Vol. II) and *The Quality of Aging* (coeditor); he is also senior editor of the *International Glossary of Social Gerontology.*

Matilda White Riley, sociologist, is Senior Social Scientist at the National Institute on Aging, NIH. She is perhaps best known for her three-volume set *Aging and Society* as well as for many age-related books and articles. The recipient of awards and honors, and now well into her eighties, she is currently directing Program on Age and Structural Change (PASC), of which the present volume is the first major publication.

Maris Vinovskis, historian. Currently on leave as Research Advisor in the U.S. Department of Education, he is Professor of History and Research Scientist at the University of Michigan. He has written widely on the history of education, including *The Origins of Public High Schools,* and *Education and Social Change in Nineteenth Century Massachusetts* (coauthor). His most recent (coauthored) book is *Religion, Family, and the Life Course.*

Preface

This book is built around a single concept, *structural lag*. Each chapter explores implications of that concept in a different domain, and all reflect the authors' shared conviction of its importance, both for social theory and for practical policy.

By structural lag, we mean the tendency of social structures and norms to lag behind people's rapidly changing lives. So defined, the concept is simple enough, but its ramifications are many and complex. They take the authors—writing from their several disciplinary perspectives—far across time and space. All social structures change, of course, but they do not develop or adapt at the same rate, nor do all individuals follow the same trajectory through the life course.

These structural and individual differences and, above all, the inertial tendency of social structures to persist rather than respond to the changing needs and characteristics of individuals, create a continuing tension between people and the structures in which their lives are embedded.

STRUCTURAL LAG

The Problem

The tendency for structural changes to lag behind changes in people's lives has become a serious problem in our own time. The nature of this lag, and the challenges it presents for both policy and scholarship, can be seen from just one example: the structural arrangements and social norms with respect to work and retirement in the contemporary United States. We have entered a historical period in which men and women live, on average, almost 20 years beyond the usual retirement age. It is also a period in which most women of working age have joined the labor force, whether or not they also have the care of children. As a result, especially for women, the long middle years of adult life are chronically overloaded with the combined activities of two-career families, child rearing, and homemaking.

In contrast to the overload of that life stage, we now have an extended period of older age that is essentially without formal structure, an entry into the time of the "roleless role." The contrast between these life stages is increasingly visible and increasingly conflict prone, especially as the economic entitlements of older people are often seen as economic burdens of the young and the middle-aged.

The legal abolition of a fixed retirement age in the United States has not solved these problems. Full-time jobs are scarce commodities and likely to remain so for a considerable time. As a nation, it is sometimes claimed, we can grow all the food we eat, and then some, with less than 5% of our labor force, and we can manufacture all we sell with less than 15% of available workers. Furthermore, older people want to lead more productive lives, but the competition for jobs is real. Moreover, to the extent that wages are seniority driven (as is conspicuously the case in academic life), it is often argued that each older person who stays on the job blocks more than one opening for younger people.

The point is not that a compulsory retirement age was an unqualified good, but that we have complex problems to solve in bringing our opportunity structures (to use Robert Merton's term) into greater congruence with what technology and medical advances have done for the way we grow up and grow old.

An Integrative Approach

This contemporary example of structural lag from the domain of work and retirement in the United States is just one of several explored in this book. The problem pervades all developed societies and threatens those not yet developed. Many other examples are still under study and could not be included here, such as a general underestimation of the capacities of young children—even the ability of babies to teach babies; the widespread lack of opportunity structures for adolescents; the constraints on education beyond the early ages.

Toward an overall integration of all such examples, whether or not treated directly in the following chapters, we set out an emerging framework for understanding changing age structures. Taken together, the Introduction and Chapters 1, 2, and 12 describe structural lag and the potentials for correcting it.

The chapters in the body of the book direct attention to varied aspects of the lag in particular domains, which range widely across disciplines and focus on the respective interests of the authors. We have read and reread each of these chapters, guiding the planning and the successive revisions to ensure their relevance to the central theme, and to identify their cross-disciplinary interconnections. The aim is to avoid a set of disparate chapters cobbled together only by indirect references to a simple idea; rather, the aim is to develop—however imperfectly—an integrative exegesis of the idea itself. Throughout this lengthy process, we have been assisted by our editorial associate Karin Mack and by John Riley, the senior editor's longtime close collaborator.

Readers

In describing structural lag, its problems and its potentials, the book addresses a wide national and international audience: to experienced scholars and graduate students in the social and behavioral sciences; to policymakers in both public and private sectors; to members of the practicing professions; to gerontologists and others interested in human development and aging; and to sophisticated readers concerned with major issues of everyday life. For readers wanting to pursue specific points in greater depth, most chapters include extensive references.

A Cumulative Body of Knowledge

The book is part of a continuing investigation of structural change conducted by Matilda White Riley, in association with Anne Foner, John Riley, Karin Mack, and a network of participating scholars. That research effort, entitled the Program on Age and Structural Change (PASC), now in its first phase, is supported by the National Institute on Aging (NIA), as was much of the research cited in these chapters. Earlier versions of some chapters were presented (as a component of PASC) at the 1992 meetings of the American Association for the Advancement of Science. Robert Kahn's research on age-related issues has been supported by the National Institute on Aging and by the John D. and Catherine T. MacArthur Foundation, through its Research Network on Successful Aging.

ACKNOWLEDGMENTS

This book, with its emphasis on structural change, rests on a long history of multidisciplinary scholarship and administrative support. Here we can only mention its original stimulus from Russell Sage Foundation (through Gilbert Brim), the Ford Foundation (through Ollie Randall), and the Social Science Research Council. Most immediately, the book is indebted to T. Franklin Williams, whose vision as Director of the National Institute of Aging brought PASC into reality; and to his successors at NIA, Gene Cohen and Richard Hodes, who have continued to encourage and sustain the program.

The book also owes much to the foresight of numerous advisors to the Behavioral and Social Research Program at the National Institute on Aging, many of whom made recent recommendations for the future agenda based on the experience of that Program during the decade of the 1980s. These advisors include Paul Baltes, Vern Bengtson, Robert Butler, David Featherman, George Maddox, David Mechanic, George Myers, Bernice Neugarten, Warner Schaie, Ethel Shanas, James Smith, Mervyn Susser, and Sherry Willis.

In addition, encouragement and suggestion in the early stages of planning the book were supplied by Ronald Abeles, Lars Anderson, Glen Elder, Carroll Estes, Linda George, Anne-Marie Guillemard, Jerald Hage, Dennis Hogan, Katrina Johnson, David Kertzer, Margaret Marini, John Meyer, John Myles, Marcia Ory, Richard Scott, Neil Smelser, Michael Wagner, David Willis, and many others. Related background papers were prepared by Nitza Berkovitch, Karen Bradley, Dale Dannefer, and Karyn Loscocco. Preparation of the manuscript was aided in many ways by members of the staff of NIA's Behavioral and Social Research Program, in particular by Tung Nguyen and

Cammy Tieu. The exacting task of seeing the book through the publication process was undertaken by Jeannette Wilson, Program Coordinator of PASC.

To all these persons and agencies, and to the literally hundreds of other scholars in the United States and abroad who have contributed to the background of PASC in general and this book in particular, we express sincere appreciation.

MATILDA WHITE RILEY
ROBERT L. KAHN
ANNE FONER

Contents

Introduction: The Mismatch between People and Structures

Matilda White Riley, Robert L. Kahn,
and Anne Foner
in association with Karin A. Mack

The chapters in this book examine the relatively unexplored phenomenon of *structural lag*, as it affects not only older men and women but also people of all ages. In modern industrial societies, the numbers of capable and long-lived people are mounting dramatically, but the *opportunity structures* that shape their lives at all ages have remained largely static or become more constrained. In many respects, the concept of opportunity structures, introduced into scientific discourse over half a century ago by Robert Merton (cf. Merton, 1957), is essential to the thesis of this book. We argue that age criteria are so built into social structures as to restrict opportunities. Put another way, there is a mismatch (to use George Maddox's term) between people and the social structures, institutions, and norms that surround them.

In the 19th century, the situation was very different. When relatively few people survived into old age, responsibilities for work and family were virtually lifelong. Years of retirement, for those who could retire at all, were few. Today, by contrast, survival into old age

1

is commonplace and many years of vigorous postretirement life are the realistic expectation. We are the beneficiaries of great gains in economic productivity and public health as well as advances in science and education.

Nevertheless, the major responsibilities for work and family are still crowded into what are now the middle years of long life, while education is primarily reserved for the young, and leisure and free time are disproportionately allocated to the later years. Despite the 20th-century metamorphosis in human lives from infancy to old age, the social structures and norms that define opportunities and expectations throughout the life course carry the vestigial marks of the 19th century. Our failure to match in social structures the rapid gains in longevity, health, and style of life has had the unintended consequence of creating a poor fit between social institutions and people's capabilities and responsibilities at every age (cf. Kahn, 1981; Riley, 1988).

The challenge for the 21st century, therefore, is to discover, invent, and bring about social changes that will mitigate the 20th century's structural lag. What kinds of future structures and institutions can lessen the burdens of middle age, prepare children for the complexities of the real world, and create opportunities for productivity, independence, and self-esteem in the added years of later life?

Answers to such large questions and their derivatives are crucial for research in the behavioral sciences and other disciplines, for public policy and professional practice, and for public enlightenment. Contributors to this volume, in exploring a variety of possible answers to such questions, go to the very heart of social change itself. From diverse disciplinary perspectives, their chapters range across time and space to examine how major age-related roles in contemporary society have come about, and how they might possibly be altered to enhance the quality of human lives.

BACKGROUND INFORMATION

Issues of Structural Change

Details of this need for understanding structural lag were foreshadowed in an essay titled "Aging and Social Change," which was published over a decade ago (Riley, 1982). That paper listed the following issues of structural change as being under debate at that time (p. 23):

- Whether to provide tax credits for home care of older people.
- How and in what direction to change laws governing custody of children.
- Whether and under what conditions to encourage uninterested students to leave high school early.
- Whether to spread work more evenly over the life course, by providing longer vacations, flexible work hours, incentives for midlife switching to new careers.
- Whether to reduce the heavy transfer payments by the middle-aged and to require that both the old and the young become more nearly self-supporting.
- How to determine the appropriate age for retirement, given the increases in life expectancy.
- How to restructure the health establishment to meet the special needs of geriatric patients.
- How to design communities, housing, shopping centers, roadways to meet the human needs that are changing over the life course.

In the intervening years, however, few such age-related structural issues have been resolved. Indeed, they have become exacerbated by serious revolutions abroad and disturbances at home. The term "social change" has become painfully commonplace, but its scientific meaning and its implications for human lives—past and future—remain obscure. In research, great emphasis has been placed on aging and human development, but the related issues of the environing social structures have been neglected, or simply accepted as "given."

Today, as the contributors to the present volume seek deeper understanding of such structural issues, they draw on a guiding principle[1] set out in that 1982 essay: *There is a dynamic interplay between people*

---

[1] This principle, and its source in several decades of previous work, is described in Chapter 1 of this book.

growing older and society undergoing change (p. 11). This interplay involves two distinct, but interdependent, "dynamisms" (or processes):

1. People in successive cohorts[2] (or generations) grow up and grow old in different ways because the surrounding social structures are changing. That is, the process of aging from birth to death is not entirely fixed or determined by biology, but is influenced by the changing social structures and roles in which people lead their lives.

2. Alterations in the ways in which people grow up and grow old, in turn, press on the surrounding social structures to change them. That is, the roles available to people at particular ages are not fixed or immutable but are reshaped by the collective actions and attitudes of the people who are continually aging, moving through the roles, and being replaced by their successors from more recent cohorts.

To repeat: People's lives are influenced by changing social structures; and reciprocally, the changes in people's lives exert pressures on social structures for still further change.

The book in which that earlier essay appeared focused primarily on the first of these dynamisms: Its title was *Aging from Birth to Death: Sociotemporal Perspectives* (Riley, Abeles, & Teitelbaum, 1982). Subsequent research, espousing this "life-course perspective" on the process of aging in successive cohorts, has yielded massive evidence of the sustained strengths, vigor, and capacities of today's long-lived people.[3] Meantime, however, the related dynamism—changing age structures—remains largely unexplored. All too little attention has been paid to the role opportunities that have not kept pace with the advances in people's lives. The structural issues identified in that 1982 publication are still issues today.

To address these issues, this book is the first major publication of the Program on Age and Structural Change (PASC), recently initiated

---

[2] The life-course experiences of each cohort of people (those born at approximately the same period of time) reflect a particular period of history. (The term *birth cohort* is preferred to *age cohort*, since members of any particular cohort "age" from birth to death.)

[3] Indeed, so much current attention is devoted to analyzing the patterns of people's lives—without explicit concern with the surrounding structures—as to approximate a "life course reductionism."

at the National Institute of Aging (NIA).[4] In its immediate focus on structural lag, PASC takes a radical approach to the long tradition of analysis of social change in general. PASC is unique in emphasizing the pressures for structural change exerted by the tensions, conflicts, inequalities, and special transition experiences involved in the unending process of new people replacing their predecessors throughout the institutions of society (Foner, 1982; Foner & Kertzer, 1979; Kertzer & Schaie, 1989). It is unique in emphasizing the interplay between social structures and the universal processes of aging and cohort flow (cf. Riley, 1973). And it is unique in emphasizing the dynamic character of the "social convoy" of significant others who surround each individual throughout a long lifetime, both giving and receiving social support (Kahn, 1979). The broad challenge to PASC is to enlarge and specify this radical approach: to develop conceptual, methodological, and substantive understanding of changes in social institutions and their linkage to people's lives, and—in so doing—to explore the pros and cons of possible avenues for improving the balance between people's capacities and the opportunities available to them.

Purpose of This Work

Authors of the following chapters were given this challenge. Thus they focus varied attention on the potentials—and the obstacles—for reducing structural lag. Their chapters are replete with innovative ideas and provocative details, aimed to stimulate discussion and thought, and to suggest practical ways of enhancing the roles available to people throughout their long lives.

The contributors use multidisciplinary approaches to examine selected aspects of age-related structural changes in work, retirement, family, education, and other social roles. As possible models for the 21st century, these authors discuss alternative organizational arrangements, some of which have existed at past times, some in other countries, and some only in projected scenarios. Already in the United States, for example, roles in work, family, and school are seen to intersect, as corporations provide education for employees, or day care for employees' children and frail parents. Affecting structural

---

[4] As described in Chapter 1, PASC, which is directed by Matilda White Riley at NIA, involves an international communications network of scholars.

arrangements in many domains of life, incipient cultural changes are discernible: Discriminatory "ageist" attitudes are increasingly challenged as invalid; and in some quarters, at least, the popular emphasis on material values and associated success as the *summum bonum* is beginning to be questioned.

The chapters in this book also suggest *how* structural changes might come about. They discuss specific mechanisms that would be required to reduce middle-age burdens of combined work and family, to unlock wider options for shaping the life course at every age, to prevent ageist discrimination against older people and children, and to enhance well-being through sustained active participation in the later years.

SYNOPSIS

Contributors—from sociology, psychology, economics, history, and anthropology—were asked to treat selected aspects of structural lag from the framework of their own disciplines. Their chapters are arranged in three Parts, according to their main emphases.

Part I describes the nature and implications of structural lag as a pervasive problem of modern societies. When applied in particular to older people, as in much of this book, the lag is a mismatch between the strengths and potential capacities of the rising numbers of long-lived *people* and the lack of productive and meaningful *role opportunities*, or places in the social structure, that can foster, protect, and reward these strengths and capacities. Part II illustrates the historical changes and cross-cultural variabilities in the fit between people and roles, detailing changes in work, retirement, education, leisure, the family, and the community. Part III, using older workers as an example, scrutinizes possible interventions to reduce the structural lag, including innovations in corporate and public policies.

The Endnote, which suggests the broad research agenda needed to guide such policies and assess their feasibility, dramatizes the broad reach of the idea of structural lag. Together with this Introduction and the chapters in Part I, this last chapter summarizes the implications of the concept from the past to the future—well into the 21st century.

There are overemphases and omissions—little on childhood and much on old age, for example. But the lacunae underscore the challenge of the book—to stimulate continuing conceptualization and specification of the unexplored issues of structural change in its relationship with the human life course.

Part I. The Dilemma of Structural Lag

Chapter 1, by the Rileys, begins with an abstract conceptual framework for understanding the current structural lag (or mismatch) between rapidly changing human lives and the surrounding social structures that have been resistant to changes that could accommodate these lives. The authors explore the mismatch throughout the life course, considering not only older people but those of all ages. Then, as one possible model for loosening age barriers and reducing structural lag across the entire society, the Rileys postulate an ideal type of "age-integrated" structure[5] and contrast it with "age-differentiated" structures that tend to perpetuate this lag. Using examples from work, leisure, and the family, they illustrate how elements of age integration are already beginning to emerge and, if developed, could improve role opportunities for people of every age and thus give new meaning to both social structures and human lives. This chapter helps to locate the concept of structural lag within the large body of past and future research on age. For the past, it notes some of the many predecessors and successors to the "aging and society" approach (described in that chapter), and the history of behavioral and social research supported over the past decade by the National Institute on Aging (Riley & Abeles, 1990). For the future, the Rileys' chapter introduces structural lag as a prelude to the Program on Age and Structural Change (PASC).

Chapter 2, by Robert Kahn, elaborates the manifestation of structural lag in sociopsychological terms.[6] Here the key concept is "goodness of fit"—or lack of it—between needs, aspirations, and abilities of individuals on the one hand and, on the other, expectations and opportunities that confront them in the social structure. Kahn presents current data on older people to document their desire to be productive in both paid and volunteer activities, and to be recognized

---

[5] In some respects, reminiscent of Bernice Neugarten's (1982) "age-irrelevant" society.

[6] Here, as in many aspects of PASC, Bernice Neugarten's wealth of sociopsychological ideas are pertinent. Thus, in her analysis of age norms, she speaks of the "lack of congruence" between personal attitudes and attitudes attributed to the "generalized other" (Neugarten, Moore, & Lowe, 1965, p. 27).

for the productive contributions they make. The data on health and effective functioning make clear the ability of older people to be productive. It is the expectations and opportunities in the social situation that must be changed. The notion of a 4-hour work module, together with more explicit recognition of unpaid productive activities, are proposed as central to such changes, and their implications for social structure and underlying values are discussed. Field experiments (like clinical trials in medicine) are recommended for the research agenda of the future, to ensure that social programs aimed to correct the structural lag be given serious trial and evaluation before their initiation on a national scale.

Part II. Directions of Change

Moving toward specification of ideas from Part I, John Henretta, in Chapter 3, assesses the long-term trend in the United States toward earlier retirement of workers from the labor force. His chapter on "Social Structures and Age-Based Careers" describes the recent shift from the post-World War II "internal" labor market pattern of "lifetime work," toward a "contingent" labor market that produces more diverse pathways of work over the life course. Henretta discusses early pension incentives, job losses, and disability laws as implicated in the trend toward early retirement. These developments and such phenomena as "bridge jobs" and postretirement work contribute to the increasing variability in retirement patterns. If these trends persist, age may become less relevant in defining work status, and there may be enlarged work opportunities for older people in the future.

Enlarging the examination of changes in retirement patterns to include both the United States and Europe (with a separate discussion of the situation in the former East Germany), German sociologist Martin Kohli, in Chapter 4, calls attention to a striking paradox: On the one hand, workers continue to retire at younger and younger ages; but on the other hand, life expectancy is increasing, stereotypes of the "unproductive older worker" are proving fallacious, and the financial viability of public pensions is being questioned. Seeking to understand this paradox, Kohli scrutinizes several hypothesized causes of the trend toward early retirement, and suggests that such "push" factors as persistent unemployment are particularly powerful. He explores possibilities for reducing structural lag through interventions in the labor market and changes in public policy that could distribute work more evenly across the age strata.

Historian Andrejs Plakans attacks the little-studied topic of leisure in Chapter 5. He shows that lifelong work patterns in premodern Western societies left little place for unstructured time, and he describes the widespread emergence and subsidization of retirement as a new life stage that provides old people with leisure time. Despite generally positive reactions to retirement, however, many old people nowadays are ambivalent and are filling this large late-life block of unstructured time with structured, worklike activities. Plakans explores this lag between time free from work and the apparently persistent, but unmet, need for structuring time.

In Chapter 6, social historian Tamara Hareven turns attention to the family. She analyzes the relationship between changes in the family and changes in society, and she makes the provocative suggestion that certain models of family behavior from the past might be adapted to contemporary needs to provide a better fit between the family and other societal institutions.

Addressing the relationship between the family and work in Chapter 7, sociologist Phyllis Moen focuses on the problems encountered by women in the United States who are mothers of infants or preschoolers and are at the same time entering, remaining in, and reentering the labor force at unprecedented rates. She traces these problems to historical changes in population aging, gender roles, and occupational opportunities for women. To deal with the resulting problems, new flexibilities are needed in societal institutions and norms regarding work and child care that can be beneficial for men as well as women raising children and for all stages of the life course.

Chapter 8, by Maris Vinovskis, which reminds us of the important structural needs of children, deals with three historical issues of relevance for understanding structural lag and structural change today: the relationship of early industrialization to the development of mass schooling; the economic productivity of education; and the relationship of education to social mobility and people's life chances. In discussing these themes, Vinovskis draws on his wide historical and political understanding of education, to explore factors leading to the expansion and reform of 19th-century educational institutions in the United States. He shows how these educational changes have been influenced by people's changing needs; and how, in turn, educational reforms have affected the course of people's lives. Today, however, educational institutions, still bearing the imprint of earlier reforms, lag behind the needs for education and training, not only for the young, but over the whole life course.

In Chapter 9, the concluding chapter of Part II, anthropologist Jennie Keith extends the gerontological investigation of structural lag into seven widely varied research sites, ranging from relatively undeveloped to modern situations. She distinguishes two types: "simple" societies, in which the constraints of physical aging are extreme while the constraints of social aging are minimal, and modern societies, where cultural age barriers overshadow the physical limitations. She uses this typology to highlight the American paradox of perpetuating social constraints of age even though physical limitations are relieved and suggests ways to reduce those social age barriers that impede the innovation and flexibility of older persons.

Part III. Current Interventions: Older Workers

Such varied probes into the nature of structural lag (Part I) and its origins (Part II) raise the critical question of what future changes might help to reduce it. Can future trends be guided through policy or practice? Can useful innovations be constructed and enacted? What are the implications—both negative and positive—of particular proposals for change? What future research is needed to assess and guide possible changes, such as field experiments to test proposed policy interventions in advance (as recommended by Kahn)? The three chapters in Part III merely hint at the possible answers. Their focus is mainly on older people in the selected domains of work and retirement. At the same time, however, they suggest more broadly how changes for people of any one age and in any particular domain can affect all ages and all related institutions throughout the society.

William McNaught, in Chapter 10, reports on a unique collection of his own empirical studies. He begins with the thesis that much could be done to increase productive opportunities for older people during the years currently assigned to retirement. In three case studies of innovative hiring and personnel practices, he demonstrates the extent to which "seniors" are already engaged in productive activities and businesses are already adapting to a changing labor force. Broadening the definition of "work" to include voluntary activities and family care, he reviews recent research findings about work preferences of older persons who no longer have jobs and the job performance of older persons who are working. Then, in a highly personal statement, he outlines his own views of the major institutional adjustments necessary to accommodate the changing attitudes, needs, and talents of older workers; and he emphasizes the important responsibility of older people themselves in pressing for such adjustments.

Moving to the level of public policy, Richard Burkhauser and Joseph Quinn, in Chapter 11, trace the economic incentives embedded in Social Security and employer pension plans, which have systematically discouraged older people's work over the past three decades in the United States. Despite such penalties, a growing percentage of people are now working after retirement and the labor force participation rates of older workers are no longer falling. This chapter first describes the current retirement system and evaluates its impact on work and retirement, and then proposes a provocative series of public policy changes that would increase work effort at older ages.

In her final overview, Anne Foner (Chapter 12) discusses the implications of structural lag reaching from the past into the future. She links the concept of structural lag to broad social theories, showing both its continuities with other theoretical perspectives and its distinctive features. She selects themes from the previous chapters that illustrate and shed light on the relationship between changing lives and structural change in many domains of social life. In particular, she points to the mechanisms, complexities, and problems involved in effecting age-related structural changes that might reduce the lag.

Foner's discussion helps to clarify the wide focus of the book, and the implications of change for scientific research, public policy, professional practice, and people's everyday lives. The adaptations that we make—or fail to make—in social structures today will affect the future lives of everyone already born, and those yet to be born, for as long as they survive into the 21st century.

REFERENCES

Foner, A. (1982). Perspectives on changing age systems. In M. W. Riley, R. P. Abeles, & M. S. Teitelbaum (Eds.), *Aging from birth to death: Vol II. Sociotemporal perspectives* (pp. 217–228). AAAS Symposium 79. Boulder, CO: Westview Press.

Foner, A., & Kertzer, D. I. (1979). Intrinsic and extrinsic sources of change in life-course transitions. In M. W. Riley (Ed.), *Aging from birth to death: Vol I. Interdisciplinary perspectives* (pp. 121–136). AAAS Symposium 30. Boulder, CO: Westview Press.

Kahn, R. L. (1979). Aging and social support. In M. W. Riley (Ed.), *Aging from birth to death: Vol I. Interdisciplinary perspectives* (pp. 77–92). AAAS Symposium 30. Boulder, CO: Westview Press.

Kahn, R. L. (1981). *Work and health.* New York: Wiley.

Kertzer, D. I., & Schaie, K. W. (Eds.). (1989). *Age structuring in comparative perspective.* Hillsdale, NJ: Erlbaum.

Merton, R. K. (1957). *Social theory and social structure.* New York: Free Press.

Neugarten, B. L. (Ed.). (1982). *Age or need? Public policies for older people.* Beverly Hills, CA: Sage Publications.

Neugarten, B. L., Moore, J. W., & Lowe, J. C. (1965). *American Journal of Sociology, 70.*

Riley, M. W. (1973). Aging and cohort succession: Interpretations and misinterpretations. *The Public Opinion Quarterly, 37,* 35–49.

Riley, M. W. (1982). Aging and social change. In M. W. Riley, R. P. Abeles, & M. S. Teitelbaum (Eds.), *Aging from birth to death: Vol. II. Sociotemporal perspectives* (pp. 11–26). AAAS Symposium 79. Boulder, CO: Westview Press.

Riley, M. W. (1988). The aging society: Problems and prospects. *Proceedings of American Philosophical Society, 132,* 148–153. Philadelphia, PA: American Philosophical Society.

Riley, M. W., & Abeles, R. P. (1990). *The behavioral and social research program at the National Institute on Aging: History of a decade* (Working Document). Bethesda, MD: Behavioral and Social Research, National Institute on Aging, National Institutes of Health.

Riley, M. W., Abeles, R. P., & Teitelbaum, M. S. (Eds.). (1982). *Aging from birth to death: Vol. II. Sociotemporal perspectives.* AAAS Symposium 79. Boulder, CO: Westview Press.

PART I

THE DILEMMA
OF
STRUCTURAL LAG

CHAPTER 1

Structural Lag:
Past and Future

Matilda White Riley and John W. Riley, Jr.

Sixty years ago, when we were first married, we began writing a book about leisure. We were impressed with the challenge of finding a new societal ethos by redefining leisure—not as rest or recreation—but in the Aristotelian sense of the serious pursuit of universal values. As the counterpart of the philosophers of ancient Athens, we saw middle-aged women as a new "leisure class" who could take up this challenge. (In 1930, only 20% of American women[1] were in the paid labor force and, beyond imposing the tasks of early child rearing, society made few demands on those not working.) After two years of effort, however, we put that book away, deciding that we "needed far more experience" to finish it.

Now, in the ninth decade of our lives, we still have had little firsthand experience with leisure or the search for new societal values (unlike most people in the industrialized world, we are not retired). During the intervening 60 years, middle-aged women have filled their time, not with leisure, but with paid work. (In the United States today, some 68% of women aged 35 and over are now in the labor

---

[1] U.S. Census report of women 35 and over who were "gainfully employed."

force.[2]) With the unprecedented increases in longevity, which mean that people spend one-third of their adult lives in retirement, it is now the older women and men who might form a new "leisure class." Yet older people's retirement, far from being devoted to any search for a new ethos, consists largely of "unstructured time" (see Chapter 5, in this book), devoid of clear institutionalized expectations and rewards, and often devoted to a leisure focused more on passive amusement and the consumption of material goods than on any type of active philosophical endeavor. While young and middle-aged adults, especially women, are deprived of free time by the doubly demanding roles of work and family, many older people tend to be surfeited with it. Yet there are few normative expectations to give meaning to this time or to their lives, and few employment or other opportunities to participate with younger people in the mainstream activities of society. Nor are the earlier years of the life course exempt from such problems: Except for the too often unrewarding tasks of schoolwork, children and young adults (especially minority youths) are offered few clear role opportunities for being, or feeling, useful.

THE PROBLEM OF STRUCTURAL LAG

Thus today, instead of returning to our aborted book on leisure, we confront a larger and more immediate dilemma: the problem of "structural lag," as changes in age structures lag behind changes in lives (Riley, 1988). In society at large, lives have been drastically altered over this century—as a consequence of increased longevity, advances in science and education, the gender revolution, improvements in public health, and other historical trends and events—but numerous inflexible social structures, roles, and norms have lagged behind. There is a mismatch or imbalance between the transformation of the aging process from birth to death and the role opportunities, or places in the social structure, that could foster and reward people at the various stages of their lives. While the 20th century has experienced a revolution in human development and aging, there has been no comparable revolution in the role structures of society to keep pace with the changes in the ways people grow up and grow old. The lag involves not

---

[2] 1992 *Current Population Survey.*

only institutional and organizational arrangements but also the many aspects of culture that, in addition to being internalized by people, are built into role expectations and societal mores and laws.[3] For the future, then, structural changes will be needed if people are to find opportunities to spread leisure and work, as well as education, more evenly over the life course, and to make room for family affairs.

To understand these changes and to explore the possibilities for reducing structural lag, we have been working during the past three decades with a network of colleagues, beginning with the "aging and society" approach,[4] and culminating in the newly developing Program on Age and Structural Change (PASC), of which this volume is a major component. Our aging and society approach rested on a massive inventory of social science findings on the middle and later years (Riley, Foner, Moore, Hess, & Roth, 1968), and drew on an accumulating body of social theory that included—to cite only three of the many early examples—essays by Parsons (1942) and Linton (1942) on age and sex as fundamental to the social system, and an overview by Tibbitts (1960; see, e.g., p. 13) of studies of old age. Our own first theoretical volume (Riley, Johnson, & Foner, 1972)[5] elaborated the interdependence between changes in people's lives and changes in age structuring—the interdependence from which the concept of structural lag derives.

The Program on Age and Structural Change thus provides a relevant focus for this chapter because matching the structural lag in society is a recent lag in research on age-related social change. There have been great advances in research on how patterns of development and aging change—approaching a "life-course reductionism"; and some attention has been paid to how these life-course patterns can *be* changed

---

[3] It is noteworthy that we use "structural lag" as a shorthand term to include cultural elements. Our concept is in some ways reminiscent of William Fielding Ogburn's (1922) classic concept of "cultural lag," in which the various elements of culture are interdependent so that a change in one element produces changes in others. In contrast, however, our emphasis is on interdependence between *people* and *roles* or social structures—*including* their cultural elements.

We also use widely the term "opportunity structure" introduced into the sociological literature by Robert Merton (1957). Merton is currently preparing a monograph showing the "emergence, diffusion, and differentiation" of the concept, which he used as early as 1938 in connection with *anomie* (personal communication).

[4] In the interim, much of the wealth of research—a good deal of it supported by the National Institute on Aging—was focused more on lives than on structures (see Riley & Abeles, 1990).

[5] Though originally called an "age stratification" approach, the implications of this designation proved to be inappropriate, as both too static and too easily confused with class stratification.

through appropriate structural interventions. Yet there is little theory or method to guide research on structural changes that can enhance the quality of aging from birth to death (as one exception, see Kertzer & Schaie, 1989).

As evidenced by the chapters in this book, structural lag and the need for change are currently most conspicuous for older people because of their protracted longevity, their increasing numbers in the population, and—save for the disadvantaged minority—their remarkably good health and effective functioning (Manton, Stallard, & Singer, 1992).[6] But analysis of older people has heightened awareness of the population as a whole. Roles performed by older people are integral parts of the structure of the total society, and enhancing role opportunities for people of one age has repercussions for people of every age. For example, providing free time for middle-aged women can open work roles for interested older people, and increasing the economic independence of the elderly can reduce the responsibilities of their middle-aged offspring. There are myriad examples of the systemic nature of changes in age structuring. As a consequence, in this chapter we deal with structural lag in general, as it impinges on people of every age.

In the following sections, we present a brief overview of our own explorations of age-related structural changes in social roles and normative expectations. We postulate that such changes could help to mitigate the problems of structural lag and could perhaps ultimately lead to new meanings for both leisure and work. We begin with an analysis—abstract, but designed to be thought provoking—of the sources of structural lag. Here we draw on general principles from the aging and society approach that define two "dynamisms" (or processes) and the interplay between them: the dynamism of *structural change* and the dynamism of *changing lives* (Riley, 1979). Then, focusing more concretely on work and family as examples, we consider some possible directions of future structural change. In exploring one set of changes that might reduce structural lag, we postulate an ideal type of "age-integrated" structure that could replace the currently familiar "age-segregated" type. We then consider some implications of such age-integrated structures for people's lives, for additional forms

---

[6] As early as 1960, Talcott Parsons spoke of our "lag" in "defining positive opportunities for persons of advanced age."

of structural integration, and for the basic values involved. Finally, we identify a few straws in the wind suggesting that age-integrated structures are not entirely visionary. We conclude by asking whether such tendencies toward age integration portend a 21st-century revolution in social structures, in which age constraints may become more flexible and wider opportunities may be open for people of every age.

SOURCES OF STRUCTURAL LAG

The problem of structural lag occurs because changes in human lives have been occurring with dramatic rapidity over the past century, whereas social structures, norms, and institutions have failed to adapt to this metamorphosis in lives. As we illustrate, the dynamism of changing human lives has been outrunning the dynamism of structural change. In analyzing the problem and the potential for reducing the lag, we make use of the conceptual framework schematized in Figure 1–1 (well-known to many students of age), which identifies these two dynamisms and the dialectical interplay between them. Here we build on three general principles and a corollary, taken from the aging

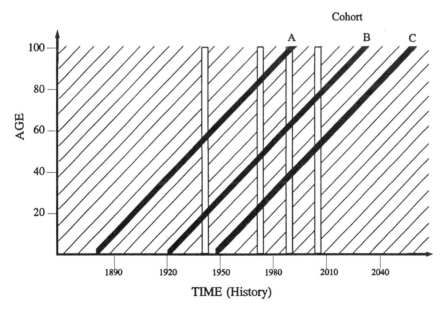

Figure 1–1 Changing Lives and Structural Change

and society approach (Riley, Foner, & Waring, 1988; Riley, Huber, & Hess, 1988), and described in further detail later in this chapter:

1. Each dynamism is a distinct and separate process that responds in its own way to broad social, economic, scientific, and other historical trends and events.
2. Though distinct, the two dynamisms are interdependent; that is, each influences the other.
3. The two dynamisms differ in timing: that is, they tend to be asynchronous.
4. Today, as a corollary, their interdependence and lack of synchrony produce a structural lag that creates pressures for new structural changes.

Two Dynamisms

These dynamisms are schematized very roughly in Figure 1–1, which is a social space bounded on its vertical axis by years of age; and on its horizontal axis by dates that index the course of history, past and future. Within this space, two sets of bars, vertical and diagonal, are continually crisscrossing each other. These bars refer respectively to our dual focus on changes in age-related social structures and in people's lives. (Here we ask the reader to think along with us.)

In respect to the *dynamism of structural change*, we start with a single moment of time, such as the year 1970, where the vertical bar indicates how social institutions and role structures are organized roughly by age, from roles open to the youngest at the bottom (as in the family or in kindergarten) to roles open to the oldest at the top (as in the "roleless role" of retirement). Age, or some surrogate for age, is built directly or indirectly into social and cultural institutions as a criterion for entering and performing in certain roles, and for relinquishing others. Sometimes these age criteria are explicit; at other times they operate subtly and indirectly. Of course, the age structuring observed at any given time is far from static. Over time, as society moves through historical events and changes, we can imagine this vertical bar moving—across the space from one date to the next. Over time, the age structures of role opportunities and norms may (or may not) be shifting, as they are subjected to the internal pressures from role occupants of every age and to external social and cultural changes.[7] For example, modified expectations for performance by older workers (or women) can serve to relax age (or gender) restrictions in hiring (as occurred during World War II). Or eliminating the requirements for "passing" from one school grade to the next can blur the age criteria and prolong the years of staying in school (cf. Angus, Mirel, & Vinovskis, 1988).

With respect to the *dynamism of changing lives,* the diagonal bars represent cohorts of people born in the same time period who are aging from birth to death—that is, moving across time and upward with age, through the successive roles in family life, school grades, work careers, retirement, and ultimate death. As society changes, the aging process also changes. In Cohort A, for example, a man born in 1890 could scarcely have looked ahead to retirement at all, but a man born in 1950 (Cohort C) can expect to spend two or three decades in retirement. Similarly, a woman born in Cohort A could scarcely expect to live long enough to see her grandchildren grow up—unlike a woman in Cohort C, who can look ahead to her great-grandchildren. Thus, as history unfolds, the shape of people's lives is continually being altered from one cohort to the next.

Interdependence

Although the two dynamisms are separate and distinct processes— each with its own response to external trends and events, its special antecedents and consequences, and its unique timing—the two are nevertheless interdependent. Within the larger age system schematized in Figure 1–1, the crisscrossing of the two sets of bars calls attention to the continuing interplay between the two dynamisms. (This interplay can only be imagined with the aid of an oversimplified diagram.) At any particular time, people of different ages in all the coexisting cohorts (the full set of diagonal bars) are moving through the age-related structures (one of the vertical bars), confronting the role opportunities and norms available in the family, the school, the workplace, or the community. These people are influenced *by,* but at the same time they are also influencing, these structures. They are

---

[7] This is the distinction between sources of role change that are endogenous and those that are exogenous to the age system, as developed in the aging and society approach (and examined in PASC; also see Foner, 1982).

continually shaping each role as they collectively act and think in their everyday lives, or as public policy or professional practice dictate. This dialectical principle that each dynamism influences the other derives its power from the fact that aging and cohort succession, and their interplay with social structures, are universal processes—persisting as long as the society persists. The principle, though general, subsumes a complex of scientific views, some that are by now widely accepted, but others that are truly radical in their implications.

Influence on Lives. In one direction of the interplay, as social structures change, the people in successive cohorts who are moving through these structures grow up and grow old in different ways. It is a sociological truism that people's lives tend to be molded by the environing social structures. And much empirical research on human development and aging has specified this theory and the mechanisms through which it operates. A mosaic of studies has demonstrated *how* people's lives have been altered over the past century by the shifting character of work and the family, and by wars, depressions, energy shortages, and the like.

Studies of interventions that alter the social environment have shown the potentiality of other changes, not yet realized (see Riley & Abeles, 1990; and Chapter 2). Even in very old age, people's functioning—already at levels far higher than commonly recognized—can be improved (cf. Kaplan & Haan, 1989). For example:

- Among elderly patients in nursing homes, social activity, immune functioning, and perhaps even survival can be enhanced—provided that the social environment is altered to increase the sense of personal control and independence (Rodin & Langer, 1977).

- Among older workers, intellectual functioning improves with age, provided that the work situation is challenging and calls for self direction (Gribbin, Schaie, & Parham, 1980; Schooler, 1987).

- Very old people, whose performance on intelligence tests has deteriorated, can be brought back to their performance levels of 20 years earlier, provided that the social environment affords incentives and opportunities for practicing and learning new strategies (Willis, 1990).

- Memory can be improved, provided that the impoverished context often characterizing retirement is altered to include the stimulation of a rich and complex environment (Park, 1991; Sharps & Gollin, 1987).
- Among very old nursing home residents (average age 90), speed and distance of walking ability can be improved, leg-muscle strength doubled, and muscle size increased, provided that length-strength training is included in the regimen (Fiatarone, Marks, Meredith, Lipsitz, & Evans, 1990).

Influence on Structures.   In the other direction of the interplay, differences in the life-course patterns of people in successive cohorts create collective pressures toward changes in social structures and roles. This is a radical postulate. There is still little understanding of the reciprocal ways in which changes in lives can, in their turn, cause structural change.

Yet there are significant conceptual beginnings. Sociologists of age (Waring, 1975) have analyzed the effects of cohort differences in size, as the "baby boom" cohorts in the United States first strained the school system and the labor force, and soon will become the "senior boom" exacerbating the inadequacy of roles for the elderly. Sociologists of age have also conceptualized "cohort norm formation" (Riley, 1978; 1986): As members of the same cohort respond to shared historical experiences, they gradually and subtly develop common patterns of response, common definitions, and common beliefs that crystallize into common norms and become institutionalized in revised social structures and roles. By contrasting modern with African age-set societies, Foner and Kertzer (1979) have dramatized "intrinsic" pressures for change engendered in any society by the strains and conflicts between the younger people in oncoming cohorts and the older people whom they are displacing. Using the social-psychological concept of "goodness of fit," Robert Kahn (in Chapter 2) examines the abilities, aspirations, and needs of individuals, as they mesh (or fail to mesh) with the structural requirements and opportunities of the work situation (see Kahn, 1979; 1981).

Asynchrony.   The most noteworthy characteristic of this interplay between changes in people and in roles is that it flies in the face of any notion that social change proceeds smoothly. For the two dynamisms contain a paradox of *timing*. Each is marching to a different drummer. Aging individuals are moving along with axis of the life course (the diagonal bars in Figure 1–1). But change in social structures (as we imagine the vertical bar moving across time) proceeds along its own axis of historical time, which—as Pitirim Sorokin (1941, p. 505) demonstrated long ago—has little rhythm or periodicity. Since these two sets of bars are continually crisscrossing each other in different directions, only rarely can they be perfectly synchronized. And it is this *asynchrony* that produces a recurring mismatch between them—a lag of one dynamism behind the other.

Under some conditions, people's lives lag behind structural change (as when unemployed workers cannot cope with the technologically advanced jobs available, or older people with the bureaucratized health care system). More critical in modern society than this "people lag," however, is the converse problem of the lag of structures behind lives addressed in this book. Changes in people's lives are ahead of the structural changes, because many structures (such as summer vacations for schoolchildren to work on the farm, or 65 as the expected age of retirement) tend to retain their earlier form. When the two dynamisms are far out of synchrony, as they are today, critical strains can eventuate—both for individuals and for society as a whole—and such strains continually press for still further changes.

Pressures for Structural Change

Implicit in these societal dynamics then, as the conceptual framework helps us to discern, are currently insistent pressures toward structural change. These pressures operate not only through the decisions made by legislators, public officials, employers, educators, and people in the practicing professions, but also through the millions of everyday thoughts and acts of men and women who are growing up and growing old. At every age, changing attitudes and styles of living are generating new norms and altering social institutions. Within the cohorts of those who are young today, many are dissatisfied with the traditional norms of the schools they attend; many of those now reaching the middle years are protesting the multiple stresses of combined work and family roles; and many in cohorts now in old age are restive in the prolonged "roleless role" of retirement. Older individuals differ widely; not all wish to remain in the labor force, but none wish to be disregarded, denigrated, dependent, or categorized as useless. They wish to be seen as responsible participants in society rather than as burdens to be borne by younger members of oncoming cohorts. Even among the terminally ill, increasing numbers of older patients seem determined to participate in controlling the timing and conditions of their own death. Such pressures for structural change as the "living will," informed consent, and greater symmetry in doctor-patient relationships all foreshadow new norms and institutional arrangements (such as the hospice) for dying. The issue of structural lag thus forces consideration of the only experience on which individuals can never directly report (cf. J. Riley, 1991).

To summarize: Tremendous numbers of capable and potentially productive older people cannot long coexist with empty role structures, nor can younger adults continue to struggle under excessive role demands, while children have little part in serious affairs. For individuals, as Robert Kahn demonstrates in this book, there is a problem of person-environment fit. For society and its institutions and groups, economic and instrumental responsibilities are unevenly distributed by age. Something will have to give. As social scientists, we seek a deeper understanding of future structural changes that might improve the fit and reduce the lag.[8]

POSSIBLE DIRECTIONS OF STRUCTURAL CHANGE

If, then, it is the neglected dynamism of changing structures that must be modified to offset the lag, what will the structural changes of the future be like? How can they occur? How might we specify the detailed structures characterizing one of the vertical bars in Figure 1–1 as at the year 2000? or 2040? In this chapter, we consider just two of the many areas of possible structural changes—work and family. As a heuristic aid, we describe alternate extreme scenarios or "ideal types" of social structures. We postulate, in contrast to age-differentiated types, which are characterized by significant structural lag, age-integrated types, which theoretically have the potential to reduce it. (In Max Weber's sense, such ideal types are precisely that: They are

---

[8] For extended examples of interventions to improve *both* lives and structures, see Riley and Riley (1989).

hypothetical and artificially simplistic. They may never exist in real life but are an idealized selection from it.)

Work

As schematized in Figure 1–2, we begin with work, with its close association with both education and leisure, and its indirect impact on the family. At the left of the chart, *age-differentiated* structures at one extreme divide societal roles and their occupants into the three familiar rigid "boxes": retirement or leisure for older people; work roles (paid or unpaid) for the middle-aged; educational roles for the young. This type of structure is commonplace today (cf. Kohli, Rein, Guillemard, & van Gunsteren, 1991). It is convenient, providing orderliness of entry and exit from roles. It is bolstered by "ageism"—the view that children are of little societal use, and the erroneous but stubborn belief in universal and inevitable decline because of growing old. That was accepted almost without question in societies where paid employment was the predominant role, achievement (or material success) the predominant value, and where paid work was the nearly exclusive province of men (thus predating the current era in which most women

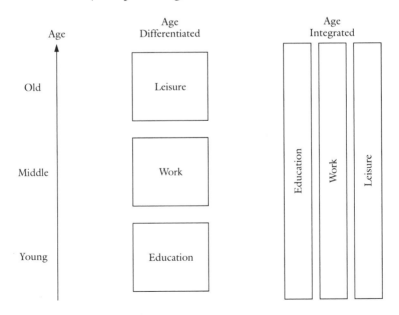

Figure 1–2   **Ideal Types of Social Structures**

carry the double load of work outside as well as inside the home). Nevertheless, these age-based structures and cultural norms can be seen as outdated vestigial remains of an earlier era when most people had died before their work was finished or their last child had left home.

At the opposite extreme, at the right of the chart, is the ideal type of *age-integrated* structures (cf. the classic pieces by Rehn, 1977; Best, 1981; also Habib & Nusberg, 1990). Here we can imagine that the age barriers are removed, so that role opportunities in all structures—education, work, and leisure—are open to people at every age. Throughout society, people of ages are brought together; that is, they are "integrated." Ideally, such flexible structures would open to older people the full range of role choices. For the middle-aged, there would be reductions in the strains imposed by multiple roles of work combined with family and homemaking. For young adults, there would be opportunities for the meaningful integration of work and school; and for children, opportunities to participate in responsibilities and decision making in family, school, and community.

A noteworthy feature of such ideal-typical age integration contributes to its feasibility: Spreading work more evenly across all ages does not depend on any necessary increase in the numbers of openings in the labor force, but merely reallocates the available openings more widely across the full age span. Thus, independent of fluctuations in the total demand for labor, age integration could lead quietly to replacement of some full-time by part-time jobs, thereby freeing time for education, leisure, family, or other activities. To be sure, reducing the hours of paid work can entail reductions in income and loss of benefits (as emphasized in several chapters in this book). However, as one drastic structural change and partial solution to such losses, Robert Kahn (in Chapter 2) postulates a "4-hour work module" as an entirely new standard on which benefits could be based, to replace the conventional 40-hour per week standard. The whole notion of age integration is indeed revolutionary.

Apart from any pecuniary losses entailed, age integration has inherent drawbacks. If flexibility of age criteria for work were pushed too far, abuses could follow: Entitlements to support relaxation, recreation, and self-fulfillment in retirement could be threatened (productivity cannot be required of everyone), or the well-known dangers of exploiting the labor of older people or children could rear their ugly heads.

Family

Parallel to these structural alternatives in work roles are ideal types of family and kinship roles (cf. Riley & Riley, 1993). At one extreme is the familiar type *differentiated* by age and also by generation. This type is similar in reality to the 19th-century structures composed of three generations: parents, their little children, and occasional grandparents. More recently, with increasing longevity, this age-differentiated type has expanded: Four generations are alive at the same time, and kin relationships have been prolonged. In reality today, a mother and her daughter are only briefly in the role of parent-and-*little* child. Today a woman and her husband are likely to survive jointly for 40 years or more—though not necessarily to remain married to each other. (Our own marriage has lasted for more than 60 years.) In this age-differentiated type, kinship ties are not only affectional but also often rest on an economic base (as in the implicit intergenerational "contract" for material support between parents and their adult offspring; cf. Riley & Riley 1993).

At the opposite extreme is an *age-integrated* ideal type of kinship structure in which the constraints imposed by age and generation have been submerged. Here we imagine a boundless network of kin and kin*like* relationships, in which people of any age—inside or outside the traditional family or household—are free to choose (or to earn the right) to support, love, or confide in one another. Or they may choose to avoid stressful or unpleasant relationships. We speak of this age-integrated type as a "latent matrix" (Riley, 1983), since many of these relationships may remain dormant until they are called on. This kinship type corresponds, not to structures that yet exist, but to many real elements in contemporary lives and behaviors. The pressures of changing lives have not yet crystallized into altered and accepted roles and norms. Institutionalized structures have not kept pace.

SOME IMPLICATIONS OF AGE INTEGRATION

Where, then, does this typology of age differentiation versus age-integration leave us? It alerts us to key elements of the age-differentiated types that reflect the reality of the past and to key elements of the age-integrated types that, as we hypothesize, may be prophetic of some real directions for the future. It alerts us to far-reaching social and cultural consequences that might eventuate from any shift toward age integration. Here we mention just three: (1) the impact on lives, (2) related forms of integration, and (3) changes in underlying values and meanings.

The Impact on Lives

Because of the principle of interdependence between the two dynamisms, structural changes would have a reciprocal effect on the ways people grow up and grow old. Age-integrated structures would predictably lead to a reconstruction of people's entire lives. The rigid life course, which was historically established by men, would be replaced with flexible life pathways, as these are already being introduced by many women. Beyond a floor of economic security for everyone, these flexible paths would allow people at all ages to move in and out of education, to change jobs or start new careers, and to intersperse leisure and family activities more evenly with other activities throughout life. People in their later years would find doors opening to the full range of role choices; and they could become popularly regarded as an asset, not a burden on society. People in their years of paid employment would have more freedom for family life, community service, self-actualization, traveling, educational advancement, cultural pursuits, development of second careers. Young people, even children, would become part of the "real world." Ideally, too, these flexible life pathways would also be diverse—allowing for the wide heterogeneity of people's preferences and attitudes (cf. Dannefer, 1987).[9]

Related Forms of Integration

In addition to its effect on lives, age integration also evokes other forms of *institutional integration* (cf. Riley & Riley, 1991). As roles in work or retirement intersect with roles in other social institutions, old structures give way to new hybrids. (Chapter 4 in this book provides

---

[9] Unless such pathways were completely optional, they could result in exploitation and abuse, reduction in needed entitlement, or denigration of those who differ from the predominant view. As Anne Foner reminds us, we certainly do not wish to revert to children in mines as in Zola's *Germinal* or in New England factories in the early 20th century; nor do we wish to emulate the lot of migrant labor families today, or high school dropouts who too often have to become drug pushers or worse.

relevant examples from former East Germany of a converse shift away from age integration.) For example, corporations become integrated with schools as they provide educational facilities for employees, and with families as they provide day care for employees' children and frail parents, or as technological advances allow jobs to be performed in the home. *Gender integration* is already being produced by the extraordinary increases in labor force participation by young and middle-aged women, so that men and women interact directly with each other at work as well as in the family (cf. Chapter 7). Even a degree of *class integration* seems possible, if the "haves" in their middle years were to have established patterns of reduced hours of paid work over a long period of future time, bringing them closer to the "have-nots"; or if new economic policies were to "level the playing field" for all ages.

Changes in Underlying Values and Meanings

Finally, a shift toward age integration would give new meanings to both individual and social life and would challenge the basic values and norms inherent in the familiar rigid structures. For example, working part-time or starting over in new careers, since they typically mean accepting periods of reduced income or loss of benefits, now tend to be regarded as signs of failure—but not so under age-integrated conditions. Flexible structures place less value on economic competition and comparative achievement and more on responsibilities and other rewards—affection from family and friends, respect from the community, esteem for contributions to science and the arts, recognition for personal fulfillment. As in Robert Bellah's (Bellah, Madsen, Sullivan, Swidler, & Tipton, 1991) view, a "good society" gives precedence to family and children over personal indulgence, and to environmental and civic concerns over private opulence. If life pathways were to become more flexible and diverse, how might individual rights be weighed against social responsibilities (as in the "responsive society" of Amitai Etzioni, 1991)? What new rewards might be attained?

AGE INTEGRATION: SOME STRAWS IN THE WIND

We have been talking about ideal types that may never exist in reality. Nevertheless there is already evidence that some forms of age integration may be imminent. Beneath the surface of our contemporary age-differentiated society, people's altered lives are creating very real pressures toward new structures. Again we illustrate from roles in family and work.

Family

In the family, the age-integrated (or "latent matrix" type) illustrates the emerging reality of complex contemporary kinship roles that, though not yet institutionalized, nevertheless cry out to *be* structured. Already manifest in many contemporary lives are kin relationships, and other kin*like* relationships, that include the profusion of step-kin and in-laws left in the wake of rising divorce and remarriage; adopted children[10] and older people adopted as foster parents; gay and lesbian families; single-mother and single-father families; cohabiting partners (in the United States nearly half of young people today have cohabited); "fictive" kin, common in ethnic communities; godchildren and countless types of elective relationships; even biological linkages to two mothers, one who donates the egg and a second who bears the child.

For such confusing relationships, there are not yet any established social structures or norms. Theories of the "family" exclude them. Unlike some other languages, English does not have names for them. One personal example (using fictitious names) will illustrate the complexity of this age-integrated type. Our granddaughter Susan (a Harvard graduate) cohabits with Jim (a Harvard astrophysicist). They are not married, but their commitment runs deep: They have bought a home, and now have a baby (our first great-grandson). Jim has been twice divorced, and has a daughter nearly the same age as Susan. Yet, Susan has close bonds to this daughter and to both exwives. The question is: How is Susan related to all these people? (Even more intriguing: How are *we* related to Jim—or to his exwives?) What is the structure—the norms and expectations—for such relationships? How does age, or generation, enter in? This account may sound humorous, but it is nonetheless real as an illustration of changes in lives, and in people's behaviors and attitudes, for which no comparable structures

---

[10] Cf. Thomas Ericsson's (1990) account of Swedish spinsters who, having developed their own businesses, adopted young workers to be their heirs.

or norms have yet been institutionalized. Lives and kinship attitudes and actions have been transformed. Yet, the lag persists.

What new norms and expectations for family roles, then, what new theories and terminologies, can replace those previously defined by age and generation? Surely, current ideological calls, as in the United States for a "return to family values," must go beyond the outworn stereotype of two parents with their *little* children. How is the "family" to be handled legally? In public policy? In taking census counts? How will norms of intergenerational responsibility or "contract" come to be redefined? Pressures to correct the structural lag are imminent.

Work

At work, evidences are emerging in the United States and elsewhere that, not only in lives but also in social structures, some elements of age integration are becoming a reality: that structures are changing, that the established age barriers are breaking down, and that deliberate interventions to offset structural lag are feasible (cf. Riley & Riley, 1989). Not only are educational roles no longer confined exclusively to the young, but work roles are no longer confined exclusively to the middle years. There has been—sometimes interrupted but sometimes fostered by periods of recession—increasing provision for older people of part-time work, flextime and flexplace arrangements, and programs of "unretirement," as well as opportunities to "moonlight" in work that is not officially reported (cf. Quinn, Burkhauser, & Myers, 1990). There are scattered signs of deliberate structural interventions that bring together people of all ages in all three domains of education, work, and leisure. For example, there are interventions to make it possible for people to move early from school to work, and later from work back again to school; to change careers; and (as workers and parents in the middle years) to include more leisure activities, rather than concentrating nearly all the "optional time" in retirement. In many countries, flexible working arrangements are challenging such established stereotypes as the rigid 40-hour week, the 8-hour day, and vacations of restricted length (cf. Henrichs, Roche, & Sirianni, 1991).

All such incipient changes can operate as pressures for still further changes toward age-integrated flexible roles. If such latent tendencies in fact coalesce toward a new societal integration, they could help to reduce structural lag and to unlock wider potentials for people's lives.

In some places, and under some conditions, then, strong pressures are already operating to alter societal structures in the age-integrated direction. For the future, it remains to be seen how the private sector will respond to such pressures, and how governments, policymakers, and practicing professionals will play their part (cf. Riley, Riley, & Johnson, 1969).

ONE SCENARIO FOR THE FUTURE

Age and Structural Lag, as a 1990s sequel to our 1930s attempt to study leisure, is quite a different book. In preparing it, we and our collaborators, after analyzing past and present changes, unabashedly propose future changes in domains far transcending leisure alone. Working with us, these collaborators attempt to probe the potentials for a new and more balanced relationship between social structures and human lives. They begin to ask whether, within the realm of possibility, we can discern a future society in which retirement as we know it today will be replaced by periods of leisure interspersed throughout the life course with periods of education and work; a society in which lifelong learning replaces the lockstep of traditional education; a society in which opportunities for paid work are spread more evenly across all ages; a society in which older people, as well as children, will be productive assets, not burdens; a society in which work is valued as much for its intrinsic satisfactions as for its economic returns; a society that can give new meanings not only to leisure but also to all of life—from birth to dying and death.

REFERENCES

Angus, D., Mirel, J., & Vinovskis, M. (1988). Historical development of age stratification in schooling. *Teachers College Record, 90,* 211–236.

Bellah, R. N., Madsen, R., Sullivan, W., Swidler, A., & Tipton, S. (1991). *The good society.* New York: Knopf.

Best, F. (1981). *Flexible life scheduling: Breaking the education-work-retirement lockstep.* New York: Praeger Special Studies.

Dannefer, D. (1987). Aging as intracohort differentiation: Accentuation, the Matthew effect, and the life course. *Sociological Forum, 2,* 211–236.

Ericsson, T. (1990). *Widows and spinsters: The demography of small business women in late nineteenth century Sweden.* Paper prepared for the June conference on the Historical Demography of Aging. Brunswick, Maine: Breckenridge Conference Center of Bowdoin College.

Etzioni, A. (1991). *A responsive society: Collected essays on guiding deliberate social change.* San Francisco, CA: Jossey-Bass.

Fiatarone, M. A., Marks, E. C., Meredith, C. N., Lipsitz, L. A., & Evans, W. J. (1990). High intensity strength training in nonagenarians: Effects on skeletal muscle. *Journal of the American Medical Association, 263,* 3029–3034.

Foner, A. (1982). Perspectives on changing age systems. In M. W. Riley, R. P. Abeles, & M. S. Teitelbaum (Eds.), *Aging from birth to death: Vol. II. Sociotemporal perspectives* (pp. 217–228). AAAS Symposium 79. Boulder, CO: Westview Press.

Foner, A., & Kertzer, D. I. (1979). Intrinsic and extrinsic sources of change in life-course transitions. In M. W. Riley (Ed.), *Aging from birth to death: Vol I. Interdisciplinary perspectives* (pp. 121–136). AAAS Symposium 30. Boulder, CO: Westview Press.

Gribbin, K., Schaie, K. W., & Parham, I. A. (1980). Complexity of lifestyle and maintenance of intellectual abilities. *Journal of Social Issues, 36,* 47–61.

Habib, J., & Nusberg, C., Eds. (1990). *Rethinking worklife options for older persons.* Jerusalem, Israel: JDC-Brookdale Institute of Gerontology and Adult Human Development, Washington, DC: International Federation on Aging.

Henrichs, C., Roche, W., & Sirianni, C. (1991). *Working time in transition.* Philadelphia, PA: Temple University Press.

Kahn, R. L. (1979). Aging and social support. In M. W. Riley (Ed.), *Aging from birth to death: Interdisciplinary perspectives* (pp. 77–90). AAAS Symposium 30. Boulder, CO: Westview Press.

Kahn, R. L. (1981). *Work and health.* New York: Wiley.

Kaplan, G. A., & Haan, M. N. (1989). Is there a role for prevention among the elderly? Epidemiological evidence from the Alameda County Study. In M. G. Ory & K. Bond (Eds.), *Aging and health care: Social science prospects* (pp. 27–51). London: Routledge.

Kertzer, D. I., & Schaie, K. W. (Eds.). (1989). *Age structuring in comparative perspective.* Hillsdale, NJ: Erlbaum.

Kohli, M., Rein, M., Guillemard, A. M., & van Gunsteren, H. (Eds.). (1991). *Time for retirement.* New York: Cambridge University Press.

Linton, R. (1942). Age and sex categories. *American Sociological Review, 7,* 589–603.

Manton, K. G., Stallard, E., & Singer, B. (1992). Projecting the future size and health status of the U.S. elderly population. *International Journal of Forecasting, 8,* 433–458.

Merton, R. K. (1957). *Social theory and social structure.* New York: Free Press.

Ogburn, W. F. (1922/1950). *Social change, with respect to culture and original nature* (New edition with supplementary chapter). New York: Viking.

Park, D. C. (1991). Applied cognitive aging research. In F. Craik & T. A. Salthouse (Eds.), *Handbook of cognition and aging*. Hillsdale, NJ: Erlbaum.

Parsons, T. (1942). Age and sex in the social structure of the United States. *American Sociological Review, 7,* 604–616.

Parsons, T. (1960). Toward a healthy maturity. *Journal of Health and Human Behavior, 1,* 163–173.

Quinn, J. F., Burkhauser, R. V., & Myers, D. A. (1990). *Passing the torch: The influence of economic incentives on work and retirement.* Kalamazoo, MI: Upjohn Institute for Employment Research.

Rehn, G. (1977). Toward a society of free choice. In J. J. Watts & R. Rose (Eds.). *Comparing public policies.* Ossolineum: Wroclaw.

Riley, J. W., Jr. (1991). Death and dying. In E. Borgatta & M. Borgatta (Eds.), *The encyclopedia of sociology.* New York: Macmillan.

Riley, M. W. (1978). Aging, social change, and the power of ideas. *Daedalus, 107,* 39–52.

Riley, M. W. (1979). Aging, social change, and social policy. In M. W. Riley (Ed.), *Aging from birth to death: Vol. I Interdisciplinary perspectives* (pp. 109–120). AAAS Symposium 30. Boulder, CO: Westview Press.

Riley, M. W. (1983). The family in an aging society: A matrix of latent relationships. *Journal of Family Issues, 4,* 439–454.

Riley, M. W. (1986). The dynamism of life stages: Roles, people, and age. *Human Development, 29,* 150–156.

Riley, M. W. (1988). The aging society: Problems and prospects. *Proceedings of American Philosophical Society, 132,* 148–153.

Riley, M. W., & Abeles, R. P. (1990). The behavioral and social research program at the National Institute on Aging: History of a decade (Working Document). Bethesda, MD: Behavioral and Social Research, National Institutes of Health.

Riley, M. W., Foner, A., Moore, M. E., Hess, B., & Roth, B. K. (1968). *Aging and society: Vol. I. An inventory of research findings.* New York: Russell Sage.

Riley, M. W., Foner, A., & Waring, J. (1988). Sociology of age. In N. Smelser (Ed.), *Handbook of sociology* (pp. 143–290). Newbury Park, CA: Sage Publications.

Riley, M. W., Huber, B. J., & Hess, B. (Eds.). (1988). *Social structures and human lives.* Newbury Park, CA: Sage.

Riley, M. W., Johnson, M. E., & Foner, A. (1972). *Aging and society: III. A sociology of age stratification.* New York: Russell Sage.

Riley, M. W., & Riley, J. W., Jr. (1989). *The quality of aging: Strategies for intervention* [Special issue]. *The Annals, 503, May.*

Riley, M. W., & Riley, J. W., Jr. (1991). Vieillesse et changement des roles sociaux. *Gerontologie et Societe, 56,* 6–14.

Riley, M. W., & Riley, J. W., Jr. (1993). Connections: Kin and cohort. In V. L. Bengtson & A. Achenbaum (Eds.), *The changing contract across generations* (pp. 169–189). New York: Aldine.

Riley, M. W., Riley, J. W., Jr., & Johnson, M. E. (Eds.). (1969). *Aging and society: Vol. II. Aging and the professions.* New York: Russell Sage.

Rodin, J., & Langer, E. J. (1977). Long-term effects of a control-relevant intervention with the institutionalized aged. *Journal of Personality and Social Psychology, 35,* 897–902.

Schooler, C. (1987). Psychological effects of complex environments during the lifespan: A review and a theory. In C. Schooler & K. W. Schaie (Eds.), *Cognitive functioning and social structure over the life course.* Norwood, NJ: Ablex.

Sharps, M. J., & Gollin, E. S. (1987). Memory for object locations in young and elderly adults. *Journal of Gerontology, 42,* 336–341.

Sorokin, P. A. (1941). *Social and cultural dynamics, Vol. IV: Basic problems, principles, and methods.* New York: American Book Company.

Tibbitts, C. (Ed.). (1960). *Handbook of social gerontology.* Chicago, IL: University of Chicago Press.

Waring, J. M. (1975). Social replenishment and social change. *American Behavioral Scientist, 19,* 237–256.

Willis, S. L. (1990). Current issues in cognitive training research. In E. A. Lovelace (Ed.), *Aging and cognition: Mental processes, self-awareness and interventions.* Amsterdam, Holland: Elsvier.

CHAPTER 2

Opportunities, Aspirations, and Goodness of Fit

Robert L. Kahn

O n a recent trip to New York I was caught in a cold rain and stepped off the curb hoping to find a taxi but expecting only a splash of dirty water from some cab already occupied by a more fortunate citizen. However, I had a double stroke of good luck: I was picked up immediately by a driver whose dashboard license identified him as Ture Olof; and in the course of our brief time together, Mr. Olof gave me a concise and unsolicited political lecture, the gist of which I recognized immediately as relevant to the topic of this chapter.

He told me that our country was in deep trouble, for reasons aggravated by fiscal corruption but having to do fundamentally with the allocation of productive work. Olof proposed to rectify the situation by first becoming mayor of New York City and thereafter President of the United States.

I am not usually attracted to conversation with strangers, and I have a strong conviction that anyone driving in Manhattan should not be diverted from the main task of preserving life and limb. The scope of Olof's ambition and his mention of work allocation, however, were irresistible; I asked him to tell me what he had in mind. His answer was a program of three points, the first two of which involved such trivial reforms as canceling all personal debts and awarding immediate ownership to all current occupants of residential units.

It was the third of his points that brought me close to our present topic. He proposed to limit all paid employment to three days a week. Anyone working for pay more than three days a week would have broken the law and could be reported for having done so by any other citizen. The penalty for this breach of Olof's legal code was to be an immediate sentence of 30 days' vacation in a nearby rural area—I think he mentioned the Catskills—to be spent outdoors, where the beauties of nature would help the miscreant to reorder his or her mistaken priorities.

Olof's proposal was too rigid to suit me, and it was universalistic rather than adapted to the changing life course. But he was in the right territory; goodness of fit between social structures and people's changing needs and capacities is the focal issue for this chapter and a central issue for the book as a whole. Moreover, as the Rileys have emphasized in Chapter 1, the relationships between social structures and human lives are reciprocal; the lines of influence, run in both directions.

That first chapter describes the nature of the linkages between changing structures and changing lives and the social forces affecting this linkage. In this second chapter, I am concerned with specifying how these linkages are experienced by people at particular ages; how the causal pathways are affected by properties of individuals—their needs, goals, aspirations, abilities, and well-being; and what mechanisms could improve the fit between persons and their environments. These emphases are complementary and together they define the multidisciplinary theoretical orientation of the chapters that follow.

All the chapters attempt to develop a deeper understanding of the relationship between the changing lives of individuals and the changing social structures that influence them and are influenced in turn. In many different life domains—education, employment, family, retirement, and generational relations—the chapters explore this connectedness between social structures and individual lives. The common discovery of those explorations is that all social structures do not develop at the same pace and, perhaps more important, that the developmental dynamics of groups and individuals are different. More specifically, at least in our time, there is a persistent structural lag; increases in human longevity and continued vitality have gone far beyond the social arrangements for education, work, and family life, most of which took their present form at an earlier time.

In this chapter, I address these issues as they are manifested in one domain, the productive activities and aspirations of older people. I present a sociopsychological schema for thinking about goodness of fit in that domain, apply that schema to the current situation of older people, and propose a set of institutional changes that would increase both their contributions and benefits. I believe that the proposed changes would enhance the quality of life throughout the entire age range.

GOODNESS OF FIT

Social scientists agree that to understand how a person will react in a particular situation or structure, facts about the situation and facts about the person must somehow be combined. They do not agree, however, about how to combine such diverse characteristics. Furthermore, the concepts, scales, and indexes that have been developed in the field of personality and individual ability are not commensurate with the descriptors used to characterize the situations or environments in which people live and work.

Elsewhere, my colleagues and I have proposed that we think of the relationship between individuals and situations as a problem in goodness of fit (French, Rodgers, & Cobb, 1974; Kahn, 1981). One aspect of goodness of fit is familiar in working life, the fit between the demands of the job and the abilities of the person who holds it. For example, if a clerical job requires the entry of 60 words per minute at a keyboard and the person holding the job can average only 40, the difference between these two measures reflects goodness of fit (or lack of it) between person and job.

The example is familiar because we are accustomed to thinking in terms of job requirements as demands and worker abilities as supplies or resources. But the concept of goodness of fit is not so one-sided. People have needs, goals, and aspirations as well as skills and abilities. To the situations in which they find themselves, they bring demands as well as resources.

Two aspects of fit are thus implied, the fit between the individual's abilities and the requirements of the situation or structure on the one hand, and on the other the fit between the individual's needs and the situation's opportunities. These are represented in Figure 2–1. The arrows in the figure indicate the lines of causality with which this chapter is primarily concerned, that is, those showing that certain properties of individuals lead to demands for resources in their immediate situation, even as the requirements of the situation (work, family, etc.) make demands on the resources of individuals. Other causal paths certainly exist—new situational opportunities may give rise to new individual goals, for example—but our emphasis is on bringing the external world into greater congruence with individual needs and abilities. The following sections briefly review the research in each of the four conceptual categories that constitute this schema.

Personal Resources: Knowledge, Skills, and Abilities

These, along with the lifelong experience of older men and women, represent their productive potential. It is a potential greatly underestimated by the larger public (cf. Riley & Bond, 1983), and the underestimation begins with the years of potential contributions. Chronological age is a poor indicator of the probable duration of such contributions; it would be more appropriate, as Victor Fuchs (1983) has suggested, to think in terms of years remaining.

Life expectancy at birth in the United States, in spite of a disgracefully high infant mortality, has increased by more than 20 years since

Figure 2–1   Goodness of Fit between Person and Situation. Adapted from J. R. Hackman & F. L. Suttle (1977), *Improving Life at Work* (p. 115). Santa Monica, CA: Goodyear. Used with permission.

1900, with corresponding gains in years of life remaining at later ages except among the oldest old. For most people, in spite of the age-related increase in chronic and degenerative diseases, most of these are years of physical vigor and mental competence (Brody & Brock, 1985; Suzman, Harris, Hadley, Kovar, & Weindruch, 1992).

Some more direct indication of the capacity of older people for productive work is apparent when we compare the age distributions for paid employment, which policy and incentives begin to discourage near age 55 and law (until recently) tended to terminate at age 65, with the distributions for unpaid work, where opportunities for participation are less age constrained. In the 10-year age groups beginning with age 55, the proportion of people in paid employment drops drastically, from 53% to 22% to 4% among men and women aged 75 or more. By contrast, the proportion of people doing unpaid work in formal organizations holds relatively constant across these age groups; it increases slightly after age 65 (from 37% to 40%), and 26% of all men and women aged 75 or more report some such unpaid work. The contrast with paid work is even more dramatic when we consider unpaid work done in the home rather than in organizational settings. The proportion of older people who provide care for friends or family members with disabilities or other chronic health problems increases after age 45, is sustained at or near 20% to age 75, and remains substantial thereafter. The proportion of such caregivers among men and women aged 75 or more (14%) is about at the average for all ages and significantly higher than among those in early adulthood (Herzog, Kahn, Morgan, Jackson, & Antonucci, 1989).

These data on unpaid productive work—that is, work performed without pay that nevertheless produces goods or services for which an equivalent market value can be estimated—tell us what older people are already doing; when we measure preferences, we obtain additional evidence for their productive potential. Most people aged 55 or more (64%) do not do unpaid organizational work, but 40% of them say that they would like to. And of those who are doing some work of this kind, 20% say that they would like to do more (Herzog & Morgan, in press; also see Chapter 10 of this book).

When people who are not volunteering say that they would like to do so, the question immediately arises: Why are they not acting in accordance with their expressed preferences? To some extent, their responses may be biased; social acceptability favors expressing some interest in voluntary work rather than admitting to having none. But the predictors of volunteer work suggest other explanations. Some of them have to do with enduring properties of individuals—socio-economic status and personality. Men and women with more years of education, higher incomes, and work experience in professional, managerial, and other white-collar occupations are more likely to do voluntary work than those in other socioeconomic and occupational categories. People who score low in neuroticism and who tend toward extroversion rather than introversion are more likely to be volunteers. Gender, race, and religion, on the other hand, do not predict voluntarism; involvement in unpaid work and, by implication, the potential for it do not differ across those lines.

Perhaps most relevant for potential increases in voluntarism, however, is one of the main reasons people give for having begun voluntary work: Somebody asked them. And the likelihood of being asked is increased by being in the presence of people who are already volunteers. Older men and women who attend church or go to meetings of voluntary organizations make themselves visible and imply some degree of interest; efforts at recruitment come next.

An additional consideration in estimating the productive potential of older people involves the relationship between paid and unpaid work. They are not mere alternatives. Among men and women aged 55 or older, the relationship between paid and unpaid work is markedly curvilinear; older people who work part-time for pay are more likely to do additional unpaid work as volunteers than are those who work for pay on a full-time basis or do no paid work at all.

It is likely that one of the factors that militate against the realization of the productive potential of older people is the perception of others that the elderly are greatly diminished in cognitive as well as physical ability and that these deficits cannot be redeemed. Experimental evidence tells us otherwise, as the Rileys point out in Chapter 1 (and describe more fully in Riley & Abeles, 1990). Laboratory experiments at the Max Planck Institute in Berlin, for example, found that short-term word recall by untrained older people averaged less than 5, and that younger people did significantly better. However, after mnemonic instruction and intensive practice, older people could recall 15 words, considerably more than young people without such training. It is also true that young people, given equivalent training, do still better—averaging a recall of 30 words. When pushed to the limits, on most dimensions youth wins. But the performance and, equally important, the ability of older people to learn and improve, were well established (Baltes & Baltes, 1990).

Moreover, in one domain at least, youth appears to offer no advantage. Baltes and his colleagues at the Max Planck Institute have done research on wisdom, in which experimental subjects are presented with vignettes that pose difficult human problems—whether a very young woman, still in school, should terminate an unwanted pregnancy or not, or how a family should deal with a life-threatening illness not fully understood by the patient. Answers to these vignettes were then rated for wisdom by a panel of judges who did not know any characteristics of the respondents. Old men and women did as well as young adults overall, and on problems that tend to occur in middle or later life rather than earlier, the older respondents did better (Smith, Dixon, & Baltes, 1988).

My interpretation is that life experience in the domain of interpersonal relations and decisions, unlike that in the domain of technology, does not become obsolescent. The wisdom of age is not universal, but it is real and in large part it remains to be utilized.

Personal Demands: Needs, Goals, and Aspirations

We have been concerned thus far with what older people *can* do; we turn now to the question of what they *want* to do—their needs, their goals, their aspirations. The raw data are clear. People now are healthier than those of earlier generations were at comparable ages and they have many more years of active life before them. Nevertheless, they leave the labor force earlier than their parents and grandparents did. As recently as 1957, 83% of all men aged 60 to 64 were in the labor force; in 1987 only 57% were employed or seeking employment. The shift is still more dramatic among men aged 65 to 69; in 1957, the majority of them (53%) were in the labor force; in 1987 the percentage was only 26. These changes in the age pattern of employment are discussed more fully in Chapters 3, 4, and 11.

Part of the answer is economic, although the allegation of universal prosperity among older people is greatly exaggerated. For the following data I have relied extensively on recent unpublished lectures (Michael Hurd, 1992).

The dollar income of elderly households (occupants 60 years of age or more) is less than two-thirds (64%) that of younger households. If adjusted for household size, however, money income is about equal for these two age groups. With a further adjustment for nonmoney income and assets, the advantage shifts to older people because of Medicare, pension entitlements, and equity in housing. The situation of older people varies greatly, however. Only 15% have financial assets in addition to those just listed, and more than 12% have incomes below the poverty line.

Many economists interpret these data as indicating a reduced need for paid employment on the part of older people, and explain their lowered labor force participation in these terms. I question the power of that explanation and two of the economic assumptions that support it—first, that employment, except for its being paid, has negative utility and second, that the fiscal motivation of older people is to "spend down" rather than save, so that the exhaustion of their assets coincides with their death. The former assumption ignores the noneconomic psychosocial motives for working and the latter assumption, the so-called life-cycle hypothesis, ignores the motivation to bequeath assets to children and others and to provide for the contingency of long-term care. In short, the economic models underestimate people's motivation to work and to know that their work is valued.

The substantial wish of older people to be active and useful is indicated by the fact that 33% of those over 55 years of age do work for pay, that a larger percentage do volunteer work of market value, and that 40% of the nonvolunteers express a wish to engage in such work. The norms expressed by older people are consistent with these facts; more than 80% agree that older people should contribute through community service and that they should continue to work as long as they are able (Herzog, House, & Morgan, 1991).

What most older people do not want, however, is full-time work at the jobs they held before retirement. Older people who work for pay average about 30 hours per week, rather than the more general pattern of 40 or more; their preference is for part-time work, if anything under 40 hours is so defined. They are not alone in this; 40% to 45% of employed workers of all ages, according to earlier nationwide studies, would prefer fewer hours even if that meant correspondingly less pay. Most people who express such preferences, however, do not believe that their employers will accommodate them (Quinn & Staines, 1979). Recent research, described in Chapters 10 and 11, shows the persistence of these attitudes and perceptions.

With these facts about the resources and demands of older people in mind, let us turn to the properties of the situation as older people experience them.

Situational Requirements

For older people who are employed, the amount and timing of work is experienced as inflexible, and recent longitudinal data bear out that impression. Among older people (50–70 years of age) working for pay in 1986, 41% wanted to work fewer hours, but three years later only about one in four (28%) of those who wanted fewer hours had managed to obtain them. At least as many (33%) of the older workers who wanted more work in fact got less, which suggests that reduced hours may be more a reflection of economic conditions and employer choice than accommodation to the wishes of employees (House, 1989).

For many older men and women who have retired from paid employment, voluntarily or involuntarily, I believe that the problem is not the magnitude of situational or structural demands but their absence. Some housework and preparation of meals are lifelong responsibilities, and for a minority of older people—women more often than men—there is the strenuous and demanding task of caring for a spouse or other person with chronic illness or disability. But the near absence of required tasks is a major element in later life, and many older people experience it as a burden rather than a blessing (Kahn, 1991; Chapter 5 in this book).

Old age in our society has been described as a roleless role, with the devaluation that the absence of role expectations implies. Physicians in geriatric practice recognize this syndrome and some recent research findings on the overuse of prescription drugs have been interpreted as reflections of the roleless state of the elderly. A Pennsylvania study of the use of Halcion, a controversial drug prescribed for insomnia, illustrates the point (*New York Times*, February 2, 1992). For low-income people 65 years of age or older, the state of Pennsylvania provides reimbursement for prescription drugs. A review of prescriptions for 14,578 older people who had received the drug showed that 85% of them had exceeded the maximum stipulated cumulative dose, and that 70% of them had exceeded the recommended duration of 2 to 3 weeks. Marshall Folstein, a psychiatrist and Alzheimer's specialist at Johns Hopkins, offered a terse interpretation: "The real problem is, they don't have anything to do when they're awake, so they want to be asleep" (sec. 4, p. 2).

For many people past middle age, the most significant situational demand that they encounter is the demand that they retire. Recent longitudinal data tell us that message is as often unwanted as welcomed. A study (sponsored by the National Institute on Aging) on the full range of productive activities showed that during the period between 1986 and 1989, 29% of all people in the age range 50 to 70 years who were employed in 1986 had retired or stopped working by 1989—14% voluntarily and 15% involuntarily. Moreover, although physical health prior to retirement was controlled, people who left paid work voluntarily reported better physical health and less depression thereafter than those whose retirement was compelled by employer policy, downsizing, and the like (Herzog, House, & Morgan, 1990; 1991).

Situational Opportunities

In describing older people's aspirations and the demand-properties of their environments, we have mentioned some of the opportunities and constraints that they encounter. We have seen, for example, that a significant proportion of all employed people would prefer to work fewer hours, even if doing so meant proportionately less pay. In the age range 24 to 54 years, 41% of all employed workers give this response, and the percentage remains quite stable until age 65 (38% for people 55 to 61 years of age, and 36% for those between 62 and 64 years). Even after age 65, when many people who would have preferred part-time work have retired, voluntarily or involuntarily, a significant minority of those who continue to work express a preference for fewer hours and less pay—25% among those 65 to 69 years old and 20% among those aged 70 or more (Herzog, House, & Morgan, 1991).

We have seen also that most people who want fewer hours of work believe that such arrangements are not feasible, and longitudinal data for the period 1986–1989 indicate that their beliefs are realistic; only 28% of those who wanted shorter hours in 1986 had obtained them by 1989. Moreover, when older people change jobs for any reason, more of them (36%) lose pay than gain or maintain income. And when older people move to part-time jobs, the losses are more severe; the tendency is toward the minimum wage.

The opportunities for working as a volunteer are undoubtedly greater; leaders of voluntary organizations, civic and religious, describe them as needing and welcoming volunteers. But the majority of older people—almost two-thirds—do not report working as volunteers; among men and women aged 55 and more, only 36% do unpaid work in organizations while almost all (93%) do some housework or home maintenance and 68% provide direct help to family members or friends.

The data we have reviewed need reconciliation. Organizations apparently need volunteers; many people who do not volunteer say that they would like to do so, and their involvement in providing nonorganizational help implies appropriate motivation and ability. Why are more older people not active as volunteers? An answer is suggested by data from a recent Gallup poll, which included a direct question to volunteers about how they came to be involved. As noted previously, the most frequent answer was simple: "Someone asked me." The image of organizations waiting for potential volunteers to offer their services and older people waiting to be invited to voluntarism has a certain plausibility; it remains to be learned how closely the image fits the facts and how broadly it applies.

GOODNESS OF FIT AND ITS EFFECTS
ON WELL-BEING

Most research on goodness of fit between individual attributes and situational characteristics has been done in work settings in which the main concern was whether the abilities of the person were adequate to the demands of the job. From the employer's point of view, it is the business of selection and placement to minimize such problems, and of training to rectify them. A study of workers in 23 occupations, however, provides more comprehensive information (French, Caplan, & Harrison, 1982). The findings show that goodness of fit has explanatory power beyond situational and individual attributes taken separately. For example, there is an inverse linear relationship between job complexity and depression; people in jobs with minimal complexity are more likely to exhibit depressive symptoms and, as Kohn and Schooler (1983) have shown, to suffer long-term losses in intellectual flexibility. But if the complexity of the job is combined with the preferences of the individual on a commensurate scale, we see a symmetrical U-shaped relationship in which depressive symptoms are minimal when job complexity corresponds to individual preferences. In similar fashion, goodness of fit predicts job satisfaction/dissatisfaction, boredom/interest, and presence or absence of somatic complaints, anxiety, and irritation (French, Caplan, & Harrison, 1982).

Comparable data are not available for people who do not work for pay, but those who do volunteer work or engage in other unpaid productive activity rate the benefit of such work, to themselves and to others, as no less than that of paid work (Herzog & House, 1991). Independent estimates of the economic value of unpaid work are consistent with these subjective ratings (Herzog & Morgan, 1992). And as we have seen, even after appropriate controls for preretirement health, older people who describe their retirement as voluntary report better health and well-being than those whose retirement was involuntary. In short, substantial gains in overall well-being can probably be realized by bringing the productive opportunities and requirements for older men and women into closer congruence with their capacities and preferences, that is, by changing the situational elements in Figure 2–1. How can this best be done? How can structural lag of this kind be reduced?

THE RECOGNITION AND ENHANCEMENT OF PRODUCTIVE BEHAVIOR

I propose two answers to those questions, each consistent with the evidence we have reviewed but both going considerably beyond it:

1. We must recognize the full range of productive activities, paid and unpaid, throughout the life course, and abandon in our national statistics and in our thinking the dangerous pretense that life consists of paid employment and a great undifferentiated residual.

2. We must modify, or rather give people the opportunity to modify, the allocation of paid employment throughout the life course.

Rationale for Proposed Changes

People who do unpaid work at home or in organizational settings rate it equal in value, hour for hour, to paid employment, but it is not so recognized. If we want to increase voluntarism, we must acknowledge its societal importance and value. People respond to recognition and approval and are discouraged by its absence.

As a first step toward changing the public mind-set and the thinking of policymakers about the value of unpaid work, we should bring it into our national statistics. In the data collections of the Census Bureau and the Department of Labor, unpaid work should be treated like paid employment; its hours, type, location, and market value should be determined at regular intervals. Unpaid work should then be included as an identifiable component of gross national product (GNP). Those who perform such work—and it is a disproportionately large part of the work done by older people—would thus be identified as societal contributors rather than burdens. That in turn may plausibly lead to an increase in the opportunities for voluntary work and in the motivation of older people to engage in it.

My second proposal refers to paid employment and is based on the concept of the work module, which is simply a time-task unit, 4 hours of work at a given task (Kahn, 1974). The 8-hour day and the 40-hour week dominate our thinking, our accounting, and our legislation. They have acquired an aura of importance and immutability that is quite out of keeping with their historical recency and their inappropriateness to modern technology and business practice. Not only do many advanced technologies require continuous operation rather than 8 hours on and 16 hours off; supermarkets and other service establishments run increasingly on a 24-hour, 7-day schedule.

We know that people's needs and preferences for paid employment differ across the life course; they do not correspond to the choice between a 40-hour package and nothing at all. Some modifications have been introduced on a limited scale—job-sharing and part-time work, for example. The very labels, however, suggest the persistence of the full-time 40-hour stereotype (cf. Chapter 5 of this book).

Movement to a 4-hour module as the standard unit of accounting would not imply the imposition of fewer hours and less work. Most people in the labor force might need and want 8-hour (that is, two-module) workdays, and some would work 12 hours or more. But the

40% of workers who tell us that they would prefer shorter hours, even at less pay, would find their preferences legitimized. Not all these people, as we have seen, are elderly, but many are. For them, the introduction of work schedules based on the 4-hour module would change the retirement experience from an externally imposed event to a self-defined and gradual process.

Overcoming Barriers to Change

In this chapter, we cannot discuss fully the barriers that prevent and the forces that oppose such changes, but we can at least acknowledge them and suggest some compensating factors.

Perhaps the most frequent objection to any proposal that would increase the number of workers in an establishment is the added cost of fringe benefits. Some employers provide certain benefits to all employees, irrespective of hours worked. Examples include life insurance, health coverage, sick leave, paid vacations, and privileges such as discount purchases.

Many employers do not offer health care or other such benefits to people who work less than "full-time." More to the point, there is no intrinsic reason why health care, which is by far the most expensive of the fringe benefits, should be contingent on employment. If health care coverage were provided on some other basis, a major objection to the 4-hour module would be eliminated.

Other fringe benefits are less costly and their costs tend to be proportional to hours worked. When a person working 4 hours a day is ill or on paid vacation, the cost to the employer is accounted on the basis of 4-hour days, not 8-hour days. Life insurance, when it is provided at all, is usually given in amounts roughly proportional to earnings, which reflect hours worked as well as hierarchical position.

The effect of the work module on claims for injury on the job or for work-related disability is difficult to estimate without experimental trials. It can be argued that such financial risks, from the employer's view, are proportional to the number of employees. But it can also be argued that these risks are proportional to hours worked and, indeed, that increasing flexibility in hours would reduce fatigue and overall time pressures, and thus reduce the risks of injury or disability.

There is, however, a third category of costs that must increase as the number of employees grows; these costs have to do with supervision, training, coordination, and scheduling. Possible additions to costs of this kind must be taken seriously, but they should not be exaggerated. The once laborious clerical functions of scheduling and payroll accounting are now done by computer, even in small establishments. Moreover, few establishments of size limit their activities to 40 hours per week. Most of them, therefore, are already piecing together individual work schedules to meet the overall and fluctuating demands of the enterprise. Adopting the 4-hour module would add employees but it would not require a wholly new scheduling process.

Finally, we must consider the costs of training, supervising, and coordinating additional employees. Those costs are real. Whether they would be offset by gains in satisfaction and motivation—that is, gains in goodness of fit between persons and job—deserves to be tested in practice. I believe that they would be more than balanced by such gains, and I look forward to field experiments that, like clinical trials in medical research, will test the effects of the work module and thus replace rhetoric with facts.

Many years ago, Donald Campbell (1969), in an article advocating such trials more broadly, expressed the hope that the United States might become "an experimenting society." It is a phrase that has been widely quoted and widely misunderstood. It does not imply that social changes should be frivolous or even frequent, but rather that we give serious trial and evaluation to major social programs before initiating them on a national scale. We would thus suffer less from fads and be more likely to benefit from wise decisions.

We are already a society that is, to a significant degree, data driven. We tend to pay attention to the things that we count—employment and unemployment, gross national product, debt and deficit, years of life, incidence of certain diseases, and on through a long list of what are sometimes called social indicators. Systematic monitoring of that kind is not a substitute for experimental evaluation; it tells us the effects of what we are already doing, rather than the effects of attempts at improvement. I believe that the combination of such monitoring with the experimental evaluation of proposed changes in policy, however, is uniquely powerful.

Bringing unpaid work into our national statistics and introducing the 4-hour module as the major accounting unit for paid work would be such a combination. Their intended effects go beyond enhancing the productivity of specific establishments, although that is important in itself. At least as important is encouraging the various forms of un-paid productive work and giving recognition to those who perform it. The resulting lifelong mix of paid and unpaid work, education and employment, and self-development and self-expression would enable people to improve the quality of their lives.

At the societal level, the nature of such gains is given by the title of this book; it is the reduction of structural lag. In terms of the schema around which this chapter is organized (Figure 2–1), that means bringing structural opportunities and role requirements into greater congruence with people's abilities and aspirations at every age. Few challenges are greater, and few hold more promise for the quality of American life.

REFERENCES

Baltes, P. B., & Baltes, M. M. (Eds.). (1990). *Successful aging: Perspectives from the behavioral sciences.* New York: Cambridge University Press.

Brody, J. A., & Brock, D. B. (1985). Epidemiologic and statistical characteristics of the United States elderly population. In C. E. Finch & E. L. Schneider (Eds.), *Handbook of the biology of aging* (2nd ed., pp. 3–26). New York: Van Nostrand Reinhold.

Campbell, D. T. (1969). Reforms as experiments. *American Psychologist, 24,* 409–429.

French, J. R., Jr., Caplan, R. D., & Harrison, R. V. (1982). *The mechanisms of job stress and strain.* Chichester: Wiley.

French, J. R., Jr., Rodgers, W. L., & Cobb, S. (1974). Adjustment as person-environment fit. In G. Coelho, D. Hamburg, & J. Adams (Eds.), *Coping and adaptation.* New York: Basic Books.

Fuchs, V. R. (1983). *Who shall live? Health, economics, and social choice.* New York: Basic Books.

Hackman, J. R., & Suttle, F. L. (1977). Improving life at work (p. 115). Santa Monica, CA: Goodyear.

Herzog, A. R., & House, J. S. (1991). Productive activities and aging well. *Generations, 15,* 49–54.

Herzog, A. R., House, J. S., & Morgan, J. N. (1990). The relation of work activity to health and well-being among older Americans: Longitudinal analyses. Unpublished manuscript, University of Michigan, Institute for Social Research, Ann Arbor, MI.

Herzog, A. R., House, J. S., & Morgan, J. N. (1991). Relation of work and retirement to health and well-being in older age. *Psychology and Aging, 6,* 202–211.

Herzog, A. R., Kahn, R. L., Morgan, J. N., Jackson, J. S., & Antonucci, T. C. (1989). Age differences in productive activities. *Journal of Gerontology: Social Sciences, 44,* S129–S138.

Herzog, A. R., & Morgan, J. N. (1992). Age and gender differences in the value of productive activities: Four different approaches. *Research on Aging, 14,* 169–198.

Herzog, A. R., & Morgan, J. N. (In press). Formal volunteer work among older Americans. In S. Bass, F. Caro, & Y. P. Chen (Eds.), *Achieving a productive aging society.* Westport, CT: Greenwood Publishing Group, Inc.

House, J. S. (1989). [Americans' Changing Lives: A project of the National Institute on Aging, #AG05561]. Unpublished raw data. University of Michigan, Institute for Social Research.

Hurd, M. (1992). Lectures at the Institute for Social Research, University of Michigan, Ann Arbor, MI. Unpublished.

Kahn, R. L. (1974). The work module: A proposal for the humanization of work. In J. O'Toole (Ed.), *Work and the quality of life: Resource papers for work in America.* Cambridge, MA: MIT Press.

Kahn, R. L. (1981). *Work and health.* New York: Wiley.

Kahn, R. L. (1991). The forms of women's work. In M. Frankenhaeuser, U. Lundberg, & M. Chesney (Eds.), *Women, work, and health: Stress and opportunities* (pp. 65–83). New York: Plenum Press.

Kohn, M., & Schooler, C. (1983). *Work and personality: An inquiry into the impact of social stratification.* Norwood, NJ: Ablex.

New York Times. (1992, February 2). *New York Times,* section 4, p. 4.

Riley, M. W., & Abeles, R. P. (1990). The behavioral and social research program at the National Institute on Aging: History of a decade (Working document). Bethesda, MD: Behavioral and Social Research Program, National Institutes of Health.

Riley, M. W., & Bond, K. (1983). Beyond ageism: Postponing the onset of disability. In M. W. Riley, B. B. Hess, & K. Bond (Eds.), *Aging in society: Selected reviews of recent research* (pp. 243–252). Hillsdale, NJ: Erlbaum.

Quinn, R. P., & Staines, G. L. (1979). The 1977 quality of employment survey. Ann Arbor, MI: Institute for Social Research.

Smith, J., Dixon, R. A., & Baltes, P. B. (1988). Expertise in life planning: A new research approach to investigating aspects of wisdom. In M. Commons, J. Sinnott, F. Richards, & C. Armon (Eds.), *Beyond formal operations: Comparisons and applications of adolescent and adult development models.* New York: Praeger.

Suzman, R. M., Harris, T., Hadley, E. C., Kovar, M. G., & Weindruch, R. (1992). The robust oldest old: Optimistic perspectives. In R. M. Suzman, D. F. Willis, & K. G. Manton (Eds.), *The oldest old* (pp. 341–358). New York: Oxford.

PART II

DIRECTIONS OF CHANGE

CHAPTER 3

Social Structure and Age-Based Careers[1]

John C. Henretta

Age structures employment careers through a complex web of state and workplace institutions that only vaguely reflect biological imperatives of growth and decline. This chapter discusses the link between social structure and age-structured employment and analyzes the effect of social change on retirement patterns of current cohorts of older workers. Social structure refers to the rules and institutions of the workplace and state that constrain the actors in the system, both employers and employees, either by limiting their choices or altering the incentives. Some aspects of social structure, such as the eligibility age for Social Security benefits, have obvious effects on age structuring. Other aspects, such as the relative growth and decline of industries, have less obvious but still quite important effects.

The chapter's central argument is twofold. First, there has always been important within-cohort variability in age patterning of work careers, and it is important to understand how this variation stems from institutional rules and structures. Second, changing structures in recent years have produced more variable age structuring of careers and increased within-cohort variability. The same factors that produce

[1] This chapter was prepared under the auspices of Program on Age and Structural Change and supported by the National Institute on Aging.

more variable work careers for persons of all ages have also produced more variation in the exit timing of older workers.

THE INSTITUTIONALIZATION OF THE LIFE COURSE

Discussion of the life course patterning of individual lives has, until recently, focused on the long-term increase in age structuring. The life-course institutionalization hypothesis summarizes this trend by arguing that the life course of successive cohorts has become less variable as more uniform age-based sequences of life events have emerged. In this conceptualization, event timing is increasingly determined by the institutions of the welfare state (Mayer & Schoepflin, 1989) and the workplace (Kohli, 1986; 1987). Highly individualized structures such as the family (Hareven, 1982) or particularistic relations in the workplace (Graebner, 1980; Jacoby, 1985) have become less important during this century as standardized age-based structures have emerged. Greater control over the life course by universal rules reduces within-cohort variability (Anderson, 1985; Kohli & Meyer, 1986; Uhlenberg, 1978).

Though the long-term trend is unmistakable, the institutionalization hypothesis has been qualified in three essential ways:

1. The relationship between state and workplace regulations and age structure is complex and need not produce unidirectional change (Riley, 1987).

2. At any one time, there is extensive within-cohort variability in age structuring (Hogan, 1981; O'Rand, 1990; Spilerman, 1977) partly due to individual career differences and partly patterned across categories of sex, race, and ethnicity (Held, 1986; O'Rand, 1990).

3. There is some evidence for a slowing and reversal of institutionalization as trends in social structure have created more variable age-based individual schedules than in the past, resulting in more diverse event timing (Guillemard, 1989; Henretta, 1992; Kohli, 1986). If correct, this trend reverses the long-term development of the institutionalized life course (Anderson, 1985) and may portend a future in which age is less relevant in defining status.

This chapter focuses on rules that produce age-structuring and recent trends that have halted its increase.

THE AGE-BASED ORGANIZATION OF
THE WORKPLACE

A number of processes related to age, such as health changes or general human capital investments, may create age patterning of employment careers. In this chapter, the more limited sense of the term "workplace age structuring" will be used to refer to patterning that arises from workplace rules that produce nontransferable entitlements accruing to seniority in a firm or craft, including such things as pension entitlements, higher wages, and job security (Spilerman, 1977). Career lines of individuals may also reflect seniority effects. Spilerman (1977) defines career lines as empirical regularities in job sequences within or across firms produced by structurally determined transition probabilities. These career lines may be complex, with multiple entry points, extensive branching, and a long series of jobs; or may be simple, with few job changes and little branching. In addition, not all career lines are age structured. For example, an unskilled job in one firm may commonly lead to a broad range of unskilled jobs with other firms; whereas in a different firm an unskilled job may lead to seniority-based, within-firm movement to more skilled jobs. Large numbers of these career lines arise from the structures of firms and industries, and some career lines are organized outside firms (Spilerman, 1977). For example, career lines within building industry craft occupations are organized by craft, not within firms, but they may still be seniority based.

Recent work by other researchers develops these ideas by arguing that age-structured and non-age-structured career lines exist side by side within firms (Belous, 1989; Noyelle, 1987) and industries (Hodson, 1983). That is, some jobs in a firm are entry portals to a seniority-based, within-firm career line while other job classifications in the same firm are not part of a within-firm career line. Hence, there is within-industry and within-firm variability in the extent, nature, and rewards accruing to seniority.

Spilerman (1977) points out that seniority entitlements arising from social structure within a firm (an "internal" market) do not always produce a "good" job—one with secure and increasing economic rewards. Seniority-based employment in a failing firm may offer declining earnings and little opportunity for advancement. The shifting industrial distribution of employment and its associated pattern of growth and decline of opportunity implies change over time in the rewards that accrue to age structuring in a firm or industry.

Lifetime and Contingent Work Organization

The distinction between "lifetime" and "contingent" work organization (e.g., Belous, 1989, 1990; Doeringer, 1990; Polivka & Nardone, 1989) elaborates Spilerman's nontransferable entitlement concept and is central to the discussion of age-structured employment. Whereas the conceptual distinction may be clear, actual employment relations may include elements of both work organization types. The model of lifetime labor in an internal labor market is one in which employers and employees invest in a long-term relationship (Belous, 1990). Nontransferable rewards, including firm-specific training, wage level, protection from layoff, job mobility, and the value of past pension rights increase with tenure (Lazear, 1979; Spilerman, 1977; Yellen, 1984).

Careers in the internal market ideally consist of a set of jobs organized in a hierarchical sequence with clear entry portals at the bottom and a strong emphasis on promotion from within the firm. Policies allowing entry only through jobs at the bottom of the hierarchy and tying increasing rewards and security to tenure produce an age-based organization of careers and discourage preretirement voluntary quits. Retirement is an institutional mechanism to define a clear exit portal for persons whose careers within the organization have been protected and age based (Lazear, 1979). However, employees who happen to lose their jobs in such firms are particularly disadvantaged. The wages and working conditions to which such employees have become accustomed are nontransferable and unlikely to be repeated by a new employer (Osterman, 1988; Yellen, 1984) because these conditions reflect firm-specific training or pure seniority effects that focus rewards at the end of the career.

The contingent or "day laborer" model of employment in an external labor market is opposite the lifetime model; it is not highly age structured by the rules of the workplace. The contingent model conforms to a spot market in a commodity in which the contract is of short duration and carries no stated or implied promise of continuation

(Quinn, Burkhauser, & Myers, 1990). The purest form of this model of work organization is the true day labor pool found in agriculture. Wages are set by the market for the particular skill needed with no premium for increased tenure that doesn't affect skill. Pension coverage and other benefits are less common. Yet, contingent work does not just include unskilled work; for example, substitute teachers have contingent employment (Polivka & Nardone, 1989). The key element is whether the job is located within an age-structured career line; standard job classifications, such as the part- versus full-time distinction, do not adequately measure age structuring. Tilly (1991) notes that although most part-time work fits the contingent model, part-time work in some industries indicates the employer's commitment to retain employees during periods of slack work (Tilly, 1991). Hence, any one indicator of contingent labor, such as part-time work, may not be inconsistent with a lifetime model of employment.

The Development and Logic of Internal Markets

Sanford Jacoby's *Employing Bureaucracy* (1985) traces the development of the lifetime model in industrial employment. Jacoby argues that regularized employment, including internal promotion ladders, clearly stated personnel policies, fringe benefits such as pensions, and limits on the power of low-level supervisors to hire and fire, developed slowly during most of this century. There were two periods of rapid change during World Wars I and II when regularized employment developed rapidly because of extreme labor shortage. Jacoby's account focuses on two processes in addition to employers' reaction to labor shortage. First, he views the development of regular employment as a victory for personnel managers who argued—even though they lacked supporting evidence—that their methods of regular and predictable employment improved productivity and reduced costs. Second, the development of increased security for workers reflected bargaining between unions and employers over appropriate working conditions.

In contrast to Jacoby's historical focus on the ideology of personnel management or the negotiation between capital and labor, the institutional economics literature focuses on the efficiency of internal markets. In this view, internal markets result from the rational choice by employers of the best employment strategy in the face of market imperfections (Bulow & Summers, 1986; Yellen, 1984). For example, to the extent employers cannot measure the effort put forth by workers, they may pay more to elicit greater effort (Bulow & Summers, 1986). Such payment leads to a "gift exchange" (Akerlof, 1982) in which workers provide more than minimum effort over their careers in return for a late-career wage above the level they would receive from a new employer. Internal markets are more likely when human capital is specific to the firm (Williamson, 1981) because employers have a large training investment.

In general, employers will prefer work organization that minimizes uncertainty (e.g., Belous, 1989). When the most uncertain characteristic in their environment is the supply of adequately trained and loyal labor, employers may develop an internal market to ensure labor availability and diligence. When technological change or market competition provide the more important sources of uncertainty, or in cases in which trained, experienced labor is not a great advantage, the lifetime model of employment may hinder adaptation. By fixing the cost of labor based on long-term implicit contracts, the internal market reduces the flexibility of the employer to control costs (Freeman, 1988). Hence, in changing markets, employers may prefer the contingent labor model for at least some jobs.

Retirement Institutions in Internal Markets

During this century, the internal market age-structured career for industrial workers became the accepted cultural model for employment. The development of pension mechanisms occurred late in this process, in the period after World War II (Jacoby, 1985), but has been an important factor in creating retirement as an exit portal from a protected career line.

Before the development of the internal market, older industrial workers followed highly variable paths to work exit, such as shifts to less demanding work, lower wage work, piecework, or ad hoc wage-setting systems with the same employer (Anderson, 1985; Graebner, 1980; Ransom & Sutch, 1986). The growth of regularized employment with a clear retirement exit portal led to decline in individualized partial exit pathways. In sum, the institutionalization of retirement was one part of a larger change in the organization of work.

THE EROSION OF AGE-STRUCTURED EMPLOYMENT

There is accumulating evidence that the social structural supports for age-structured employment are eroding because of diverse yet interrelated changes, ranging from a more competitive marketplace that has led to changes within firms, a relative shift of employment from manufacturing to services, and a changing regulatory environment for pensions.

Belous (1989) provides some indicators of the growth in contingent labor. He defines contingent labor as temporary workers, part-time workers, the self-employed, and business service workers (e.g., computer, stenographic, or advertising services). Based on these rough indicators, he estimates that the number of contingent workers grew from approximately 23% to 27% of the civilian labor force in 1980 to between 24% and 30% in 1988. Contingent work organization has always characterized a substantial minority of jobs; hence, it has always defined variable age patterning by workplace institutions. With either Belous' lower or upper estimate, however, the contingent labor force is growing faster than the total U.S. labor force.

Within-Firm Changes

Osterman (1988) argues there is an increasing rate of change in industry produced by introduction of new technology and increasing foreign competition. As a result, employers are choosing to keep a smaller proportion of their employees in the core lifetime-employment labor force and employ more persons in the peripheral contingent labor force (Belous, 1989; Noyelle, 1987; Osterman, 1988). They may accomplish this goal either by changing the mix of employment contracts within the firm or through subcontracting part of production to external domestic or foreign firms. As discussed in the next section, this process may shift the categorization of some jobs from manufacturing to service categories.

Belous (1989) and Noyelle (1987) both present case studies of firms in diverse industries that increased their use of contingent labor in recent years. Both find examples across a range of industries, and

Belous argues that in many cases increases were not part of any strategic plan but emerged at the division or line level to address cost and other pressures. As a result, there may be variability in the use of contingent workers among the divisions of a firm.

Added to the evidence of increased contingent labor use from case studies, there is survey evidence that employers are becoming more concerned with the cost of labor. Freeman (1988) and Belous (1990) report the result of a Conference Board survey on wage-setting policy. In 1978, employers ranked "industry patterns" and "local labor market conditions and wage rates" as the first and second factors used in setting wages. By 1983, the same employers ranked these considerations fourth and third respectively. "Productivity or labor cost trends in this company" and "expected profits of this company" had moved from third and fourth to first and second over the period. This shift is consistent with an increasing use of contingent labor because it implies increased focus on cost issues in employment.

Though the solution of using more contingent labor may be attractive to employers, Osterman (1988) argues that there are limits on how much it can grow. First, women have provided an important source of contingent labor during the postwar period, but in recent years, their preferences have shifted away from contingent labor. Hence, there may not be an adequate supply of contingent workers to meet industry's demand. Second, there is a limitation on the amount and type of work a firm will wish to entrust to contingent workers.

Shifts in Industrial Structure

In addition to change of emphasis within firms, there has also been a relative shift from manufacturing to service employment. Manufacturing employment in 1989 was roughly equal to its 1970 level while the broadly defined sector of private service-producing industries (retail and wholesale trade; finance, insurance, and real estate; and services) provided most of the growth in employment. As a result, manufacturing dropped from 27.3% to 18% of total employment (*Economic Report of the President*, 1991, Table B-43). The distinction between lifetime and contingent employment is not the same as the difference between manufacturing and services (Belous, 1989; Hodson, 1983; Noyelle, 1987). Nonetheless, firms in the service sector tend to be smaller, are less likely to be unionized, often must adjust to varying demand, and tend to be in highly competitive markets. Hence, the service sector has higher levels of contingent employment and its growth has increased the number of contingent workers.

One reason for the shift from manufacturing to services is a basic shift in employment structure in a "post-industrial" economy with high relative demand for particular services. For example, between 1970 and 1989, employment in the retail trades almost doubled and now equals manufacturing employment (*Economic Report of the President*, 1991, Table B-43). In addition, the growth in service employment partly results from the shifting of employment required in the manufacturing process from manufacturing to service industries. Though manufacturing employment has been static, the real value of manufacturing production has continued to increase (*Economic Report of the President*, 1991, Table B-11). The disparity between stagnant employment and growing production results from productivity increases and the shifting of manufacturing-related jobs into services as firms become less vertically integrated (Cohen & Zysman, 1987; Weidenbaum, 1988). During the first half of the 1980s, the proportion of industries utilizing subcontracting increased, at least modestly, across a range of industries and services (Belous, 1989). Subcontracting of peripheral functions, such as groundskeeping, and of less skilled production work decouples wages of the changed job categories from those of the firm's core workers (Belous, 1989). Hence, unskilled workers may be removed from the incentive system used to retain highly skilled workers. This process may sever career lines within the firm—unskilled jobs that previously were portals to training and skilled jobs may no longer provide entry to an age-structured career.

Changing Pension Arrangements

Changes in pension plans reinforce the evidence for a weakening of the emphasis on age-structured employment. The postwar increase in pension coverage has meant that successive cohorts of retirees have higher levels of pension receipt. Among workers, pension coverage increased until 1975 and has been static since then (Quinn & Burkhauser, 1990). One reason for the lack of increase has been relative growth of service industries, which produces a compositional effect on coverage. Manufacturing has relatively high pension coverage (75.8% in 1987). While some services, such as finance (70.5%) and professional services (75.0%) have high pension coverage, others such as retail trade (46.8%) have lower coverage (Short & Nelson, 1991). Most workers with pensions are in defined benefit plans, but defined contribution plans have become more common in recent years. The proportion of active pension plan participants in defined contribution plans increased from 9.6% to 20.3% between 1977 and 1985 (Clark & McDermed, 1990). Defined benefit plans usually compute pensions using a combination of length of service and final years' earnings. This benefit structure provides a disincentive to leave the current job, unless the new job carries a substantially higher wage, since the pension entitlement resulting from early-career years is based on the worker's final earnings with the firm (Clark & McDermed, 1990; Quinn, Burkhauser, & Myers, 1990). Final earnings generally rise with later exit from the firm. Therefore, the value of past service increases with seniority, producing one aspect of an age-structured career.

In contrast, defined contribution plans promise a stated, current-year contribution with future investment risk borne by the employee. There is generally no disincentive for a late-career switch to another employer (Clark & McDermed, 1990). Employers increasingly choose defined contribution plans because they have lower administrative costs accruing from less government regulation (Clark & McDermed, 1990). In addition, defined contribution plans require less employer assumption of risk and more predictable costs. While employers have not necessarily switched to defined contribution plans because they wish to deemphasize age structuring of employment, the shift has that effect.

Continuing Change or One-Time Shift?

Just as a number of processes led to an increase in the age structuring of employment during the first half of this century, a number of factors that limit age structuring now seem to be at work. These include within-firm efforts to address changing competition, shifting industry patterns of employment, and changing pension arrangements. While most workers continue to work within age-structured internal labor markets, there is accumulating evidence that the prevalence of such arrangements has at least peaked and may be receding.

An unsettled issue is whether the "flexible" organization of work, of which age-structuring is only one part, is a cyclical adjustment to the economic dislocations of the 1970s and 1980s (Dunlop, 1988) or is part of a continuing, long-term pattern of change (Freeman, 1988). Answering this question requires a longer time perspective. Yet, the disparate changes that affect age structuring today are unlikely to be reversed at the same time.

SHIFTING WORK ORGANIZATION AND LATE-LIFE WORK EXIT

Explanations of retirement timing have often emphasized age-dependent changes in the individual. Work-related resources may decline as health declines and skills become obsolete. Concomitantly, there is age increment in pension and social welfare eligibility. The firm plays a secondary role in this general perspective, affecting individual trajectories through the level of pensions, seniority-based careers, and employer investment in training (Graebner, 1980; Kaufman & Spilerman, 1982; Pampel & Weiss, 1983). These same themes are also central to economic explanations (for a recent review, see Hurd, 1990).

It is likely, however, that firm-based changes in the organization of work are increasingly important contributors to the within-cohort variability in retirement timing. As within-firm employment is organized to utilize more contingent workers or as firms and industries adjust to changing employment patterns, some older workers are likely to exit lifetime jobs at earlier ages through routes other than "regular" retirement after age 62. Since the process differs by firm, industry, and job classification, the use of irregular pathways may increase variability in career endings. Among U.S. workers, the three major early exit routes are job loss, early and regular pensions, and disability (Sheppard, 1991).

Job Loss

The growing literature on the effects of industrial growth and decline (e.g., Birch, 1987; Greene, 1982) focuses on change in the distribution of jobs induced by constant processes of job creation and destruction. Job elimination and creation constantly reshape the workforce. Their rate may be increased by changes in work organization and industry distribution of employment. Industrial contraction, one part of dynamic adjustment, has important effects on older workers. Herz

(1991) finds that experienced older workers were slightly less likely than younger workers to lose their jobs because of plant closings, slack work, or abolition of positions; yet, 7.6% of employed workers 55 to 64 years old lost their jobs between 1979 and 1983 and 6.5% between 1985 and 1989. Hence, over the decade, about 14% of older workers lost jobs (assuming no double counting). Factory workers were strongly overrepresented among displaced workers, especially between 1979 and 1983. The significance of the continued job loss during the latter period, which was one of economic expansion, is that job loss is not limited to periods of economic decline. Though Herz does not provide data on reemployment by age, the overall characteristics of those reemployed suggests use of "bridge jobs" discussed later in this chapter. For example, half of those displaced between 1985 and 1989 and reemployed by 1990 changed industries, one-quarter received wages at least 20% below their former jobs, and nearly one-tenth held part-time jobs.

Based on other research, there are also indications that job exits for older workers may be permanent ones. Hausman and Paquette (1987) use LRHS data to estimate that 86% of men 58 to 62 who lost their previous job did not find another. Opportunities for new jobs decline with age (Hutchens, 1988), and evidence of difficulties in finding substitute jobs and the decreased wage offers to many workers who previously held internal-market jobs (Cohen & Zysman, 1987; Yellen, 1984) imply late-career job losses may become permanent. In addition, the availability of early pension or disability benefits to some workers (Osterman, 1988; Sheppard, 1991) also encourage permanent work exit.

Pensions

Even though most firm pensions today are highly age-structured defined benefit pensions, their use in recent years has produced some early exits. First, more members of successive cohorts have been eligible for increasingly generous regular-age private pensions. Many large pension plans provide regular options for retirement at 60 or younger; and almost all pensions offer early retirement options (Ippolito, 1990; Schulz, 1985). Quinn, Burkhauser, and Myers (1990) review extensive research showing that many pension plans contain strong incentives for exit at earliest possible pension eligibility.

A second important pension trend has been the increased use of early retirement incentives that may be offered to only some of the firm's workers, have a limited acceptance period, or include extra incentives for retirement. These incentive plans illustrate the uses of pension plans to adjust to changing markets, new technology, or a changing mix of lifetime and contingent workers. The outcome is an early exit for some older workers. During the 1980s, about 40% of U.S. firms with more than 1,000 employees offered special early retirement incentives (Meier, 1986). These offers continue. LaRock (1992) reports that 23% of employers offered incentives in 1986 and 16% did so in 1991. Early pension offers are highly variable within a firm; their targets vary by production technology in use and management's need to retain certain skills (Kohli, Rosenow, & Wolf, 1983), thus creating within- and between-firm variability.

Bridge Jobs and Returns to Work

Patterns of job loss and early pension offers produce more variable paths out of the labor force. Some workers are affected, whereas others are not. Early exit may occur before the individual is ready to retire, and some early exiters may return to work in new jobs. Researchers have become more interested in this issue in recent years and have developed a range of evidence that suggests late-life job exit and entry patterns characterize a significant and increasing minority of older workers.

The concept of bridge jobs (Doeringer, 1990; Ruhm, 1990) focuses on jobs held after a career job (defined as the individual's longest job) and used as a "bridge" to retirement. Sometimes these postcareer jobs (as defined earlier) are part of an age-structured career and have higher wages (e.g., a professor moving to a new university appointment), but more often they are jobs in different occupations and industries and carry lower wages. Using the Longitudinal Retirement History Study (LRHS), Ruhm, (1990) estimates more than half the workers in the 1906–1911 birth cohort left their career job by age 60, but only 1 in 9 had retired. Quinn, Burkhauser, and Myers (1990) analyze late switches to bridge jobs. They analyze LRHS workers who left a full-time job after age 58, had at least 10 years' tenure on the job, and were observed at least 4 years after exit. About one-quarter of wage and salary workers had some labor force experience after that exit. Part- or full-time work on a different job was the most common pattern.

There is some evidence that irregular exits are becoming more common. Elder and Pavalko (1993) use the Terman data to compare men's late-life work exit patterns in the 1900–1909 and 1910–1920 cohorts. The Terman data collection began in the 1920s and included high-ability children. The data have limited generalizability, but provide rich comparative material on two cohorts. Elder and Pavalko find that the proportion of men retiring by permanent and abrupt exit declined between the two cohorts, whereas the number of complete exits and later returns increased. Some further evidence comes from Hayward, Grady, and McLaughlin's (1988) comparison of exit and entry rates between 1972 and 1980. Using Current Population Survey data, they find that the volume of early exits and reentries was larger in 1980, particularly in unskilled, high physical demand occupations.

This evidence is important because it challenges the conventional view of career jobs ending in regular retirement and suggests that significant segments of the workforce follow highly diverse pathways to labor force exit. Further, the data on increased use of returns to work is consistent with the trends toward earlier exit, job loss among older workers, and greater use of contingent labor. Still, the evidence on bridge jobs may overstate the degree of disruption in late careers since some late job shifts are normal parts of career lines that are organized outside firms.

THE ROLE OF THE STATE IN RETIREMENT

Though this chapter emphasizes age structuring by the workplace, the institutions of the state also affect age structuring. Workplace social structure has its effect in the context of state regulation, and it is not possible to discuss increasing within-cohort variability without considering the state role. For example, state pension regulation affects the type of pensions offered by employers. However, the state's influence is seen most directly in two important pathways to work exit that are sponsored by the state: disability benefits and Social Security retirement benefits.

Disability

The Social Security disability program has grown in recent years, though not in a monotonic way. The number of new awards peaked in 1975, declined until 1985, but then rose 13% between 1985 and 1989 (Social Security Administration, 1990: Table 6.A1). Disability benefits may be paid at any age, but about 65% of those who become entitled to disability benefits are over age 50 (Hennessey & Dykacz, 1989). Those surviving to age 65 and not recovering automatically convert to regular retirement benefits. Of those who qualify after age 50, 62% eventually convert (Hennessey & Dykacz, 1989). The disability pathway is an important early route out of the labor force. Of those first receiving retirement benefits in 1989, 11% were converting from disability (Social Security Administration, 1990: Table 6.A4). Hence, roughly 10% of recent cohorts follow this pathway to final labor force exit.

Since disability qualification is an individual event, it introduces additional variability into early labor force exit (Henretta, 1992). There is considerable evidence that disability benefit receipt reflects a variable administrative process, not changing levels of older workers' health. Disability benefits require subjective administrative certification (Mezey, 1988), are awarded to highly variable proportions of applicants from year to year (Social Security Administration, 1983); and awards are not always correlated with disability level (Berkowitz, Johnson, & Murphy, 1976).

Retirement Programs

Changes in Social Security benefit ages and amounts have had an important effect on retirement age. Hurd (1990) reviews the evidence and concludes that Social Security's higher benefit levels beginning in the early 1970s have led to earlier retirement, but there is disagreement among empirical estimates of the size of the effect. Nonetheless, it is likely that Social Security changes, combined with increases in employer pensions (Quinn & Burkhauser, 1990) are very important in the decline in retirement age. Unlike other exit pathways, Social Security reduces variance because of its nearly-universal eligibility at a uniform age (Henretta, 1992).

VARIABILITY IN EXIT TIMING

The decline in retirement age in successive birth cohorts is the most visible change in retirement patterns. For example, 75% of men in the 1906–1910 birth cohort were in the labor force at ages 60 to 64 while 55.5% of men in the 1926–1930 cohort were in the labor force at that age (Gendell & Siegel, 1992). Retirement ages have declined for both men and women; declines were greatest in the 1970s, and there has been little change since 1985 (Gendell & Siegel, 1992).

Less visible but more important for discussions of age-structured life course institutionalization is evidence for increasing diversity in the timing of early retirement. Henretta (1992) examines variability in the time cohorts of men require to complete the retirement transition, defined by the time required for the proportion of a cohort out of the labor force to increase from 25% to 75% (the interquartile range).

The analysis shows a definite decline in the overall interquartile range for successive cohorts born between 1900 and 1920. Yet, over the cohorts examined, there are divergent patterns for the periods before and after median exit age. Exit after the median age occurs over a shorter period than in the past, whereas exit before the median age occurs over a very slightly longer period.

Declining levels of labor force participation at each age and increasing variability in early exit are linked. With nearly half a cohort exiting before age 62, the first half of a cohort exits before universal eligibility for Social Security retirement benefits. Labor force exit at these ages is more affected by the highly variable structure of the workplace and the Social Security disability program. The small increase in early exit variance may result from greater variability in the workplace, or solely from a higher proportion of the before-median exits occurring at ages when workplace factors are most important. In either case, workplace variance is more important as higher proportions of successive cohorts exit before Social Security retirement benefit eligibility.

At the same time, the overall trend toward less variance qualifies claims that labor force outcomes (measured by cohort exit) have become more diverse. Social Security benefits with their increasing level and near-universal eligibility have reduced the third quartile times, after median exit. Hence, there is a divergence in effects of universal state benefits and highly diverse workplace arrangements (Casey, 1989).

CHANGING SOCIAL STRUCTURE AND THE PATTERN OF INDIVIDUAL LIVES

The life course perspective seeks to link individual trajectories to social structure. Period-specific social structure and age interact, producing cohort differences in the effect of social change. This chapter argues that today's older workers are completing their work careers in a changed environment. Drawing the picture in very broad strokes, today's new retirees entered the labor force during the postwar era. At least for men, this period was the peak of the use of internal market labor organization though a significant minority held contingent jobs. The cohort is retiring at a time when internal market organization is under pressure. For older workers, this trend produces more diverse exit patterns from age-structured careers while younger cohorts experience fewer opportunities to enter such careers. Popular discussion of employment changes often focuses on a decline in the quality of work life; another, and important, analytic perspective focuses on the increase in differentiation between and within cohorts in career trajectories.

Patterns of institutionalization of the life course are likely to be domain- and period-specific. Trends discussed in this chapter do not necessarily imply a broad and long-lasting trend toward greater individuation of people's lives. To the extent that there is a broad social trend toward greater institutionalization or individuation, it is supported by a large number of trends in diverse aspects of the social structure. Growing individuation of exit from employment is an important example of this process. There are diverse trends in firm organization, the industrial structure of the economy, and pension structure that together seem to be diminishing the pattern of age-structured careers that grew up during the first half of this century. The short-term effect is likely to be greater individuation of employment careers. At the same time, it is important not to draw long-term conclusions based on an extrapolation of current trends because work careers may span as many as 40 years, making it common for a cohort to retire in a social, political, and economic environment very different from the time of their labor force entry. While greater variance in exit appears to be the effect for today's older workers, it is far too early to draw conclusions about the retirement fate of those now entering the labor force.

Moreover, the social structure of the workplace overlays other patterns of variability, creating a complex mosaic of career patterns across sex and race categories. Hence, the changing workplace constitutes only one factor affecting the pattern of individual lives. Women have always been more likely to be in contingent jobs. Their entry into employment during the 1970s was an important factor in the growth of contingent labor during this period (Osterman, 1988; Tilly, 1991). Major gender differences are likely to remain, but the trends discussed here may reduce gender structuring of employment as more women have greater lifetime labor force participation and as more men are in the contingent labor force (see O'Rand, 1988; 1990 for a more extensive discussion of women's labor force careers). Blacks and Hispanics have also always been overrepresented in the contingent labor force. Hence, their retirement patterns have never conformed to the model of the internal market exit portal (Gibson, 1987; Zsembik & Singer, 1990). Unemployment is often hard to distinguish from retirement, and exit occurs in diverse ways. William J. Wilson (1987) argues that decline in the availability of industrial, internal market jobs as well as change in the types of jobs available in urban areas has played an important role in increasing variability in the economic fate of blacks, particularly younger cohorts, along skill lines. In the long run, these changes may lead to greater variability in late-life work exit patterns among blacks.

IMPLICATIONS FOR STRUCTURAL LAG

Since declining lifetime age-structured employment implies less security and expanded use of irregular retirement paths, a standard conclusion is that reduced age structuring is undesirable. Overemphasis on this view, however, does not do adequate justice to the complexity of careers. First, large numbers of jobs remain in internal markets, and those workers have increasing protection with age. Second, large numbers of workers have always been in contingent jobs; and Osterman

(1988) argues that the internal market job structure has been maintained during the postwar period by a large contingent labor force, including many women, who provide a buffer allowing firms to maintain their protected workforce.

In addition, although changing employment policies lead to less secure jobs and earlier-than-desired work exit for some workers, a larger number of temporary and part-time jobs provide some opportunities for older and younger workers who do not wish full-time career employment. The growth of contingent employment is cold comfort to an older worker who has lost a full-time, high-wage job through downsizing and is not yet ready to retire. But, some retirees may view temporary or part-time jobs as desirable opportunities to supplement pension income without a full-time career commitment. Workers at all levels of skill may have greater opportunities for part-time or temporary work than in the past. Employers are less likely to discriminate against older workers in part-time or temporary work because such jobs are not entry portals to careers carrying fringe benefits, training, and implicit commitments.

An important effect of workplace changes, including increasing proportions of contingent jobs, is likely to be greater within-cohort variability in career patterns at all ages. This change will reduce age-based expectations and stereotypes. Age will still structure employment careers, but not to the extent that it did in the past. Most observers will applaud reduced age constraints, but it is also important to consider ways to reduce the costs borne by individuals affected by workplace changes.

Current institutional arrangements, primarily the employment-based provision of social welfare in the United States (Titmus, 1969; O'Rand, 1988), do not make adequate allowance for the portion of a cohort affected by shifting workplace arrangements. Both health insurance and pensions are tied to employment; and one reason employers use more contingent labor is to reduce fringe-benefit costs (Belous, 1990). In recent years, pension coverage has been stagnant, and growing numbers of Americans of all ages lack health insurance. The employer-based welfare system is likely to decrease life course coherence (cf. Kohli, 1987) for that portion of a cohort exiting in irregular ways—for example, through unemployment.

Health insurance provides an important example because most workers exit the labor force before age-65 Medicare eligibility.

Medicare was designed in an era when retirement came later than it does today, and its underlying assumption is that younger persons are covered through employer-based arrangements. While most early retirement incentive plans do provide for continuation of employer-paid health insurance until Medicare eligibility (LaRock, 1992), some workers "slip through the cracks." In addition, some workers exit from jobs that do not provide health insurance for any of their employees. The lack of universally available institutional arrangements to bridge the gap between early exit and regular retirement age is produced by the U.S. dependence on variable, employer-based early exit provisions (Casey, 1989; Sheppard, 1991). In an era of increasingly variable career and retirement patterns, the result is unexpected breaks and disruption in late-life transitions for some cohort members.

REFERENCES

Akerlof, G. A. (1982). Labor contracts as partial gift exchanges. *Quarterly Journal of Economics, 97,* 543–569.

Anderson, M. (1985). The emergence of the modern life cycle in Britain. *Social History, 10,* 69–87.

Belous, R. S. (1989). *The contingent economy: The growth of the temporary, part-time and subcontracted workforce.* Washington, DC: National Planning Association.

Belous, R. S. (1990). Flexible employment: The employer's point of view. In P. Doeringer (Ed.), *Bridges to retirement* (pp. 111–129). Ithaca, NY: ILR Press.

Berkowitz, M., Johnson, W. G., & Murphy, E. H. (1976). *Public policy toward disability.* New York: Praeger.

Birch, D. L. (1987). *Job creation in America.* New York: Free Press.

Bulow, J. I., & Summers, L. H. (1986). A theory of dual labor markets with application to industrial policy, discrimination, and Kenysian unemployment. *Journal of Labor Economics, 4,* 376–414.

Casey, B. (1989). Early retirement: The problems of 'instrument substitution' and 'cost shifting' and their implications for restructuring the process of retirement. In W. Schmahl (Ed.), *Redefining the process of retirement* (pp. 133–150). Berlin: Springer.

Clark, R. L., & McDermed, A. A. (1990). *The choice of pension plans in a changing regulatory environment.* Washington, DC: American Enterprise Institute.

Cohen, S. S., & Zysman, J. (1987). *Manufacturing matters: The myth of the post-industrial economy.* New York: Basic.

Doeringer, P. B. (Ed.). (1990). Economic security, labor market flexibility, and bridges to retirement. *Bridges to retirement* (pp. 3–22). Ithaca, NY: ILR Press.

Dunlop, J. T. (1988). Have the 1980s changed U.S. industrial relations? *Monthly Labor Review, 115*, 29–34.

Economic Report of the President. (1991). Washington, DC: U.S. Government Printing Office.

Elder, G. H., Jr., & Pavalko, E. K. (1993). Work careers in men's later years: Transitions, trajectories, and historical change. *Journal of Gerontology,* in press.

Freeman, A. (1988). How the 1980s have changed industrial relations. *Monthly Labor Review, 115*, 35–38.

Gendell, M., & Siegel, J. S. (1992). Trends in retirement age by sex, 1950–2005. *Monthly Labor Review, 115*, 22–29.

Gibson, R. C. (1987). Reconceptualizing retirement for Black Americans. *The Gerontologist, 27*, 691–698.

Graebner, W. (1980). *A history of retirement: The meaning and function of an American institution, 1885–1978.* New Haven, CT: Yale.

Greene, R. (1982). Tracking job growth in private industry. *Monthly Labor Review, 105*, 3–9.

Guillemard, A. M. (1989). The trend towards early labour force withdrawal and the reorganization of the life course: A cross-national analysis. In P. Johnson, C. Conrad, & D. Thomson (Eds.), *Workers versus pensioners: Intergenerational justice in an aging world* (pp. 163–180). Manchester: Manchester University.

Hareven, T. K. (1982). *Family time and industrial time.* Cambridge: Cambridge University.

Hausman, J. A., & Paquette, L. (1987). Involuntary early retirement and consumption. In G. Burtless (Ed.), *Work, health, and income among the elderly* (pp. 151–181). Washington, DC: Brookings.

Hayward, M. D., Grady, W. R., & McLaughlin, S. D. (1988). Changes in the retirement process among older men in the United States: 1972–1980. *Demography, 25*, 371–386.

Held, T. (1986). Institutionalization and deinstitutionalization of the life course. *Human Development, 29*, 157–162.

Hennessey, J. C., & Dykacz, J. M. (1989). Projected outcomes and length of time in the disability insurance program. *Social Security Bulletin, 52*, 2–41.

Henretta, J. C. (1992). Uniformity and diversity: Life course institutionalization and late-life work exit. *The Sociological Quarterly, 33*, 265–279.

Herz, D. E. (1991). Worker displacement still common in the late 1980s. *Monthly Labor Review, 114*, 3–9.

Hodson, R. (1983). *Workers' earnings and corporate economic structure.* New York: Academic.

Hogan, D. P. (1981). *Transitions and social change: The early lives of American men.* New York: Academic.

Hurd, M. D. (1990). Research on the elderly: Economic status, retirement, and consumption and saving. *Journal of Economic Literature, 28,* 565–637.

Hutchens, R. M. (1988). Do job opportunities decline with age? *Industrial and Labor Relations Review, 42,* 89–99.

Ippolito, R. A. (1990). Toward explaining earlier retirement after 1970. *Industrial and Labor Relations Review, 43,* 556–569.

Jacoby, S. M. (1985). *Employing bureaucracy.* New York: Columbia University.

Kaufman, R. L., & Spilerman, S. (1982). The age structures of occupations and jobs. *American Journal of Sociology, 87,* 827–851.

Kohli, M. (1986). The world we forgot: A historical review of the life course. In V. W. Marshall (Ed.), *Later life: The social psychology of aging* (pp. 271–303). Beverly Hills, CA: Sage.

Kohli, M. (1987). Retirement and the moral economy: A historical interpretation of the German case. *Journal of Aging Studies, 1,* 125–144.

Kohli, M., & Meyer, J. W. (1986). Social structure and social construction of life stages. *Human Development, 29,* 145–149.

Kohli, M., Rosenow, J., & Wolf, J. (1983). The social construction of aging through work: Economic structure and life-world. *Aging and Society, 3,* 23–42.

LaRock, S. (1992 August). Both private and public sector employers use early retirement sweeteners. *Employee Benefit Plan Review,* 14–20.

Lazear, E. (1979). Why is there mandatory retirement? *Journal of Political Economy, 87,* 1261–1284.

Mayer, K. U., & Schoepflin, U. (1989). The state and the life course. *Annual Review of Sociology, 15,* 187–209.

Meier, E. L. (1986). *Early retirement incentive programs: Trends and implications* (Research Paper 8604). Washington, DC: AARP Public Policy Institute.

Mezey, S. G. (1988). *No longer disabled: The federal courts and the politics of Social security disability.* New York: Greenwood.

Noyelle, T. J. (1987). *Beyond industrial dualism: Market and job segmentation in the new economy.* Boulder, CO: Westview Press.

O'Rand, A. M. (1988). Convergence, institutionalization and bifurcation: Gender and the pension acquisition process. In G. L. Maddox & M. P. Lawton (Eds.), *Annual review of gerontology and geriatrics* (pp. 132–155). New York: Springer.

O'Rand, A. M. (1990). Stratification and the life course. In R. H. Binstock & L. K. George (Eds.), *Handbook of aging and the social sciences* (pp. 130–148). New York: Academic Press.

Osterman, P. (1988). *Employment futures.* New York: Oxford.

Pampel, F. C., & Weiss, J. A. (1983). Economic development, pension policies, and the labor force participation of aged males: A cross-national longitudinal approach. *American Journal of Sociology, 89,* 350–372.

Polivka, A. E., & Nardone, T. (1989). On the definition of "contingent work." *Monthly Labor Review, 112,* 9–16.

Quinn, J. F., & Burkhauser, R. V. (1990). Work and retirement. In R. H. Binstock & L. K. George (Eds.), *Handbook of aging and the social sciences* (pp. 308–327). New York: Academic Press.

Quinn, J. F., Burkhauser, R. V., & Myers, D. A. (1990). *Passing the torch: The influence of economic incentives on work and retirement.* Kalamazoo, MI: Upjohn Institute for Employment Research.

Ransom, R. L., & Sutch, R. (1986). The labor of older Americans: Retirement of men on and off the job, 1870–1937. *Journal of Economic History, 46,* 1–30.

Riley, M. W. (1987). On the significance of age in sociology. *American Sociological Review, 52,* 1–14.

Ruhm, C. J. (1990). Career jobs, bridge employment, and retirement. In P. B. Doeringer (Ed.), *Bridges to retirement* (pp. 92–110). Ithaca, NY: ILR Press.

Schulz, J. H. (1985). *The economics of aging.* Belmont, CA: Wadsworth.

Sheppard, H. L. (1991). The United States: The privatization of exit. In M. Kohli, M. Rein, A. M. Guillemard, & H. van Gunsteren (Eds.), *Time for retirement: Comparative studies of early exit from the labor force* (pp. 252–283). Cambridge: Cambridge University.

Short, K., & Nelson, C. (1991). Pensions: Worker coverage and retirement benefits, 1987. *Current Population Reports, P-70,* no. 25. Washington, DC: Bureau of the Census.

Social Security Administration. (1983). *Characteristics of Social security disability insurance beneficiaries.* Washington, DC: U.S. Government Printing Office.

Social Security Administration. (1990). *Social security bulletin: Annual statistical supplement.* Washington, DC: U.S. Government Printing Office.

Spilerman, S. (1977). Careers, labor market structure, and socioeconomic achievement. *American Journal of Sociology, 83,* 551–593.

Tilly, C. (1991). Reasons for continuing growth of part-time employment. *Monthly Labor Review, 114,* 10–18.

Titmus, R. M. (1969). *Essays on the welfare state.* London: Allen & Unwin.

Uhlenberg, P. (1978). Changing configurations of the life course. In T. K. Hareven (Ed.), *Transitions: The family and the life course in historical perspective* (pp. 65–97). New York: Academic.

Weidenbaum, M. (1988). *Rendezvous with reality.* New York: Basic.

Williamson, O. E. (1981). The economics of organization: The transaction cost approach. *American Journal of Sociology, 87,* 548–577.

Wilson, W. J. (1987). *The truly disadvantaged.* Chicago, IL: University of Chicago Press.

Yellen, J. L. (1984). Efficiency wage models of unemployment. *American Economic Review, 74,* 200–205.

Zsembik, B. A., & Singer, A. (1990). The problem of defining retirement among minorities: The Mexican Americans. *The Gerontologist, 30,* 749–757.

CHAPTER 4

Work and Retirement: A Comparative Perspective[1]

Martin Kohli

THE PROBLEM: EARLY EXIT FROM WORK

The decrease in the age of exit from gainful work has been one of the most profound structural changes in the past 25 years. It has occurred—albeit to differing degrees—in all Western societies, irrespective of their institutional regimes. In the recent history of these societies, there are few trends as consistent and homogeneous as this one. The period spent in gainful work is shrinking, with early exit at the upper and the extension of schooling at the lower end of the work life contributing to this outcome from both sides. The period spent in retirement is lengthening from both sides as well, with early exit at the lower and increasing life expectancy at the upper end. Thus, what has been the "normal

---

[1] Parts of this chapter are based on a recently published comparative study of early exit from work in Europe and the United States (Kohli, Rein, Guillemard, & van Gunsteren, 1991), and specifically, on the introductory chapter written together with Martin Rein, and on the chapter that documents the labor force participation trend written together with Klaus Jacobs and Martin Rein. I am grateful to my colleagues for their continued contributions, which go much beyond the texts that we have produced together.

life course" is massively reorganized, and the relations between age groups and generations are redefined.

Moreover, the trend is (on first sight at least) highly perplexing and even paradoxical. In a period of increasing life expectancy, of increasing concern with the financial viability of the public pension systems, and of increasing admonitions from gerontologists about the fallacy of age stereotypes regarding work performance and productivity, why should there be such a pervasive tendency to leave work earlier and earlier? The paradox defies easy explanations; by posing the question of how life phases and the boundaries between them—especially the all-important boundaries between work and nonwork periods—are socially constructed, it is perhaps the most explicit challenge for life course theory. It also challenges most current assumptions about the effects of social policy by contrasting the explanatory potential of theories that focus on the state as the key actor and those that focus on actors in the economic sphere. Thus the trend toward early exit not only presents an explanatory task by itself but is also a theoretical window on the social construction of aging and the life course in general, and on the articulation of the economy and the polity.

The consequences for social policy concern the public old-age insurance system as well as some of the other welfare programs that have been created to cover the financial risks associated with not being able to work, such as unemployment and disability insurance. With the decreasing age of exit from work, these programs that were originally aimed at exceptional risks are now increasingly being used to manage the normal transition phase, and are therefore put under increasing strain.

The strain for the welfare state is intensified by the process of population aging that all Western societies face. Old-age insurance—which has long been the most popular and least controversial part of modern social welfare, and thus a cornerstone of the "moral economy" of these societies (cf. Kohli, 1987)—is becoming a focus of political controversy. The questions of intergenerational equity take on a new urgency, and some observers predict that the competition for resources between age groups or generations will emerge as one of the main arenas of social conflict (cf. Johnson, Conrad, & Thomson, 1989). In this situation, reversing the trend of early exit seems to offer an easy solution. In the United States, Germany, and Japan, measures to raise the age limit of eligibility for public pensions have been passed, and in other countries, they are under discussion. There are also many proposals for creating more flexible and gradual forms of transition from work to retirement.

But the knowledge base of this discussion is still inadequate. For delineating the possibilities and the likely consequences of raising the pension age, it is necessary to get a clear picture of what has happened so far. This is the main purpose of this chapter. In the following sections, I will (1) give some comparative evidence of the trend, (2) address how it can be explained, (3) explore the effects of the massive form of early exit now occurring in the transformation of Eastern European economies, and (4) assess the options for the future.

THE COMPARATIVE EVIDENCE

In confronting the paradox of early exit from work, each country has tended to believe that it is special. The trend toward early exit has thus usually been interpreted as the consequence of some particular twist of the particular country's social welfare system. For instance, much of the U.S. literature assumes that the only phenomena to be explained are those within the United States itself; this perspective simply ignores the experience of other countries. Germany, as another example, has a tradition of viewing its development in terms of a "special path" (*Sonderweg*) to modernization and thus is easily misled into beliefs of uniqueness.

What is required instead is a rigorously comparative approach. There is now a small but growing body of comparative studies of welfare regimes (e.g., Esping-Andersen, 1990; Flora, 1986; Gordon, 1988; Ritter, 1989), and of old-age security as an important part of them (e.g., Williamson & Pampel, 1993). But while in many respects these studies can serve as a model for the questions to be asked and the answers to be expected, they do not go sufficiently deep into the changing balance of work and retirement.

Exit from Work

For a comparative analysis of early exit, data on participation in pension programs are not sufficient because there is a wide range of intermediary arrangements between work and retirement proper (in the sense of drawing an old-age pension). These arrangements can be thought of as institutional pathways from work into retirement (cf. Kohli & Rein, 1991). They are to a large extent functionally equivalent but not easily comparable in institutional terms.

A better account of the exit process can be obtained by using data on labor force participation. These data have been made available by the Organization for Economic Cooperation and Development (OECD) for a number of countries since the mid-1960s. In principle, they are produced by following a common measurement concept, which considers as employed all persons who gainfully work at least one hour per week. In practice there are some difficulties, especially with regard to very low hours of work where results are affected by the form of measurement. But as comparative data go, the labor force participation data are certainly among the more reliable.

The basic data on male labor force participation for the six Western countries included in our study (Kohli, Rein, et al., 1991) are presented in Figures 4–1 to 4–3. (For a more detailed analysis, cf. Jacobs, Kohli, & Rein, 1991; OECD Employment Outlook, 1992; Chapter 5.) The group of men ages 60 to 64 (Figure 4–2) documents best how retirement has been redefined. Age 65 cannot be regarded as the "normal" age limit any longer if less than one-third (France, West Germany, The Netherlands) or only about one-half (United Kingdom, United States) of the male population between 60 and 64 are still part of the labor force. The highest rate—almost two-thirds—is found in Sweden; but it has shown a distinct decline as well. And it has to be kept in mind that with the labor force participation rates (which include unemployment), we obtain a conservative estimate. The levels are even lower and the downward trend is even stronger if we examine only those who are employed (employment activity rates, Figure 4–4).

The data for women at first sight differ considerably from those for men, and are also quite different across countries. Participation rates for women below 65 have declined in some countries but remained stable or even increased in others. Thus, there seems to be no trend toward early exit. Such a conclusion, however, is an artifact produced by the cross-sectional data presented so far. When the data are arranged by cohorts, women also tend to leave the work force at increasingly younger ages. At least for West Germany (Figure 4–5), the cohort data document that there are two overlapping trends: increasing general

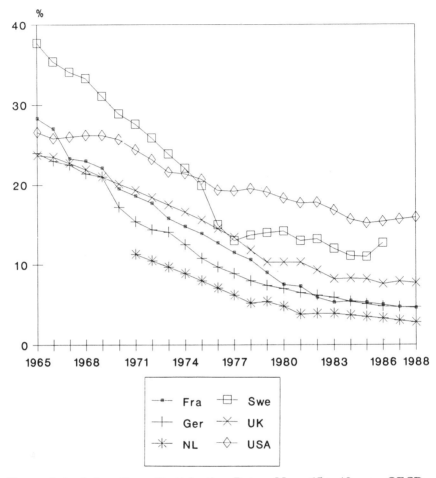

Figure 4-1 Labor Force Participation Rates: Men, 65+ (*Source:* OECD Labour Force Statistics, Paris, 1984/1989)

labor force participation as well as early exit. Each successive cohort starts the exit process from a higher level, has a steeper decline, and reaches age 61 on a lower level.[2]

Obviously, the shortening of the work life has been a key mechanism of adaptation to the shrinking demand for and/or the increasing supply of workers. To be sure, it has not been the only such mechanism—it

---

[2] For France, the picture is somewhat less clear but similar, while for the United States, there are almost no differences across successive cohorts.

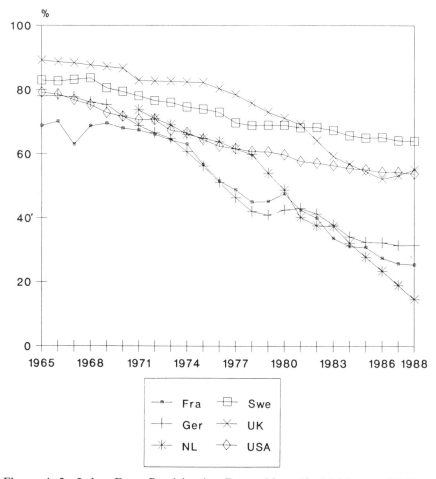

Figure 4-2   Labor Force Participation Rates: Men, 60–64 (*Source:* OECD Labour Force Statistics, Paris, 1984/1989)

has been paralleled in some countries by a shortening of yearly work time (cf. Hinrichs, Roche, & Sirianni, 1991). But the tripartition of the male life course into a period of preparation, one of "activity" in the sense of gainful work, and one of retirement has remained in place. The early exit of older workers has been instrumental in maintaining this basic structure of the modern life course. As for women, their growing labor force participation means that they, too, are increasingly integrated into this life course pattern. The extent to which early

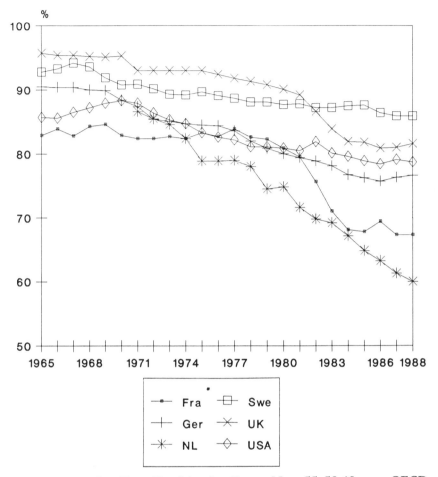

Figure 4-3 Labor Force Participation Rates: Men, 55–59 (*Source:* OECD Labour Force Statistics, Paris, 1984/1989)

exit has changed the balance of work and retirement can be illustrated by the fact that in West Germany, the median age of exit for males (as measured by the aggregate participation rates) dropped, between 1960 and 1985, by roughly 5 years (from 65 to 60). Given that life expectancy at age 60 rose somewhat (for males, roughly from 15¹/₂ to 17 years) during this period, the mean duration of retirement has increased by almost two-thirds.

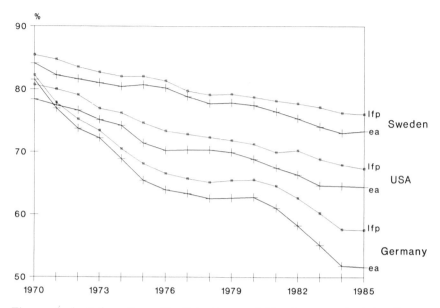

Figure 4–4 Labor Force Participation and Employment Activity Rates: Men, 55–64 (*Source:* OECD Labour Force Statistics, Paris, 1986, and calculations by K. Jacobs)

Work to Retirement Transition

The aggregate data presented here show that work and retirement remain distinctly set off against each other but that the transition period between the two has become longer and institutionally more diffuse. There is increasing universality of the occurrence of the transition to retirement, but also increasing variability of its timing, indicating a tendency toward greater individuation (Henretta, 1992).

The transition period is shaped by the institutional repertoire of labor market and social policies available in each country, and for individuals, by the interplay between working conditions and work incomes, social security, and private resources. In rough outline, several national patterns can be distinguished (cf. Rein & Jacobs, 1993):

- In the welfare systems of continental Western Europe (France, West Germany, The Netherlands, etc.), male workers usually move directly from full-time work to full-time nonwork, with

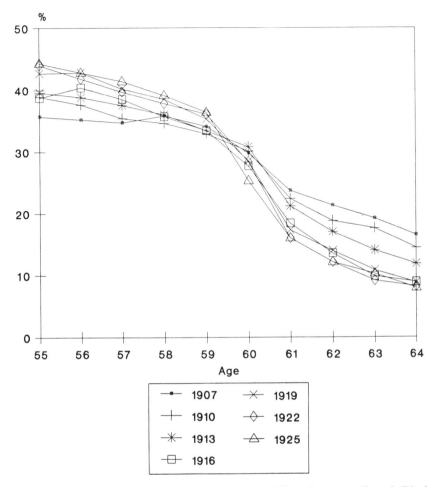

Figure 4-5 Labor Force Participation Rates in West Germany: Female Birth Cohorts by Age (*Source:* Calculations by K. Jacobs)

the public pension systems providing for fairly high income replacement rates. There is a large variety of institutional pathways between work and retirement, but they are mostly used for creating a one-time transition.[3]

---

[3] In West Germany, partial retirement was offered as an option by the preretirement program instituted in 1984, but it was almost universally rejected. This has also been the case with the program that replaced it, and with other partial or gradual ("gliding") retirement schemes: they have either not been taken up or turned around and "subverted" to allow for full exit at

- In Sweden, there is a high (but recently decreasing) incidence of combining a partial job (usually with the former employer) and a partial pension. It is made possible by a specific (and rather costly) public partial pension scheme and also depends on a labor shortage that serves as an incentive for firms to create jobs for partial employment.

- In the United States, the transition from work to retirement is strongly individualized. The public pension scheme has a relatively low income replacement rate, which does not allow for a continuity of lifestyle from work into retirement. Occupational pensions are an important component of retirees' total income; they are highly diversified among firms, and often take the form of lump-sum payments. Individual-level longitudinal studies show that, after exiting from their career jobs, a substantial minority of older people return to some form of jobs (Burkhauser & Quinn, 1989; but cf. Hurd, 1990, p. 596). These jobs are usually with less pay and are made available by an economy with a substantial proportion of low-income, low-qualification, low-security jobs.

- In Japan, where public pension replacement rates are again rather low, the end of "life-time employment" in the large firms also means demotion to some less desirable job. This job, however, is often arranged with the help of the former employer in the network of semidependent subsidiary firms maintained by the large firms (cf. Kii, 1987). As in the United States, this process may be seen as one form of labor market segmentation, with the marginal segment being denied the high employment security and salary typical for the core segment. The *teinen* age (at which life-time employment is regularly terminated) has traditionally been set at about 55, well below the age of eligibility for public pensions (cf. Schulz, Borowski, & Crown, 1991). Recently, there has been some public pressure on firms to raise their teinen age to the public pension age so that the gap between the two would disappear.

the earliest possible moment. Although partial retirement is recommended by many psychologists (e.g., Lehr, 1984) to ease the transition to retirement, those in charge of the transition seem to view it differently. Most companies so far have no interest in it, and neither have most workers (in part because for many it would mean being moved from their workplace and losing their seniority prerogatives).

- Still another transition had emerged in Hungary before the recent changes (Szalai, 1991), with the workers retiring from the "first" (state-controlled) economy to take up or expand some gainful activity in the "second" (informal or "shadow") one. Retirement from the state-controlled economy had been a positive event: it had meant getting more autonomy as well as being able to gain more money, with the pension topped up by incomes from the shadow economy. The possibility to retire rather early—with state pension ages set at 60 for men and 55 for women—had been conceded by the state as a measure of appeasement: as part of the new social compromise between the leadership and the working population that had been developed since the 1970s.

Thus, in a comparative view on work and retirement, it is the structure of the transition period that varies most across countries. The evolution of early exit as such, on the other hand, is highly similar.

LEVELS OF EXPLANATION

The drop of the age of exit from gainful work has come at a time when many factors seemed to point in the opposite direction. The "hardest" one has already been mentioned: Life expectancy (even at age 60) has considerably increased during this period. Also, the newer cohorts of aged people have increasingly better health and better educational resources. There have also been dramatic changes in the cultural "software" of aging. One has been the steady stream of gerontological literature since around 1960 arguing over and over again that the process of aging is not necessarily associated with a loss of functional capacity and productivity (at least not in the age bracket at issue here) and that the commonly held "deficit model" of aging should therefore be abolished. Another is the increasing emphasis on activity and social participation as being beneficial for "successful" aging. And finally, fixed age limits as criteria for the exit from gainful work and for the allocation of welfare benefits are increasingly seen as being alien to the universalistic normative regime of modern societies, with their emphasis on achievement instead of ascription, and even as being a violation of basic constitutional rights. In the countries of Western Europe, this resistance to age-based criteria has not yet had much institutional impact, but in the United States it has become institutionalized in the legislation against mandatory retirement as well as in a broad discourse on whether to replace chronological age by "functional" age as the basic criterion (cf. Neugarten, 1982).

Why then this paradoxical evolution? Explanations of the patterns of transition from work to retirement so far tend to be either on the macrolevel or on the microlevel, with very few studies that seriously try to bridge the gap. Explanations on both levels typically avoid many of the thorny issues of comparative research and therefore can be quite elegant in their simplicity.

Macrolevel Explanations

The macrolevel approach (e.g., Clark & Anker, 1990; Pampel & Weiss, 1983) usually takes a sample of nations for which the requisite data are available, and analyzes the relationship between exit from work and societal variables such as urbanization, shifts between economic sectors, economic growth, or demographic dependency rates. The underlying concept is often one of modernization theory—a theory (or family of theories) that has been in ill repute for some time but is gaining new interest as a consequence not only of theoretical refinements but also of real-world developments, especially the collapse of "real socialism." With such an approach, there is no need to go into the details of comparative work: Researchers can take the variables from a data handbook, hope that the measurements are sufficiently reliable, and treat all problems of context as "noise."[4]

This type of explanation works to the extent that the basic societal processes that are picked up by the indicators are sufficiently powerful. How does it fare with the data? For the decline of labor force participation over 65, which has been fairly continuous, a long-term societal explanation in terms of modernization or "industrialism" seems well suited.[5] For the trend toward early exit, however, the explanatory potential of this approach is more limited.

---

[4] More recent work has incorporated some contextual variables such as degree of corporatism and strength of left parties, and has complemented the cross-national regression analyses with historical case studies (Williamson & Pampel, 1993).

[5] This decline is part of the broader historical process that I have termed the "institutionalization of the life course" (Kohli, 1986): the evolution of a chronologically standardized sequence of life phases and life events, and of a set of biographical perspectives.

Microlevel Explanations

Microlevel explanations in contrast focus on the behavior of individuals. In the microeconomic approach, which has gained much prominence in recent years, individual retirement decisions are modeled as the result of the work and transfer income situation, and of the trade-off between work and leisure (cf. Hurd, 1990, for an overview). The relationship between social policy and work supply is seen as antagonistic; since any rational person chooses leisure over work in the effort to maximize personal utility, the more generous the benefits of the transfer system, the weaker must be the inclination to work. In these individual-level studies, institutional factors are considered only in terms of incentives or disincentives in the personal decision-making process. Much of the American research literature follows this approach, often implicitly presented as the only possible way of conceptualizing the transition to retirement. In my view, as in the view of the editors of this book, the approach is deficient in two respects: It is not able to explain how the institutions themselves have changed, in other words, its chains of causality are much too short; and even when treating the institutions as given (e.g., Boaz, 1988), it is insufficient as an explanation of the massive shift toward early exit because of its overly narrow model of decision making (cf. Hurd, 1990, p. 605). To mention just one important point, decisions are not the product simply of the retiring individuals themselves but also of the firms from which they retire (as becomes evident in the frequent cases of forced unemployment and in the widespread conflicts about who controls the exit process).

Bridging Macrolevels and Microlevels

An approach that bridges the gap between these two levels of explanation has to focus on the institutions and their sociopolitical context. It is this approach that we have followed in our own analysis (Kohli, Rein, et al., 1991), which emphasizes both the institutional pathways for early exit, and the "actors" (including firms, unions, and individuals) that have produced them (cf. also Schulz et al., 1991). The pathways as such do not provide a complete explanation of the exit process because they do not systematically follow the institutional structure down to the level of firms and individuals. But by documenting how the institutions have been created and changed by the aggregate actors in the fields of industrial relations and of labor market and social policy, our analysis shows how the process is regulated and to what economic and political conditions it responds (in line with the aim of Program on Age and Structural Change, PASC, as discussed in the Introduction and Chapter 1).

Here the most general issue in the debate on early exit is about the role of pull and push factors. On the institutional level, this refers above all to pension policy incentives and labor market constraints. Accordingly, there are two contrasting theories. The "pull-view"—the one underlying most studies so far—assumes that early exit is the result of social policies that have created attractive exit possibilities, for example, by lowering the age boundaries and opening new institutional pathways. There are two variants of this pull view: Proponents of the welfare state tend to see the process as an achievement, in line with long-standing demands (e.g., of unions), whereas neoclassical economists tend to see it as the undesirable outcome of a perverse incentive system that undermines the willingness to work. According to this pull theory, we should expect substantial differences among national policy regimes: Countries that have not developed the necessary social policy infrastructure will have low rates of early exit. But the data falsify this assumption.

The theoretical alternative is a structural perspective focusing on the "push factors" generated by the social organization of work—on the level not of long-term societal evolution but of middle- and short-term labor market changes. In this view, early exit takes place regardless of the available institutional pathways. Social policy cannot stop early exit from unfolding. It may be important in other respects, by molding the exit process so that it is more acceptable to some actors (corporate and individual) than others. Thus, social policy can alter the distribution of costs among actors, but it cannot altogether undo the process. Central to the structural view is the belief that if some actors are able to block access to early exit through one social policy pathway, this will force other actors to open alternative pathways. There is a process of instrument substitution (Casey, 1989); if one instrument is eliminated, another will be used to bring about the same ends.

This structural perspective is better able to deal with the empirical data, but in the preceding simplified form, it is still unsatisfactory.

The availability of institutional exits, and thus of legitimate pathways out of the labor force, has an impact: It makes early exit attractive for individual workers, and it makes it easier for firms to deal with an oversupply of labor and with the need to increase productivity. If no institutional pathways were available, early exit would occur on a much smaller scale. But institutions need not be well developed to produce early exit; even in rather limited public welfare regimes, such as the United States and (increasingly) Great Britain, early exit continues. Blocking all institutions that make early exit possible would pose major risks for industrial relations and the social contract more generally; hence it is unlikely to be attempted, much less to succeed.

The temporal pattern of early exit lends support to the push perspective. Even without a formal time-series analysis, some links with labor market changes are obvious. All six countries included in our study have been characterized by a collapse of GNP growth after 1974 in the wake of the first "oil shock," a recovery with positive growth rates in the late 1970s, and a fall to zero or even negative growth again in the early 1980s. Aggregate unemployment rates have (except for Sweden) closely followed this course, with a sizable increase after 1974, a plateau phase in the late 1970s, and another large increase in the early 1980s.

The early exit pattern thus reflects the sharp and persistent rise of unemployment. The early exit of older workers from the labor force has been one of the "bloodless" ways of coping with unemployment. This has been valid for retirement more generally; one of the most important functions of retirement is "control of unemployment" (Atchley, 1985). And it is by no means a new strategy; it was already promoted after World War I and especially during the Depression years, with slogans such as "Make room for the young!" in Germany, or "Incomes for the old, jobs for the young!" in the United States. But with the expansion of the welfare state in the meantime, the potential for such a strategy has multiplied; at the same time, the problems encountered by Keynesian economic regulation have put policies of employment stimulation in disrepute, so that early exit has become one of the few remaining alternatives for aggregate labor market management (Esping-Andersen, 1990). In other words, since economic policy is less and less able to increase the demand for workers, it falls to social policy to reduce the supply of workers.

On the level of institutional pathways, reducing the supply of workers has been achieved partly by lowering the public pension age limit (as, e.g., in France), partly by creating new instruments (e.g., special preretirement programs in France, West Germany, and The Netherlands), but mostly by extending and twisting existing instruments such as unemployment or disability insurance. These instruments were originally created for dealing with rather restricted special risks (e.g., unemployment during the economic growth phase of the 1950s and 1960s). Now they have been alienated from their original purpose and subverted to move entire cohorts out of the labor force. For purists, this obviously represents a breakdown of the orderly categories into which social policy instruments are meant to fit. I would rather see it as a success—as an example of creatively using the institutional repertoire to cope with a new situation of hitherto unknown proportions. It is the type of institutional "bricolage" that is well known from other policy domains as well, whether we prefer to call it an incremental policy style or (with a less upgraded term) a policy of muddling through.

In summary, the basic comparative pattern of early exit is thus one of different causes but similar outcomes. For a more complete explanation, the causes would have to be specified as to the processes and actors involved. The actors here are not only the elderly workers themselves but also (and more importantly) corporate actors such as the firms, the unions, and the state. Such an analysis is beyond the scope of the present chapter. Its main elements have been presented elsewhere (cf. Kohli, 1992). An important result is that contrary to many beliefs, early exit is broadly popular with most of the actors involved. It is usually the result of a cooperative "effort" of firms, unions, and the older workers themselves, with the state either actively creating institutional pathways for acceptable forms of early exit, or at least letting the other actors use existing social welfare schemes for that purpose.

EARLY EXIT IN THE TRANSFORMATION OF SOCIALIST ECONOMIES: THE CASE OF EAST GERMANY

The current sudden transformation of Eastern European economies from "real socialism" to some type of market system provides a laboratory for examining age-related changes and their possible implications for offsetting the structural lag that is the focus of this book.

This transformation gives another striking example as well as a contrast to what has been said so far: an example of how early exit is again used to reduce unemployment, and a contrast in terms of the massive extent and speed of this process. This is especially visible in the former East Germany (GDR) where, due to the full economic union with the West, the crash in production and employment has been most dramatic. But it is likely that the same pattern will be seen in the other Eastern European countries as well, with age and gender as the main dimensions of employment loss.

Pretransformation

In pretransformation Eastern Europe, the economic differences between countries were substantial, not only in the level of economic development but also in labor organization (e.g., ownership patterns or size of the informal economy) and in social policy institutions (e.g., age thresholds and replacement levels of public pensions). But in important respects, they could be considered as exemplars of a common structural type—with East Germany used here as the type case—characterized by a low degree of differentiation among society, economy, and polity as well as within these subsystems. One of the most striking features was the extent to which work and the social welfare system were fused. This link was achieved by a policy of full employment, and by channeling a substantial part of social welfare directly through the firm.

Much more than was true for the West, these countries were "work societies" even though productivity was low, and work motivation doubtful. The centrality of work was expressed and maintained ideologically through its symbolic valuation and even heroizing of the GDR as a "workers' and peasants' state." More importantly, it was realized through the two processes just mentioned: high labor force participation and distribution of resources through the firm.

Labor force participation was higher than in the West in two dimensions: for women and for the elderly (cf. Figure 4–6). In 1989, female labor force participation rates in East Germany, immediately before the transition almost reached the level of males; in West Germany, they still lagged substantially behind, and also still showed a slight bimodal distribution, indicating the persistence of the three-phase model of female formal work careers. For the elderly, the drop in labor force participation started later than in the West. Of the 5-year groups just

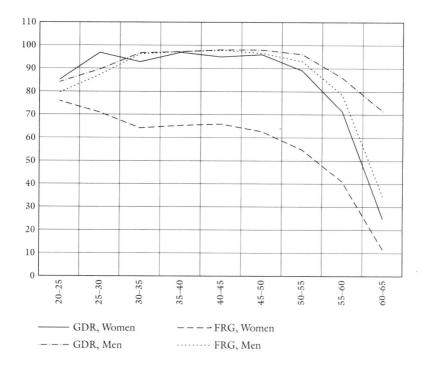

Figure 4-6 Labor Force Participation Rates (East and West Germany, 1989) by Age and Sex (Reprinted from Brinkmann & Engelbrech, 1991)

below the public pension age (60–64 for men, 55–59 for women), more than three-quarters were still in work, while for West Germany, the corresponding figures were around one-third. The available East German data on the evolution up to 1989 show that there was also a (modest) trend toward earlier exit and that female labor force participation had started at much lower levels in the first decades of the socialist economy, and had only later risen to the level of full employment. The same patterns hold for the other countries, with some differences due to the larger size of the informal sector in Hungary and Poland, for example, where the available data on labor force participation rates (which pick up participation in the formal economy only) give the impression of much earlier exit (cf. Keyfitz, 1992).

Employment of retirees was usually with their former firm. In a context of chronic labor shortage and with soft budget constraints, it was advantageous for firms to retain their retirees, especially as a "reserve army" for managing the frequent production breakdowns due to equipment failure or inadequate supplies. That retirees should be kept in the workforce was part of the "right to work" written into the GDR constitution. In addition, East German gerontological research produced a number of studies showing that work was favorable to personality development. On the side of the retirees, motivation to work was helped along by rather low pension levels.

The distribution of resources through the firm resulted in what may be called a "firm-centered social policy." In East Germany, the firm was a center of "sociation" (or social participation) in a very broad sense. It was a political unit, with the state party being organized more around firms than around local communities. It was a cultural unit, with many cultural activities (including theatricals and concerts) being sponsored by it. And it was above all a material unit: a distributor of scarce goods and services ranging from housing and vacation places to medical and child care.[6] Such distribution was especially important in an economy where markets were highly restricted—where money did not generally give access to goods but only the right to queue up for goods. The firm-centered social policy was of course not least an instrument of social control, and probably served to some extent as a compensation for the low level of control over workers on the shop floor that seems to have been typical for socialist firms. Even the nonworking elderly remained partially integrated into this form of "sociation." They could participate in what the union—in a telling reference to the militarization of work—called its "veterans' organizations," which made them eligible for the same benefits as the active workers. But its salience went beyond these material aspects; it also provided the veterans with a social link that seems to have been valued in its own right.

Posttransformation

The process of transition from a socialist economy has changed most of this. Many firms have disappeared, and the remaining ones have been forced by hard budget constraints to externalize costs both through shedding large parts of their workforce and through getting

---

[6] It was even a starting point of the informal economy—by giving workers access to goods that could be "privatized" and fed into the networks of reciprocal exchange.

rid of activities not directly related to production. In East Germany, the economic union with the West—with the immediate free availability of Western goods, and a rise of production costs to Western levels—has resulted in a collapse of the labor market of hitherto unknown proportions. The other Eastern European countries have been able to manage the transition in a somewhat smoother way, but for them also, unemployment is now rising rapidly (cf. OECD Employment Outlook, 1992, Chapter 6).

The evolution (or rather involution) of the East German labor market can now be documented by some aggregate data (cf. *Employment Observatory East Germany,* No. 2, May 1992). In 1989, the labor force comprised 9.932 million employed persons. By April 1992, this number had shrunk to 6.365 million, less than two-thirds. About half a million had moved; another half million were commuting to West Germany; 1.196 million persons were registered as unemployed; 0.507 million were participating in publicly funded training programs; and 0.780 million were in preretirement. Of those still employed, 0.404 million were in workplaces with wage subsidies (usually between 80% and 100% of full wages), and another 0.466 million were on "short-term work," a program of temporary and/or partial unemployment compensation.

This labor force involution has been managed through large-scale social transfers under the West German regime of social insurance and social assistance that has now been extended to the East. There is a range of programs with different eligibility rules and replacement levels, and again a high amount of program switching (and related institutional "bricolage") has resulted in a policy process of muddling through. Many programs (e.g., preretirement) have deadlines that have been extended several times in line with the labor market data showing that, contrary to predictions, the floor of the downswing has not yet been reached.

With most of the registered unemployed receiving a compensation in addition to all those in the special programs just mentioned, roughly 3.2 million people in April 1992 were living fully or partially on incomes paid by the public labor market agencies. Some of these income transfers—the training and wage subsidy programs—can be considered as active labor market policy, while the others are passive: They compensate people for not working. Women, who made up 49% of the 1989 labor force, have a disproportionately low share in active labor market programs (e.g., 39% of those with wage subsidies), and a disproportionately high share of unemployment (63%). As to the elderly, those in preretirement—a program starting at age 55, with a replacement level originally of 70% and now of 65% of previous net incomes—are topped up by those in retirement age who were still working in 1989, and who have now practically disappeared from the labor market. All in all, early exit has reduced the 1989 work force by about one-tenth.

These data show how strongly the removal of workers from the workforce has been structured along the lines of gender and age. The extent of early exit is visible in more detail in Table 4–1 (with the more realistic labor force activity rates instead of participation rates). In 1989, the men aged 55 to 59 were still almost fully engaged in the labor force, and over three-fourths of those aged 60 to 64. In 1992, their activity rates had decreased to less than one half and less than one-fifth, respectively. For the elderly women, the decrease has been even more dramatic. Within three years, the labor market had lost most of the people over 60, and a majority of those between 55 and 59. Never before has the use of early exit as control of unemployment been put into focus so sharply. In addition to the quantitative labor market balance, there are also qualitative issues

Table 4–1
Labor Force Activity Rates (%) in
East Germany by Age and Sex

		\multicolumn{3}{c}{*Age*}		
		55–59	*60–64*	*65+*
Men	1989	93.7	77.2	12.5
	1990	86.7	71.0	8.3
	1991	67.9	29.1	4.0
	1992	47.7	19.1	2.9
Women	1989	77.8	29.7	4.6
	1990	71.5	26.1	4.0
	1991	35.0	6.5	1.0
	1992	24.8	4.4	1.1

Source: Socio-Economic Panel (East) (for 1989: retrospective data from the 1990 Panel); own calculations.

I am grateful to Peter Krause (German Institute for Economic Research) for providing me with the detailed data.

with regard to weeding out those deemed unfit for the new market economy as well as those who are politically incriminated.

Among the consequences, the most obvious is money. Here, the main problem is insecurity about the future—about whether a person will be able to live with what he or she gets in an environment of steeply rising prices. Even though the preretirement compensation, like the pension itself, is indexed to the evolution of wages, those forced into preretirement are left with claims based on their former GDR incomes and will not be able to bolster their pension with additional income.

A second consequence is in terms of social participation (or "sociation"). The firm-centered social policy of East Germany did have its negative aspects: It was an instrument of social control that could make access to scarce resources contingent on good behavior. Today, these resources have been turned over to the market where they can be bought without political and moral costs. But on top of the question of whether all this will remain affordable is the fact of being cut off from the main areas of social activity. There are new forms of self-organization aimed at substituting for some of the activity and participation that had been organized around the workplace, but they are difficult to sustain in a climate of resignation and retreat.

Finally, there are moral consequences. In West Germany, early exit has to a large extent been a positive goal, and seen as a morally justified compensation for a life of work and for the special hardships of reconstructing the social wealth after the war. In the East, early exit has come as a sudden and largely involuntary process that has not become "normalized" socially. It deprives people of the chance to contribute to the new economic reconstruction, and devalues their lifetime accomplishments. The state and economy to which they have contributed have disappeared, and the new order has no demand for them any more. What matters here is not only age but also cohort or generation. Members of the cohorts now facing preretirement are the ones who had started their adult life in the first years of the GDR. Their personal active life course overlaps with the life course of that state, and comes to an end with it.

The situation of preretirees may still be preferable to that of the long-term unemployed who do not yet have the possibility of exit into retirement. But it is very different from that of preretirees in West Germany, not least because of this simultaneity of personal and societal biography. Extreme structural discontinuities such as now experienced in the East are likely to create high generational inequalities. Social policy that is centered on material transfers only (even when adequate) is not sufficient.

OPTIONS FOR THE FUTURE

In conclusion, it should be recalled that early exit sharpens the issues of intergenerational exchange and redistribution; the salience of these issues has become dramatically evident with the prospect of population aging and the financial squeeze of the welfare state. In the public discourse, these issues are increasingly greeted with alarming overtones; for example, "The rapid aging of the populations of all industrial countries over the next forty years will be an economic and social transformation of vastly greater magnitude than the 1970s oil price shock or the 1980s recession" (Johnson et al., 1989, p. 1).

In the light of these prospects, early exit seems highly undesirable. Although it is a popular solution for coping with (some of) the oversupply of labor, it is questionable on other grounds (see Chapter 1; cf. Riley & Riley, 1991). In the long run, a solution that concentrates the available work on an ever shorter proportion of the life course and keeps an ever larger proportion of the population completely out of work does not seem reasonable. There are good reasons—psychological and physiological ones concerning activity and competence, sociological ones concerning social participation and integration, and economic ones concerning the financing of social security—for preferring the opposite scenario of age integration, or of trying to distribute work more evenly among all age groups. Mechanisms to accomplish this goal are proposed in this book: further decreasing weekly work hours, encouraging part-time work among the "active" population, spreading the jobs that are available across all ages, and opening the possibility for sabbaticals or periods of "retirement" over the whole life course. Aging societies face a massive structural lag: a mismatch between the growing numbers and competence of elderly people and the lack of meaningful roles for them (cf. Riley, 1993; Riley & Loscocco, 1993).

The problem is that good reasons alone do not produce the preferred outcome; it is the dynamics of interests among the actors involved that is decisive. These interests in turn depend on the labor market conditions. They have to be taken into account if the sociological and political imagination is to be effective. Only by closely monitoring the existing structures will it be possible to create the appropriate institutional incentives for change.

In all aging societies, the supply of potential young entrants into the labor market is declining rapidly. It is usually argued that this will lead to a labor shortage as well as to a financial crisis of the pension (and health) system. The most obvious way out of this demographic trap—as mentioned at the beginning—would seem to be by raising the age limit of retirement. However, whether the elderly workers would indeed be absorbed by the labor market is still an open question. A few years ago, it was generally predicted in West Germany that with the decreasing size of the entry cohorts, the oversupply of labor would disappear at the beginning of the 1990s. Then, the predictions—even before the prospects of unification—moved this date to the year 2000 or beyond. Now, the unification process has created, in the East, mass unemployment on an unprecedented scale, and again early exit is used to cope with (some of) it. And for West Germany, it remains to be seen whether the effects of the demographic change will outweigh the effects of job loss through rationalization. If the retirement limit for entry into the public pension system is raised (as has been enacted by the recent pension reform) and the labor market does not offer jobs to the elderly, then the legislation simply initiates a process of shifting the burden between the different welfare programs and the elderly themselves.

Labor shortages and financial strains for the welfare system may moreover be alleviated by an increasing labor force participation of women (which in Western countries is likely to continue) and by immigration (cf. Gillion, 1991). In Germany, the events of the past 5 years have demonstrated the fragility of the assumption of a closed system; and in Western Europe more generally, the perception is slowly sinking in how difficult it will be to insulate these aging and rich populations from the pressures of mass migration.

If this perspective seems to offer little hope for integrating the growing elderly population into the main societal concerns, and at the same time for keeping the generational contract balanced, two points need to be recalled. On the one hand, early exit from formal work is not tantamount to exclusion from all meaningful activities: It also creates the room for increasing rates of activities such as unpaid volunteer work, self-help activities, intensified household production, or more demanding hobby work (see Chapter 2). Already, the economic value of such activities by the elderly is substantial (cf. Herzog, Kahn, Morgan, Jackson, & Antonucci, 1989). And their psychological and social value as sources of competence, social participation, and identity has been broadly demonstrated as well.

On the other hand, changing the intergenerational distribution of formal work by raising the age limit may become more easily possible in the long run. The comparative record presented here shows that social policy alone has limited effects. But it would be premature to conclude that policy does not matter. It is instead a question of identifying the handles on which it can make a difference. Social policy has to be complemented by interventions into the labor market, and into the schedules and conditions of work. In the long run, changes in manpower policy over the whole life course may create room for extending the transition to retirement and making it more flexible through, for example, shorter weekly and yearly working hours (reducing the labor supply) and regular periods of requalification (increasing the human capital value of older workers). By these same changes, such an extension may also become more generally acceptable, as a possible means of reducing the structural lag.

REFERENCES

Atchley, R. C. (1985). Social security-type retirement policies: A cross-national study. In Z. S. Blau (Ed.), *Current perspectives on aging and the life cycle* (pp. 275–293). Greenwich: JAI Press.

Boaz, R. F. (1988). Early withdrawal from the labor force. *Research on Aging, 9,* 530–547.

Brinkmann, G., & Engelbrech, G. (1991). Erwerbsbeteiligung und Erwerbstätigkeit von Frauen. In G. Wagner, B. von Rosenbladt, & D. Blaschke (Eds.), *An der Schwelle zur sozialen Marktwirtschaft* (pp. 23–26). Nürnberg: IAB.

Burkhauser, R., & Quinn, J. (1989). American patterns of work and retirement. In W. Schmähl (Ed.), *Redefining the process of retirement: An international perspective* (pp. 91–113). Berlin: Springer.

Casey, B. (1989). Early retirement: The problems of "instrument substitution" and "cost shifting" and their implications for restructuring the process of retirement. In W. Schmähl (Ed.), *Redefining the process of retirement: An international perspective* (pp. 133–150). Berlin: Springer.

Clark, R. L., & Anker, R. (1990). Labour force participation rates of older persons: An international comparison. *International Labour Review, 129,* 255–271.

Employment Observatory East Germany. (1992). No. 2., May. Bruxelles: European Commission.

Esping-Andersen, G. (1990). *The three worlds of welfare capitalism.* Oxford: Polity Press.

Flora, P. (Ed.). (1986ff). *Growth to limits: The Western European welfare states since World War II,* 5 vols. Berlin: De Gruyter.

Gillion, C. (1991). Ageing populations: Spreading the costs. *Journal of European Social Policy, 1,* 107–128.

Gordon, M. S. (1988). *Social security policies in industrial countries: A comparative analysis.* Cambridge/New York: University Press.

Henretta, J. C. (1992). Uniformity and diversity: Life course institutionalization and late-life work exit. *Sociological Quarterly, 33,* 265–279.

Herzog, A. R., Kahn, R. L., Morgan, J. N., Jackson, J. S., & Antonucci, T. C. (1989). Age differences in productive activities. *Journals of Gerontology, 44,* S129–S138.

Hinrichs, K., Roche, W., & Sirianni, C. (Eds.). (1991). *Working time in transition: The political economy of working hours in industrial nations.* Philadelphia, PA: Temple University Press.

Hurd, M. D. (1990). Research on the elderly: Economic status, retirement, and consumption and saving. *Journal of Economic Literature, 28,* 565–637.

Jacobs, K., Kohli, M., & Rein, M. (1991). The evolution of early exit: A comparative analysis of labor force participation patterns. In M. Kohli, M. Rein, A. M. Guillemard, & H. van Gunsteren (Eds.), *Time for retirement: Comparative studies of early exit from the labor force* (pp. 36–66). Cambridge/New York: Cambridge University Press.

Johnson, P., Conrad, C., & Thomson, D. (Eds.). (1989). *Workers versus pensioners: Intergenerational justice in an aging world.* Manchester: Manchester University Press.

Keyfitz, N. (1992). *Retirement in industrial societies: East and West.* Paper prepared for workshop on social protection and economic transformation, Laxenburg (Austria), June 11–13.

Kii, T. (1987). Retirement in Japan. In K. S. Markides & C. L. Cooper (Eds.), *Retirement in industrialized societies* (pp. 231–269). Chichester: Wiley.

Kohli, M. (1986). The world we forgot: A historical review of the life course. In V. W. Marshall (Ed.), *Later life: The social psychology of aging* (pp. 271–303). Beverly Hills, CA: Sage.

Kohli, M. (1987). Retirement and the moral economy: A historical interpretation of the German case. *Journal of Ageing Studies, 1,* 125–144.

Kohli, M. (1992). Labour market perspectives and activity patterns of the elderly in an ageing society. In W. van Den Heuvel, R. Illsley, A. Jamieson, & C. Knipscheer

(Eds.), *Opportunities and challenges in an ageing society* (pp. 90–105). Amsterdam: North-Holland.

Kohli, M., & Rein, M. (1991). The changing balance of work and retirement. In M. Kohli, M. Rein, A. M. Guillemard, & H. van Gunsteren (Eds.), *Time for retirement: Comparative studies of early exit from the labor force* (pp. 1–35). Cambridge/New York: Cambridge University Press.

Kohli, M., Rein, M., Guillemard, A. M., & van Gunsteren, H. (Eds.). (1991). *Time for retirement: Comparative studies of early exit from the labor force.* Cambridge/New York: Cambridge University Press.

Lehr, U. M. (1984). Pensionierung. In W. D. Oswald, W. M. Herrmann, S. Kanowski, U. M. Lehr, & H. Thomae (Hg.), *Gerontologie* (pp. 318–329). Stuttgart: Kohlhammer.

Neugarten, B. (Ed.). (1982). *Age or need? Public policies for older people.* Beverly Hills, CA: Sage.

OECD. (1984–1989). *Labor force statistics.* Paris: OECD.

OECD. (1992). *Employment outlook.* Paris: OECD.

Pampel, F. C., & Weiss, J. A. (1983). Economic development, pension policies, and the labor force participation of aged males: A cross-national, longitudinal approach. *American Journal of Sociology, 89,* 350–372.

Rein, M., & Jacobs, K. (1993). Ageing and employment trends: A comparative analysis for OECD countries. In P. Johnson & K. F. Zimmermann (Eds.), *Labor markets in an ageing Europe.* Cambridge: Cambridge University Press.

Riley, M. W. (1993). The coming revolution in age structure (Pepper Institute Working Paper Series P1-93-1). Tallahassee, FL: Florida State University.

Riley, M. W., & Loscocco, K. (1993). The changing structure of work opportunities: Toward an age-integrated society. In R. P. Abeles, H. C. Gift, & M. Ory (Eds.), *Aging and the quality of life.* New York: Springer.

Riley, M. W., & Riley, Jr., J. W. (1991). Vieillesse et changements des rôles sociaux. *Gérontologie et Société, 56,* 6–13.

Ritter, G. A. (1989). *Der Sozialstaat: Entstehung und Entwicklung im internationalen Vergleich.* München: Oldenbourg.

Schulz, J. H., Borowski, A., & Crown, W. H. (1991). *Economics of population aging: The "graying" of Australia, Japan, and the United States.* New York: Auburn House.

Szalai, J. (1991). Hungary: Exit from the state economy. In M. Kohli, M. Rein, A. M. Guillemard, & H. van Gunsteren (Eds.), *Time for retirement: Comparative studies of early exit from the labor force* (pp. 324–361). Cambridge/New York: Cambridge University Press.

Williamson, J. B., & Pampel, F. C. (1993). *Old-age security in comparative perspective.* Oxford: Oxford University Press.

CHAPTER 5

The Democratization of Unstructured Time in Western Societies: A Historical Overview

Andrejs Plakans

I n the 20th century, Western industrial societies contain substantial numbers of people who have withdrawn from long-term employment, a practice that represents a sharp break with much of the Western European past. As a social historian, I seek further understanding of this major change by tracing historical patterns of work, retirement, and leisure.

TIME AND RETIREMENT AS HISTORICAL QUESTIONS

A quarter century ago in their inventory of research on aging and society, Riley and Foner (1968, p. 421) suggested that the human consequences of not being gainfully employed needed to receive more attention than they had been accorded to date. This chapter is meant to contribute to the considerable amount of scholarship that has followed that invitation by focusing on one common facet of historical changes in work, retirement, and leisure: the question of time.

The formal withdrawal from gainful employment by large numbers of people has been facilitated by mechanisms allowing or requiring them to do so. Most have taken this step in the later years of life, knowing that in the welfare and quasi-welfare states of Western society disengagement from the world of work is not generally a life-threatening step. Indeed, some modern Western economies, having become saturated with employable persons, have deliberately diminished access to the world of work for older people and have initiated various exclusionary policies based on age and other criteria (cf. Gaullier, 1982; Guillemard, 1983; Moller, 1987).

The release of large amounts of disposable time, particularly in the later years of the life course, is striking when considered against the background of the long centuries during which work in the Western world was an absolute necessity for survival for most, and hard work was held to be a virtue. The didactic literature of the West, its folklore, and its mores perceived nonwork as the breeding ground for sin, and required waking hours not filled by work to be filled either with preparation for work or rest from it. Work and self-esteem were closely linked, not only in a person's productive years as we might expect, but also in the later years of life when physical and mental capacity was understood to have diminished. In the colonial United States, for example, the Puritan cleric, Increase Mather, complained, "It is a very undesirable thing for a man to outlive his work" (quoted in Haber, 1983, p. 18). His plaint was understandable for, as Haber also suggests, the Puritans looked on labor as serving both God and community, whereas leisure in their eyes did not. Even the old were expected always to keep busy, if only with "good works and deeds" (Haber, 1983, p. 19).

There is scattered evidence that such attitudes—the well-known "work ethic"—were not limited to Puritan New England but could be found throughout the Western world, not only among Protestants but also among Catholics and nonbelievers. These attitudes were prevalent among the mass of people for whom work was tied to survival and also among such hard-working state-building monarchs as Philip II of Spain, Elizabeth I of England, and Frederick the Great of Prussia (to name only a few) as well as those segments of the landowning classes (the "improving landlords") who disdained court life and spent most of their time among their animals and crops. Even at court, ritual and aristocratic leisure—arguably work of a kind—could be arduous, especially if maintenance of status depended on its correct execution (cf. Kohli, 1988, p. 383). The very thin layers of the wealthy are a poor sample for statements about general Western attitudes, but their inclusion does suggest that work was revered and performed among many who did not need it for survival.[1]

From the foregoing, we infer that the waking hours of most people in the past were filled with work: These hours were, in other words, *structured* by the tasks at hand. This situation contrasts with what research and first-person accounts tell us about how disposable time is experienced in the contemporary world among those whose connections with the world of work have lapsed. One description is suggested in Guillemard's (1982) research on retirement in France. Among the varied retirement experiences she found, one type is noteworthy— "withdrawal retirement"—involving virtually total disassociation from ongoing society:

> In this practice, everything takes place as though, with the arrival of retirement and the removal of all the demands associated with work, *time ceased to be structured by any but biological need* [emphasis added]. The term "social death" describes this practice, which is seen as biological survival dissociated from any social meaning. (p. 230)

The term "social death" may be an extreme way of describing one pattern of retirement, but it suggests how time (the waking hours) is experienced and how under certain circumstances time *ceases to be structured* by socioeconomic involvements. If we now contrast the concept with our previous portrayal of the distant past, we arrive at the structured/unstructured time typology.

My argument is that the socioeconomic structural changes that have produced the modern condition of retirement can also be viewed

---

[1] Direct testimony about these matters from the distant past is scarce, particularly about the later phases of the life course (Laslett, 1984). First-person accounts can be expected only from the literate relatively late in Western history: As researchers have recognized, "later life from the inside" (Thomson, Itzin, & Abendstern, 1990, p. 252) is difficult to describe in any event; and until the 20th century, "the elderly seldom [spoke] for themselves" (Pelling & Smith, 1991, p. 2).

as an historical break in the characteristics of disposable time. Whereas in earlier centuries, the waking hours could not escape being filled (structured), persons who now withdraw from the world of work find themselves confronted with the personal challenge of finding content for them. Not all people can do this equally well, but individual differences in adjustment have not received as much attention among gerontologists as might be expected (Braithwaite & Gibson, 1987, p. 2). In her study of the French retired, Guillemard (1982) also observed:

> The working class reaches the threshold of retirement less well equipped than the other classes for converting free time into leisure. Now, retirement is characterized precisely by the access it offers to socially nonrestricted time. Retired persons from the working class are, therefore, the least well armed for controlling and organizing their free time in retirement according to their own inclinations; this free time then becomes *empty time* [emphasis added]. (p. 239)

STRUCTURED AND UNSTRUCTURED TIME

"Structured" and "unstructured" time—"full" and "empty" time— these nonspecific categories may seem worlds removed from the precisely datable patterns of historical change, but they are nonetheless useful for examining one dimension of the advent of retirement in the world of work. Among other researchers calling for more careful attention to the time dimension, Ostor (1984) suggested a decade ago the need to link the "cultural categories of time and age":

> In order to understand age in our own societies, it is not enough to invoke generation, social time, life crisis, and the like, favorite though unexamined categories of social science today. What has been the effect of economic and other changes on the links between person and time in the advanced industrial societies? Again we have no direct answers in the face of wide gaps in the literature. (p. 289)

And Hendricks and Cutler (1990, p. 90) wrote more recently about the need "for the development of a sociological calendar, a means of capturing socially relevant qualitative and quantitative units of time that *structure* [emphasis added] the times of our lives."

From the anthropological perspective, "work, time, person and society are linked together in systematic cultural terms" (Ostor, 1984, p. 300), a proposition that historians can accept. The specific forms of these linkages, however, have to be teased out of sketchy historical evidence, with present-day first-person accounts thought of as historical evidence about the current phase.

In reviewing contemporary reflections, it is remarkable how often descriptions of the personal experience of retirement in the modern world, offered by persons used to self-articulation and by those who are not, draw on synonyms for the terms Guillemard has formalized as research concepts. Alan Olmstead, on retiring, started a diary about his experience when for the first time he faced a day unstructured by work demands. Among his varied day-by-day reactions, he notes that time needed to be "filled up" and "structured"; he had to develop an "imitation of a new routine"; he resented that the "outside world no longer needed or expected anything from [him]." He began to do "some of the little things that never would get done if [he] didn't do them"; and he discovered that "the system no longer really has any compulsion over [him]. . . . [He did] not have to be on Standard Time, or Daylight Saving Time, or any other kind of time except [his] own time" (Olmstead, 1975, pp. 3, 4, 60). In coming to grips with this new experience, he ultimately concluded:

> Leisure, the freedom, is like all freedoms in that it cannot exist except in relation to fixed occupations, duties, and obligations. . . . Leisure ceases to exist unless it keeps bumping itself against and reinforcing itself through contact and conflict with things that must be done. To begin to plan for leisure time, then, one aims first to make sure of a continuing context of chore or obligation. . . . To find leisure, look for work. (pp. 212–213)

This almost Orwellian conclusion—leisure requires work—finds echoes in the experiences of others not given to expressing themselves in terms of irony and paradox. Interviews of English subjects, for example, reveal frequent mention of confrontations with unstructured time. A retired nurse observed, "Well—suddenly—you have no company any more . . . and you miss that terribly. . . . You are alone. . . . And you have to think of something to *fill the day* [emphasis is added]: give yourself a little company" (Thompson, Itzin, &

Abendstern 1990, p. 146). An ex-miner who was an "unstoppable worker" but was forced into retirement at age 68, said: "You miss the company. . . . I would say old age begins when ye're forced to retire . . . *I could fill up time now* [emphasis added], oh aye. But if ever a job came, I would definitely take it" (Thompson et al., p. 144). Carworkers and shipbuilders who ceased working "felt terrible and lay in bed in the morning puzzling about '*how to fill me time in*' [emphasis added]" (p. 10).

Some social scientists studying retirement also use variants of this terminology. Kaplan (1979), for example, observes:

> Studies of work motivation and satisfaction point out the human or social elements of the working situation—relating to other people, performing a social function, obtaining a response, contributing to a task, and so on. The absence of these constitutes a *serious void* [emphasis added] upon retirement. What becomes the reality of retirement is the absence of a schedule, a job, and a social apparatus all at once. (p. 18)

And Parker (1982, p. 142) speaks of the need among some persons for "some kinds of revised *structure* to be imposed on daily activities when employment ceases."

Though the phrase "unstructured time" is a metaphor, it points to the recent entry into modern human lives of a dimension that earlier was relatively scarce, but now has become far more plentiful and therefore problematic. A question for historians is the extent to which the structured/unstructured conceptualization of time helps our understanding of the changes that have occurred and whether the typology might assist the organization of the research that remains to be done.

STRUCTURED TIME BEFORE THE NINETEENTH CENTURY

Finding out about time in premodern societies involves much guesswork, in contrast with the fine-grained inquiries that are possible today. Cribier's decade-old observation (1981, p. 53) about how little is known concerning the experiencing of retirement even in historically well-researched France and England is only somewhat less true now, and relevant historical data for the rest of Europe is further behind.

We lack a large collection of detailed local studies and must make do with a series of general and imprecise statements that suggest some continuities over a long period of historical time.

Troyansky (1989, p. 91), for example, suggests that in the classic Greek and Roman periods the definition of old age was associated with the idea of sufficient wealth to support retirement and, he believes, that association was still alive in the 18th century. In other words, as far back as evidence reaches, unstructured time was connected with wealthy elites and its entry into the life course appears not to have been precisely age-graded. Roebuck (1975, p. 417) believes that in premodern England "most people seem to have acted on loose, and very varied definitions" of old age. And Minois (1989, pp. 245–247) notes that the idea of retirement was "catching on" in the later medieval period, with the term becoming more widespread in the documents pertaining to wealthier strata of society.

Speculative as these statements are, as long as we focus on the vast majority of people, there is a plausible argument that, prior to the 19th century, unstructured time was a relatively rare experience. And having disposable time was affected by people's social standing.

The Elite

According to Laslett (1987, p. 139), among the wealthy, retirement—most often taking up of permanent residence in country homes "at any convenient point in their careers"—was an established feature of the life of the upper orders in England. It was probably the same on the Continent. The upper orders were supported in the main by the labor of others (as in the case of serf-owning landed nobles) or by various rental agreements (where peasant land was rented or leased). Yet even these privileged social groups may have had less unstructured time than might be deduced from their position. As suggested earlier, the wealth that exempted the landed aristocrats from doing physical labor did not absolve them from having to plan systematic and organized activities to uphold their standing among their peers and in society in general. Not to attend to such matters meant to risk loss of status, and therefore upkeep of status could easily become a full lifetime of demands and duties from which the elite did not "retire." The idea of "my station and its duties" certainly played an important role in reducing unstructured time among the crowned heads of Europe.

Monarchs who took the responsibilities of rule lightly would soon see the diminution of their country's internal and external power. With respect to another numerical minority—those associated with the Church—evidence is sparse. Minois reports that in medieval monasteries even superannuated monks did not escape being assigned tasks: They did odd jobs and they were also directed to eat with the abbot to assure that this prestigious person remained humble by having at his table an ever-present reminder of his own mortality (Minois, 1989, p. 131). The churches generally imposed very strict discipline on the lives of both their secular and regular clergy.

The Middle Strata

Among the socioeconomic groups standing between the nobilities and peasantries in the social hierarchy, the "middle classes" or the "bourgeoisie" were even less likely than the aristocracies to find unstructured time an important part of their lives. Guilds regulated both the working and nonworking hours of their members punctiliously. Urban corporations did not hesitate to point out publicly to residents of the city that their "idleness" was bringing disrepute to their families or the city as a whole, and the hours that these citizens did not devote to their work were as strictly regulated by ritual as those of the nobility. Even more than for the nobles, status anxieties forced these "middling classes" to diminish their free time and did not allow for much relaxation from wealth-creating activities. If unstructured time among the nobles was diminished to maintain status, among these "middling groups" it was severely diminished by efforts both to maintain the status they had and to acquire higher standing.

Peasant Elites

Elsewhere I have written (Plakans, 1989) that retirement as understood in modern terms did not exist in the preindustrial European peasantry. To be sure, those few individuals who had achieved a position of prominence in the rural community—such as headship of a farmstead—were likely to "step down" from it in old age either voluntarily or under pressure from their successors, although even these peasants were not invariably under obligation to do that or to sever attachments to the world of work. It is among these heads—a small but privileged elite in peasant society—that we have the first indications of formalized withdrawal from work in the now widely cited "retirement contract" (Gaunt, 1983), which outlined the conditions under which a head surrendered that status to his successor. But even where these contracts were regularly in use, there was no indication that physical labors ceased entirely when the contracts were implemented. Former heads continued to work alongside those who did not have headships, but in diminishing amounts and at chores that placed no great strain on their fading physical abilities. There does not seem to be any evidence that this transition was linked to a strictly specified age within the later years of life (Kohli, Rosenow, & Wolf, 1983, p. 25).

Peasants and Workers

By descending the social hierarchy of traditional Europe, we come to those immense subpopulations for whom unstructured time was made impossible either because of their subordinate standing or by their near-subsistence level of life. Before the industrial revolution, this means the peasantries; afterward, it means the small but growing population of factory laborers as well.

The everyday lives of the *peasants* for most of the year were regulated by the calendar of the growing season: Involvement in work was from sunup to sundown. Only in the winter months were there blocks of unstructured time, but the weather and the need to repair equipment and replenish necessities still severely restricted the peasants' freedom to do as they wished. The holidays of the busy season were dedicated to work, and the ritualistic activities that punctuated them further limited the extent to which they could be regarded as being at the person's disposal. This structuring of time lasted until death.

Among the *subpopulations touched by the development of industry* were rural people caught up in so-called protoindustrialization (manufacturing activity of various kinds as well as mining), located in the countryside. The penetration of the countryside by nonagricultural work of this kind was not widespread and tended to be located in Western and central Europe. While the additional income brought to peasant households was useful, it was decidedly not utilized to create leisure for the old. Work on the loom and the spinning wheel, done now not for purposes of self-sufficiency but to create a product deliverable to the organizer of the system, tended to be integrated with ongoing agricultural labors and, if anything, extended the hours of the working day.

A somewhat more dramatic transformation was experienced by the first and second generations of industrial workers in England (the first industrial nation), who came to be subjected to the discipline of what Hareven (1982) calls "industrial time." We cannot speak of the experience of these earlier generations as typical of the period before 1800: Industrial laborers only became a small but growing population in England by the early decades of the 19th century and were virtually unknown on the continent until the middle decades of that century. But it is probable that these early generations were the first distinct labor force where every member encountered not only the new industrial discipline but also mandatory retirement, sometimes with a small pension. There is insufficient research about whether they were also the first to experience a period of unstructured time at the end of their lives; more than likely, most of them continued to work to supplement the inadequate pensions they received. But disengaging from the labor force may not always have come at some "retirement" age: Evidently some workers "retired" before they were physically decrepit and some of these worked on into their 70s (Thomson, 1991, p. 206).

One subpopulation to which historical research has repeatedly adverted is the *laboring poor* in the countryside from the mid-18th century on and, after the turn of the century, in expanding European cities as well. They were on the margin of the labor market, working at odd jobs, continually underemployed and frequently unemployed, with the tasks of sheer physical survival pressing down on them in every waking hour. Among them, there was no question of unstructured time that could be transformed into leisure; life at the margins of existence did not permit much of either. Nor can there be a question of retirement in any modern sense of the term because they seldom were involved in any activity long enough for its cessation to constitute retirement.

The Variable Presence of Unstructured Time

In summary, then, for most people, regardless of age, unstructured time was a scarce commodity in the West before the 19th century. It was distributed unequally, with the aristocracy and the unemployed poor probably having more time to fill than the social groups in between. Nor was income the only basis of variations in unstructured time. The young tended to have more than the middle-aged and the old; men more than women; and people in urban areas more than those in the countryside. Yet for most people, especially in rural areas, "work often lasted until death, but a gradual disengagement could be arranged. . . . Retirement, if it could be afforded at all, required negotiation rather than a bureaucratic arrangement between an individual of a prescribed age and an institution" (Troyansky, 1989, p. 126).

SUBSIDIZING UNSTRUCTURED TIME: THE NINETEENTH CENTURY

The patterns just described began to change in the 19th century as a result of socioeconomic developments associated with industrialization, urbanization, agricultural modernization, and the further growth of the state. Interest began to shift to finding national-level solutions to a host of problems, including support for those not working. Even in the 18th century, intellectuals such as the "enlightened" French administrators Necker and Turgot had called for national-level systems of relief for the poor and the old (Troyansky, 1989, pp. 192–193). The 19th-century shift I speak of, however, was not the result of centralized planning and could not have been, given the relative weakness of national governments and the general suspicion of government intrusion into the private sphere. Sociopolitical changes scrambled systems of European self-classification, rendering everyone a "citizen" and creating large populations of diverse social backgrounds whose incomes depended increasingly on working for someone else, in a process called "proletarianization" (Levine, 1984).

For the development under scrutiny here, the growing significance of this process was that increasingly larger, though still minuscule, proportions of the labor force were entering into work situations from which (assuming they stayed in them for a long time) they could be "retired," and were thus presented from that point onward with an unbroken block of unstructured time to do with as they wished. A growing proportion of employment of this kind carried with it pension schemes.

In the final quarter of the 19th century, particularly in the newly unified Germany, the national government, controlled by landed conservatives, became interested in social policy aimed to better the lot of ordinary workers so as to reduce the appeal of socialist politics. In other words, 19th-century changes had systemswide ramifications. Ostor (1984, pp. 289, 300–301) suggests, "Market, time, person, work, and ideology are integrally linked throughout the emergence of the capital-intensive economy," and proposes the possibility that "capitalism, Protestantism, and changing work patterns *created retirement* [emphasis added] and its attendant problems" such as the barriers to work beyond a certain age, incompetence (at least for production), retirement, and the separation of the old.

Precursors to national pension schemes had appeared gradually. In England, for example, some form of retirement for men of property, as mentioned earlier, was an accepted practice even in early modern times, and the merits of extending pensions to those on salaries were debated from the late 17th century on; leading advocates included Daniel Defoe and later the radical Thomas Paine of the French Revolution years (Thompson, Itzin, & Abendstern, 1990). The first to be provided with pensions were the lower-paid naval warrant officers in 1672, and then customs officers. In 1749, a scheme for master merchant mariners was created. The pioneering general pension scheme, however, was for the Civil Service in 1810. By 1859, a full pension scheme allowed retirement at age 60.

The first commercial companies to establish pensions for a narrow group of loyal white-collar employees were public utilities, such as some railway and gas companies in the 1840s. A sustained campaign for pensions for manual workers began only in the second half of the 19th century, with the national Old Age Pensions scheme for persons over 70 not being created until the 20th century.

The 19th century represented not an absolute turning point, but rather a long period of transition during which old and new assumptions were intermingled. New schemes were created and old schemes took on new meaning. According to Thomson (1991), the Poor Law in England—in existence since the 16th century—served in the 19th century as a pension law as well:

> Once granted a pension in his or her mid-to late 60s, a person very seldom lost it before death. . . . The proportions of the population who received such public support as they moved through old age were high. . . . Marital status and personal living arrangements made some difference to the rates at which

payments were granted, though these distinctions were not rigid or very pronounced. . . . Extra payments were not infrequently granted for often quite extended periods of special need. . . . The poor law was little concerned with the settlement laws as these affected the elderly. . . . Transfer payments to meet the cost of the pensions were arranged between one poor law area and another. (pp. 202–203)

The upshot of these developments was that an increasingly larger proportion of a given population—though still substantially less than half—became recipients of subsidized unstructured time, mostly at the end of formal working life. Three aspects are important here. First, judging by recorded pension levels during the 19th century, it was far more likely than not for people on pensions to remain somehow connected to the work force, by part-time labor of one kind or another. Thus their subsidized unstructured time could not at this point be fully transformed into "leisure" without threat to survival. Second, by the latter half of the 19th century, though longevity was increasing, the increase had not yet produced a substantial difference between the average age of retirement and the average age of death, so that the duration of "empty time" could not have been long. Third, the growing belief that the working population should receive subsidized unstructured time was very unevenly distributed throughout continental Europe and the new societies European emigration had created. Indeed, over wide areas of the continent there had been very little change in traditional patterns even by the end of the 19th century: Most people, especially in rural areas, continued to be involved in work in some fashion until the very last moments of their lives. In the United States, "the timing of a worker's retirement remained linked to his own health and capabilities. Usually, the laborer would resign only when he was no longer physically able" (Haber, 1983, p. 109).

THE DEMOCRATIZATION OF UNSTRUCTURED TIME: THE TWENTIETH CENTURY

Only in the 20th century was there a systematic increase in the proportion of the labor force covered by private pensions and by national pensions schemes. *Entry* into private employment was to be regulated by child labor laws. At the *exit* end, there stood retirement that in principle was to initiate a long period of unstructured time entirely under the control of the individual. Thus the unstructured time earlier enjoyed by some elites was democratized in the private and public sectors, with the number of persons formally retiring growing with each passing decade. At the same time, unstructured time began to lose its episodic nature and became concentrated in the final decades of life (cf. Jeffries, 1989). The geographic distribution of these new patterns was very uneven across Western societies and has remained so in the 20th century. The institutionalization of mandatory retirement and increasing longevity expanded the period in later life that people were not believed to be able to structure for themselves. Correspondingly, in Western societies, these changes sparked the development of enterprises designed to help people with such efforts. A leisure industry as well as professions emerged that dealt with the problems associated with unstructured time.

In these developments, Western society was making a radical break with its past. Freely disposable time unstructured by work demands, had once been suspect on the assumption that people with a great deal of unstructured time were ignoring their moral duty to be self-supportive or supportive of others. The idea that long segments of time in a person's life would remain unstructured in this sense was in the past hardly credible. In the 20th century, however, the social policy of organizations and governments came to take it for granted that employees, and more generally, all inhabitants of a given state should receive an income even when they were not engaged in productive labor, however defined. It can be said that, whereas before this change people were not thought to be entitled to an income that would give them time to use as they wished, now they are commonly perceived as having just such an entitlement.

Yet because of cost and because not everyone agreed with the premise, these developments had to be fought for, even in 20th-century United States. Haber (1983, p. 113) reports that in the *private* sector in the United States, the first old-age pensions were proposed by the American Express Company in 1875, followed by the Baltimore and Ohio Railroad in 1884. By 1910, only 49 pension plans had been devised, and there were about 350 by 1925. The firms with pensions tended to be larger and more complex, with 73% of the businesses with pensions having more than 1000 workers.

The *national* government in the United States began to consider systematically connecting old age to pension payments only after the turn of the century. However, according to Orloff and Skocpol (1984, p. 728), there was an earlier development: the expansion of Civil War pensions after the 1870s, from first compensating combat injuries of veterans and dependents of the dead or disabled; then to paying veterans who had served 90 days in the Union military (injured or not) if they became disabled for manual labor; and eventually at age 62 being considered a permanent disability. These authors estimate that, in 1910, 30% of all men over 65 in the entire nation were receiving pensions. Haber (1983) describes presidential decisions and laws as starting in 1904 to define those beyond 70 as overaged. The leading historian of the history of retirement, Graebner (1990), writes:

> The national government again asserted its preferences for youth and efficiency by creating a retirement system for its own civil service employees. During the Depression, the magic of retirement was applied to the sick industry of railroading—using the mechanisms of federal law—and in 1935, when Congress passed the Social Security Act, the national government affirmed the importance of retirement for much of the American population. Private pensions came under the direct supervision of the national government in laws passed in 1947, 1958, and 1974. The Retirement Act of 1978 represents an attempt to roll back what was now seen as a very expensive, complex, and inefficient instrument of public policy. (pp. 266–267)

At the policy level, the democratization of unstructured time, therefore, did not arrive in the United States or anywhere else as a widely accepted idea. Quadagno (1982) suggests that the "strong values of voluntarism and thrift" impeded this development and when a "national pension plan was finally enacted [in the United States] it reflected our society's ambivalence about redistributing income without incorporating some test of need. The Social Security Act was a complex mixture of nearly every social welfare device known and included poor law criteria for eligibility in its old age assistance title" (p. 150).

In spite of such lingering doubts, however, modern societies have gone from deep suspicion of unstructured time to subsidizing it and, indeed, to the democratization of subsidized unstructured time where democratization is taken to mean making something available to an increasingly larger proportion of a given population. In the post-World War II period, especially in the United States, the attitudinal change appears to have become entrenched. Foner and Schwab (1983, pp. 77, 80–82) observe, "Since the 1950s, attitudes toward retirement (in the U.S.) have changed dramatically as workers have increasingly come to define retirement as a right earned after a lifetime of employment." Thus "leisure [has become] as important as, and perhaps more important than, money, at least beyond the subsistence level."

In England, however, the debate about the meaning of retirement has continued in the 20th century. Townsend (1981) has argued that mandatory retirement, encouraged or enforced by state pension schemes, constitutes a deliberate attempt to marginalize the old, to place them in a situation of "structured dependency." By contrast, Smith (1984, p. 413), calling for an expanded time frame for considering the question, suggests that late industrial society did not create the problem and that we have to recognize "a long series of endeavors to resolve persistent questions concerning the duties of the individual, the family and the community in provision for the less fortunate, of which the twentieth century saga of state pensions is but one chapter" (summarized in Macinol & Blaikie, 1989, pp. 22–23).

Perhaps retirement has increased because people find it attractive. Along these lines, Johnson (1989) has argued that the "structural dependency" hypothesis overemphasizes control and "[pays] little attention to the responses of the group being controlled, in this case elderly people, who are assumed to have little if any room for maneuver . . . [the hypothesis] inevitably focuses attention on employers and the state, and diminishes the importance of choice exercised by elderly people themselves" (pp. 65–66).

COPING WITH UNSTRUCTURED TIME: CURRENT DILEMMAS

Economists argue that scarcity increases and a ready supply decreases the value of a commodity, and therefore we might expect an inverse relationship between generally available unstructured time and the intensity with which people seek to acquire it. As indicated by the first-person interviews noted earlier, many people have had unstructured time thrust into their lives when they would have preferred to have continued remunerated labor of some kind. Currently, the availability of such time for increasingly larger numbers of people especially during their later years has generated what can only be called an ambivalent response. Personal reactions have been less celebratory than we might have expected from listening to the proponents of private and national pension schemes. The fact that over one hundred countries have social welfare programs mixed with private pension plans makes the nature of responses a worldwide phenomenon (Riley & Schrank, 1972, p. 178). To the social historian, the democratization phase of disposable time seems to be marked less by the triumph of the "leisure" concept than by the search (among both recipients and grantors) for ways for recipients to maintain connections with the world of work.

Responses to Unstructured Time

According to Achenbaum (1978), responses to mandatory retirement in the United States appear to have been mixed, though positive attitudes outnumber negative ones: "Roughly a quarter of all retired workers admit feeling obsolete; retired women often express this feeling more intensely than men. Most, however, report no significant sharp decline in life satisfaction, health, and activity after retirement" (p. 156). While the proportion of dissatisfied persons may be relatively small, their absolute numbers add up. Parnes and Less (1985, pp. 206–207) note that men who continue to work full-time beyond the age at which they can collect retirement benefits are only 18% of the category aged 62 to 74 and 12% of those aged 65 to 74. Nonetheless, these relatively small proportions constitute some three-quarter million persons, and their numbers are very likely to increase over the next 35 to 40 years (Kingson, 1982). As we might expect, farmers are particularly overrepresented among older age groups in the labor force; and farmers seem to be opposed to the idea of retirement more than people in other occupational groups (Goudy & Dobson, 1985, pp. 60–61).

The demand for time structured from the traditional sources suggests there has been an ambivalent response to unstructured time. For example, in the former Soviet Union, state-sponsored social gerontology until recently placed central importance on devising ways the retired could continue physical activity and social involvement (Howe,

1988), while the state stood ready to "mobilize pensioners" whenever labor shortages loomed (Porket, 1983). And in the United States, Wilson (1980) observes, in language that may well serve as the central research theme for the democratization phase of unstructured time, that "the 'free time' won by the American worker has been reinvested in activities work-like in their demands" (p. 24). Indeed, the retired continue to think of the unstructured time now at their disposal in terms of the lives they had been leading—creating, among other things, a conflict with leisure providers who "develop a social interest in treating leisure as a separate sphere" (p. 36). But leisure is not deployed in a social vacuum, and the retired frequently have no wish to withdraw to a separate sphere.

Factors Influencing Retirement Adjustment

General orientations to leisure aside, adaptations to unstructured time are affected by a number of factors such as whether or not it is voluntary, and whether there has been previous experience with blocks of free time. Riley and Schrank (1972) conclude, for example: "One interpretation that seems compatible with much of the available evidence is that acceptance of retirement depends strongly upon whether departure from work was perceived as voluntary or coerced" (p. 184). In the 1960s, Gordon (1961) noted that state and private pension schemes, if accompanied by an obligatory age of retirement, met with considerable opposition among many of those who were forced to retire in order to get a pension.

Advance preparation may also affect adaptation to retirement. For example, writing about a German village, Weatherford (1981, p. 156) observed that retirement appears to be brought into older workers' lives piecemeal. Senior workers already had much free time in their work because of very liberal vacation policies amounting to two months a year. In addition, sick leave included preventive rest and recuperation and long visits at health spas. Weatherford sees these as mechanisms for a gradual transition that also included work for those who wanted it even in their 70s. Writing about the United States, Kaplan (1979, pp. 18–19) speaks of the problems of "confront[ing] bulk or block time—whole days, weeks, months, years," and observes that adjustment to retirement may come easier to those who have already managed to obtain throughout their working years many periods of "miniretirement"—shorter working days, longer weekends, vacations, sabbaticals, leaves of absence. At the same time, certain halfway measures have not been free of problems. In Sweden, partial pension schemes that allowed people to continue to work in some way created role ambiguity because, in this half-attachment to the world of work, people did not feel either to be valued employees or to be fully retired (Blyton, 1984, p. 81).

In addition to the nature of the retirement process, other factors affect adaptation to it. The character of family roles is undoubtedly important. In Poland, "among older people living with their children, there was a larger proportion of people feeling lonely than among people living separately" (Synak, 1987, p. 28). Economic considerations can also play a part. In the German village referred to earlier, regardless of the size of people's pensions, there was still the fear that the combination of pensions, savings, and assistance from children would not guarantee self-sufficiency; therefore to turn away from remunerated labor entirely was thought to be foolhardy.

Important as they are, then, pensions can be doubled-edged in their effects. According to Foner (1984, pp. 218–219), "The old are sometimes pressured into ceding property ownership to qualify for government benefits," thereby standing to lose managerial status, property, and prestige. But among the Western Apache, "old people who received monthly pensions were often the wealthiest members of their families, and younger relatives came to them for money. The very frail old also usually received better care."

DEMOCRATIZATION OF UNSTRUCTURED TIME: UNINTENDED CONSEQUENCES

What I have called the democratization of unstructured time has had unintended consequences: "In imposing retirement as a universal goal for all workers, contemporary industrial societies not only have unwittingly extended poverty among their older citizens but also are throwing away an economic contribution to their general prosperity which many of them would gladly make" (Thompson, Itzin, & Abendstern, 1990, p. 142).

The need for cross-cultural study of the elderly is patent (Midre & Synak, 1989; Taylor, 1985);[2] but the linear-historical perspective is also significant as it traces continuities in people's desire to remain attached to the world of work or to worklike activities. The apparent need for structured time among those with unstructured time may seem disappointing in light of what has been believed about the possibilities of leisure and self-actualization in societies that combine abundance, high technology, and strong welfare-state policies. Yet given the long centuries of Western history during which work suffused human lives and structured virtually all waking hours, the continuing desire, even in less harsh conditions, to retain this relationship is not so surprising. Perhaps the question with which I began—what are the human consequences of not being gainfully employed?—has received an answer (at least for the time being): namely, that humans will act so as to replicate in the time dimension of their lives the structuring effects of gainful employment. It is then the job of historians and cultural anthropologists to say whether societies that *appear* to allow "time free from work" (Riley & Schrank, 1972, p. 192) are in fact doing just that, or have only permitted the emergence of different tasks that will satisfy the historically continuing desire among most people to have their time structured. The current experience with unstructured time suggests that the arrival in the West of a true leisure society has been postponed—that the structural lag persists.

REFERENCES

Achenbaum, W. A. (1978). *Old age in the new land: The American experience since 1790*. Baltimore, MD & London: Johns Hopkins University Press.

Blyton, P. (1984). Partial pensions scheme insights from the Swedish partial pensions scheme. *Ageing and Society, 4*, 69–83.

Braithwaite, V., & Gibson, D. (1987). Adjustment to retirement: What we know and what we need to know. *Ageing and Society, 7*, 1–18.

Cribier, F. (1981). Changing retirement patterns: The experience of a cohort of Parisian salaried workers. *Ageing and Society, 1*, 53–71.

---

[2] For a comparative analysis of the amount and use of free time in contemporary society, see Olszewska and Roberts (1989).

Foner, A., & Schwab, K. (1983). Work and retirement in a changing society. In M. W. Riley, B. Hess, & K. Bond (Eds.), *Aging in society: Selected reviews of recent research* (pp. 71–113). Hillsdale, NJ: Erlbaum.

Foner, N. (1984). *Ages in conflict: A cross-cultural perspective on inequality between old and young.* New York: Columbia University Press.

Gaullier, X. (1982). Economic crisis and old age: Old age policies in France. *Ageing & Society, 2,* 165–182.

Gaunt, D. (1983). The property and kin relations of retired farmers. In R. Wall, J. Robin, & P. Laslett (Eds.), *Family forms in historic Europe* (pp. 249–280). Cambridge: Cambridge University Press.

Gordon, M. S. (1961). Work and patterns of retirement. In R. Kleemeier (Ed.), *Aging and leisure: A research perspective into the meaningful uses of time* (pp. 16–53). New York: Oxford University Press.

Goudy, W. J., & Dobson, C. (1985). Work, retirement, and financial situations of the rural elderly. In R. Coward and G. Lee (Eds.), *The elderly in rural society: Every fourth elder* (pp. 57–81). New York: Springer.

Graebner, W. (1980). *A history of retirement: The meaning and function of an American institution, 1858–1978.* New Haven, CT: Yale University Press.

Guillemard, A. (1982). Old age, retirement, and the social class structure: Analysis of the structural dynamics of the latter stage of life. In T. Hareven & K. Adams (Eds.), *Aging and life course transitions: An interdisciplinary perspective* (pp. 221–243). London: Guilford Press.

Guillemard, A. (1983). The social dynamics of early withdrawal from the labor force in France. *Ageing and Society, 3,* 381–412.

Haber, C. (1983). *Beyond sixty-five: The dilemma of old age in American past.* Cambridge: Cambridge University Press.

Hareven, T. (1982). *Family time and industrial time.* New York: Cambridge University Press.

Hendricks, J., & Cutler, S. J. (1990). Leisure and the structure of our life worlds: Forum. *Ageing and Society, 10,* 85–94.

Howe, A. (1988). Themes in Soviet social gerontology. *Ageing and Society, 8,* 147–169.

Jeffries, M. (Ed.). (1989). *Growing old in the twentieth century.* New York: Routledge.

Johnson, P. (1989). The structured dependency of the elderly: A critical note. In M. Jeffries (Ed.), *Growing old in the twentieth century* (pp. 62–72). New York: Routledge.

Kaplan, M. (1979). *Leisure: Lifestyle and lifespan. Perspectives for gerontology.* Philadelphia, PA: Saunders.

Kingson, E. (1982). Current retirement trends. In M. Morrison (Ed.), *Economics of aging: The future of retirement* (pp. 98–135). New York: Van Nostrand.

Kohli, M. (1988). Ageing as a challenge to sociological theory. *Ageing and Society, 8,* 367–394.

Kohli, M., Rosenow, J., & Wolf, J. (1983). The social construction of ageing through work: Economic structure and life-world. *Ageing and Society, 3,* 23–42.

Laslett, P. (1984). The significance of the past in the study of ageing: Introduction to the special issue on history and ageing. *Ageing and Society, 4,* 379–389.

Laslett, P. (1987). The emergence of the third age. *Ageing and Society, 7,* 133–160.

Levine, D. (Ed.). (1984). *Proletarianization and family history.* Orlando, FL: Academic Press.

Macinol, J., & Blaikie, A. (1989). The politics of retirement, 1908–1948. In M. Jeffries (Ed.), *Growing old in the twentieth century* (pp. 21–42). New York: Routledge.

Midre, G., & Synak, B. (1989). Between family and state: Ageing in Poland and Norway. *Ageing and Society, 9,* 241–259.

Minois, G. (1989). In S. Tenison (Trans.), *History of old age from antiquity to the Renaissance.* Chicago, IL: University of Chicago Press. (French original work published 1987.)

Moller, I. H. (1987). Early retirement in Denmark. *Ageing and Society, 7,* 427–442.

Olmstead, A. (1975). *Threshold: The first days of retirement.* New York: Harper & Row.

Olszewska, A., & Roberts, K. (Eds.). (1989). *Leisure and life-style: A comparative analysis of free time.* Newbury Park, CA: Sage.

Orloff, A., & Skocpol, T. (1984). Why not equal protections? Explaining the politics of public social spending in Britain, 1900–1911, and the United States, 1880s–1920. *American Sociological Review, 49,* 726–50.

Ostor, A. (1984). Chronology, category, and ritual. In D. Kertzer & J. Keith (Eds.), *Age and anthropological theory* (pp. 281–304). Ithaca, NY: Cornell University Press.

Parker, S. (1982). *Work and retirement.* London: Allen & Unwin.

Parnes, H. S., & Less, L. J. (1985). Shunning retirement: The experience of full-time workers. H. S. Parnes & L. J. Less (Eds.), *Retirement among American men* (pp. 175–208). Lexington, MA: Lexington Books.

Pelling, M., & Smith, R. (1991). Introduction. In M. Pelling & R. Smith (Eds.), *Life, death, and the elderly: Historical perspectives* (pp. 1–38). New York: Routledge.

Plakans, A. (1989). Stepping down in former times: A comparative assessment of 'retirement' in traditional society. In D. Kertzer & K. W. Schaie (Eds.), *Age structuring in comparative perspective* (pp. 175–195). Hillsdale, NJ: Erlbaum.

Porket, J. (1983). Income maintenance for the Soviet aged. *Ageing and Society, 3,* 301–323.

Quadagno, J. (1982). *Aging in early industrial society: Work, family and social policy in nineteenth-century England.* New York: Academic Press.

Riley, M. W., & Foner, A. (1968). *Aging and society: Vol. I. An inventory of research findings.* New York: Sage.

Riley, M. W., & Schrank, H. (1972). The work force. In M. W. Riley, M. Johnson, & A. Foner (Eds.), *Aging and society: Vol. III. A sociology of age stratification* (pp. 160–195). New York: Sage.

Roebuck, J. (1975). When does old age begin? The evolution of the English definition. *Journal of Social History, 12,* 416–428.

Smith, R. (1984). The structured dependence of the elderly as a recent development: Some skeptical historical thoughts. *Ageing and Society, 4,* 409–428.

Synak, B. (1987). The elderly in Poland: An overview of selected problems and changes. *Ageing and Society, 7,* 19–35.

Taylor, R. (1985). Studying the aging cross-culturally: Review article. *Ageing and Society, 5,* 207–222.

Thompson, P., Itzin, C., & Abendstern, M. (1990). *I don't feel old: The experience of later life.* Oxford: Oxford University Press.

Thomson, D. (1991). The welfare of the elderly in the past: A family or community responsibility? In M. Pelling & R. Smith (Eds.), *Life, death and the elderly: Historical perspectives* (pp. 194–221). New York: Routledge.

Townsend, P. (1981). The structured dependence of the elderly: A creation of social policy in the twentieth-century. *Ageing and Society, 1,* 5–14.

Troyansky, D. G. (1989). *Old age in the old regime: Image and experience in eighteenth-century France.* London: Cornell University Press.

Weatherford, J. M. (1981). Labor and domestic life cycles in a German community. In C. Fry (Ed.), *Dimensions: Aging, culture and health* (pp. 145–161). New York: Praeger.

Wilson, J. (1980). Sociology of leisure. In A. Inkeles, N. Smelser, & R. Turner (Eds.), *Annual review of sociology* (Vol. 6, pp. 21–40). Palo Alto, CA: Annual Reviews, Inc.

CHAPTER 6

Family Change and Historical Change: An Uneasy Relationship

Tamara K. Hareven[1]

T hrough much of the American past, the family has been seen as the linchpin of the social order and the basis for stable governance. Thus the family, unique among the social structures discussed in this book, serves as a broker between individuals and other social processes and institutions. Yet, the role of the family and the values governing its comportment and relationship to the community have been subjected to various paradoxes, which have rendered adaptation to change and realization of the family's responsibilities to individual members exceedingly difficult (Demos, 1970; Hareven, 1977b).

The concept of structural lag, defined in this book as the mismatch between changing lives and changing social structures (see Chapter 1), is remarkably applicable to understanding the social changes involving the family and the anxieties surrounding its future. The conceptual framework helps identify the dilemma the family is facing in

[1] The author acknowledges with gratitude the valuable editorial suggestions from Jack and Matilda Riley, Anne Foner, and Jenifer Dolde.

contemporary society in light of the contradictions surrounding its role. Because of the power of these contradictions, I will differentiate between a structural and a cultural lag.[2] The cultural component concerns the myths and stereotypes in American society that govern expectations from the family, and that are used as a yardstick for the assessment of "normal" or "deviant" family behavior. Since these myths and stereotypes about the family have had a strong impact on individuals, institutions and policy, it is important to examine how the cultural, as well as the structural, lag is exacerbating the misfit between social change and individual and familial needs (Hareven, 1981). One of the main problems affecting the family's ability to discharge its responsibilities is a mismatch between social and economic change, on the one hand, and the pace of family change and the ideologies governing its role, on the other hand.

The lag affecting the family does not involve a simple linear change and a carryover of 19th-century patterns into the present. Those aspects of change at dissonance with contemporary social needs involve developments that have occurred since the late 19th century. By contrast, certain earlier family and life course patterns (in the preindustrial era and in some periods in the 19th century) would be more compatible with complex social conditions in the 1990s, than contemporary patterns. The late 19th-century family patterns that are at odds with contemporary societal needs include the ideal of domesticity involving the view of motherhood and homemaking as full-time pursuits; the ideal of privacy enshrining the segregation of the family from the community and the larger society; and the diminution of interaction between the nuclear family unit and the wider kin group.

At the same time, earlier historical patterns more compatible with contemporary needs and developments are still surviving in certain groups of the population. If those were to be recognized and supported, a better fit between other contemporary structures and the family could be achieved. Such patterns include flexible and creative use of household arrangements involving coresidence with nonfamily members as well as with kin; instrumental relations among nuclear family members and extended kin; diversity in family forms; kinship

---

[2] In this book, cultural values and normative expectations as institutionalized in structures are treated, for parsimony, as components of structural lag.

networks including complex configurations of kin and surrogate kin; acceptance of married women's employment as part of a collective family effort in the working class; "erratic" flexible timing of life course transitions; and a closer integration between family and community. A historical consideration of such family patterns helps us assess the uniqueness of contemporary conditions and distinguish between long-term trends and temporary aberrations. From a historical perspective, this chapter explores family patterns in American society that have been affected by both a structural and a cultural lag resulting from the social and cultural construction of the role of the family. It examines changes in the family in relation to cultural and structural lags in the following areas: the organization and role of the household; interdependence among kin; privacy and sentimentality in family relations and the family's relationship to the community; women's work and the ideology of domesticity; and the timing of life transitions.

MYTHS ABOUT THE PAST

A series of myths about family life in the past cloud popular understanding of contemporary problems. According to these myths, three generations lived together happily in the same household, families were intimate and close-knit units, and single-parent households rarely existed. This belief in a lost "golden age" has led people to depict the present as a period of decline in the family. Nostalgia for a nonexistent past has handicapped policymakers in assessing realistically the recent changes in family life (Hareven, 1990). For example, the efforts in the late 1970s early 1980s to legislate changes in family behavior that would return the family to "the way it once was," are a striking example of policymakers' presumptions of what the family was like in the past. (See *Family Protection Act,* 1979; 1981.)

Despite persistence of this stereotype, historical research has dispelled the myths about the existence of ideal three-generational families in the American past. A nuclear household structure has predominated since the 17th century. There never existed in American society or in Western Europe an era when coresidence of three generations in the same household was the dominant pattern. The "great extended families" that became part of the folklore of modern society were what William Goode (1963) referred to as a product of

"Western nostalgia" (p. 6). Early American households were simple in their structure. Three generations seldom lived together in the same household. Given the high mortality rate in preindustrial societies, most grandparents could not have expected to overlap with their grandchildren. It would thus be futile to argue that industrialization destroyed the great extended family of the past, when such a family type rarely existed (Demos, 1970; Greven, 1970; Laslett & Wall, 1972).

Internal household arrangements in early American society differed, however, from those in our times. Even though households did not contain extended kin, early American households did include unrelated individuals, such as boarders, lodgers, apprentices, and servants, as well as dependent members in the community (Demos, 1970; Modell & Hareven, 1973). The tendency to include nonrelatives in the household was derived from a different cultural concept of family life. Unlike today, when the household—"home"—serves as a private retreat for the family and is, therefore, primarily a site of consumption, the household in the past was the locus of a broad array of functions and activities that transcended the more restricted circle of the nuclear family. In this respect, the historical households would be more suitable to serving today's social needs, as explained later in this chapter.

THE MALLEABLE HOUSEHOLD

Despite an overall commitment to residence in nuclear households, which was practiced by members of various ethnic groups and native-born Americans alike, the nuclear family included kin in times of need or at the later stages of the life course (Anderson, 1971; Hareven, 1977a). Household space was an important resource to be shared and exchanged over the life course. It was shared with boarders and lodgers in exchange for services or rent, or with children who had already left home and married, but who, during economic crises, housing shortages or when the parents became too frail to live alone, returned with their spouses to reside with their parents in exchange for services or supports. Since the household was considered an economic resource, its membership changed in relation to the family's economic opportunities and needs over the life course. Households were like a revolving stage on which different family members appeared, disappeared, and reappeared at their own initiative or under the impact of external conditions such as migration, labor markets, or housing shortages (Hareven, 1982).

Household members engaged in direct exchanges across neighborhoods, as well as over wide geographic regions. As some members went out into the world, newcomers moved in. Individuals whose families were disrupted by migration or death were often absorbed into other people's households. Young people were able to move to new communities, confident that they would board or lodge with relatives or strangers. Working mothers were able to place young children in the homes of relatives or strangers, and dependent elders, who had become too infirm or poor to live alone, moved into their children's or other people's households. Such exchanges among relatives, neighbors, or complete strangers were laced through the entire society, as the family performed its function as broker between individuals and other social structures (Hareven, 1982; 1990).

The greatest flexibility in the use of household space was in the taking of boarders and lodgers. Throughout the 19th century and the early part of the 20th century, one-third to one-half of all households took in boarders or lodgers at some point over their head's life course. In the later years of life, boarding and lodging served as the "social equalization of the family," a strategy by which young men or women who left their parents' home communities moved into the households of people whose own children had left home (Modell & Hareven, 1973). This practice provided young migrants to the city with surrogate family arrangements, middle-aged or older couples with supplemental income, and families with young children with alternative sources of income and child care. The income from boarders and lodgers provided the necessary supplement for new homeowners to pay mortgages and for wives to stay out of the labor force. The taking in of boarders and lodgers, a practice more widespread than admitting extended kin, thus made it easier for families to adhere to their traditional values without slipping below the margin of poverty.

Despite preferences for nonkin, families also took kin into the household, though usually for limited periods during times of need, or at specific stages in the life course. Only about 12% to 18% of all urban households in the late 19th and early 20th centuries contained relatives other than members of the nuclear family (Hareven, 1977a). The proportion of households taking in kin increased to 25% over the

20th century, and declined to 7% by 1950 (Ruggles, 1987). Sharing the family's household space with kin was nevertheless an important migration and life course strategy. In urban industrial communities, which attracted large numbers of migrants from the countryside or immigrants from abroad, there was a visible increase in coresidence with extended kin over the 19th century. Newly arrived migrants usually stayed with their relatives for a limited time period—until they found jobs and housing. Then they set up separate households (Glasco, 1977; Hareven, 1982). They, in turn, took others into their own households when the need arose, but again on a temporary basis. Coresidence with extended kin was most common in the later years of life, when aging parents shared their coveted household space with their newlywed children, who delayed establishment of an independent household because of housing shortages (Chudacoff & Hareven, 1978; 1979).

Continuing to head their own household was an almost sacred goal in American society among native as well as foreign-born couples. Older people, especially widowed mothers, avoided at all cost living in their children's homes. Parents usually prepared for old age by requiring their youngest daughter to postpone her marriage and stay with them; if that was not possible, they took in boarders and lodgers. Only if all these failed did they move in with a child or another relative. In these cases, the child who took in the parents headed the household; whereas in the case of newlywed couples, the parents continued to head their own household (Chudacoff, 1978; Chudacoff & Hareven, 1978, 1979; Hareven & Adams, 1994).

For older people in urban society, holding on to the space and headship of their household in exchange for future assistance in old age was a life course strategy reminiscent of the contracts between inheriting sons and rural older people in preindustrial Europe and Colonial New England (Demos, 1970). In the past, these types of accommodations encouraged greater flexibility in household arrangements than in contemporary society.

INTERDEPENDENCE AMONG KIN

The role of kin in the past has been central in individuals' functioning and adaptation to new social and economic changes and in coping with critical life situations. The viable historic patterns of kin assistance could provide an important model for the present, as new configurations of kin and surrogate kin have been emerging. Even though the nuclear family resided separately from extended kin, its members were enmeshed in kinship networks that provided reciprocal assistance over the life course. Kin served as the most essential resource for assistance and security and carried the major burdens of welfare functions for individual family members. Contrary to prevailing myths, urbanization and industrialization did not break down traditional kinship ties and patterns of mutual assistance. Historical studies have documented the survival of viable functions of kin in the 19th century, especially their central role in facilitating migration, in finding jobs and housing, and in assistance during critical life situations, particularly in the later years of life (Anderson, 1971; Hareven, 1978; 1982). Patterns of kin assistance were pervasive in neighborhoods and extended back to the communities of origin of immigrants and migrants. Contemporary research has documented continuity in the viable roles of kin in modern American society (Litwak, 1960; Shanas et al., 1968; Sussman & Burchinal, 1962).

In a regime of economic insecurity, and in the absence of welfare institutions, kin assistance was the only constant source of social security. Kin carried the major burden of welfare functions, many of which fall now within the purview of the public sector. Reciprocity among parents and children and other kin provided the major, and sometimes the only, base for supports during critical life situations, especially in the later years. Mutual assistance among kin, although involving extensive exchanges, was not strictly calculative. Rather, it expressed an overall principle of reciprocity over the life course and across generations. Individuals' sense of obligation to their kin was a manifestation of their family culture—a commitment to the survival, well-being, and self-reliance of the family, which took priority over individual needs and personal happiness (Hareven, 1982). Autonomy of the family, essential for self-respect and good standing in the neighborhood and community, was one of the most deeply ingrained values.

Individuals who subordinated their own careers and needs to those of the family did so out of a sense of responsibility, affection, and familial obligation, rather than with the expectation of immediate gain. Such sacrifices were not made, however, without protest, and at times involved competition and conflict among siblings on issues such as who should carry the burden of support for aging parents. The salient role of kin, and the strong sense of obligation and reciprocities that kin carried toward each other, have shaped early cohorts' expectations for supports and sociability in the later years of life. This type of integration with kin is still present in the life experience of those early cohort members who are now among the "old old" (Hareven, 1982). More recent cohorts, on the other hand, were inclined to turn to new bureaucratic agencies rather than to kin as their major sources of economic support in old age (Hareven & Adams, 1994).

The increasing separation between the family of orientation and the family of procreation over the 20th century, combined with a growing privatization of the family, occurred in the context of changes in the quality of relations with extended kin. The major historical change has not been in the decline of coresidence with kin, but rather in the nature of kin interaction and supports. The gradual erosion of the interdependence among kin has tended to increase insecurity and isolation in old age, especially in areas of need that have not been met by public programs. The difference lies in the extent of individuals' integration with kin and their dependence on mutual assistance. While more intensive patterns of kin interaction have survived among first-generation immigrants and working-class families, there has been an overall erosion of instrumental kin relations and an increasing focus on the private, nuclear family. This pattern differs, however, among various ethnic groups.

The historic shift of major responsibility for the material well-being of older people from the family to the public sector has generated some ambiguity in the expectations for support and assistance for aging relatives from their own kin. On the one hand, it is assumed that the welfare state has relieved children from the obligations of supporting their parents in old age. On the other hand, these public measures are often insufficient in meeting economic need, nor do they provide the kind of supports and sociability in areas that had been traditionally carried by the family. It is precisely this ambiguity, along with the failure of American society to consummate the historical process of the transfer of some major functions of welfare from the family to the public sector, that has become one of the major sources of the problems currently confronting older people. Even today, in the small fraction of families where the older person is severely disabled, most care is provided by the spouse, a daughter or daughter-in-law, or other relative, but at a high price to the caregiver (Brody, 1981). However, any kind of plans to return the major care for aging relatives to the family cannot be carried out realistically without providing supports to the family that would enable it to meet such expectations.

Despite the survival of some traditional patterns of kin assistance among certain ethnic groups, it would be unrealistic to expect that kin could carry the major burdens for the care of aging relatives, for several reasons. Except for the baby boomers, future cohorts will have fewer kin available to them when they reach dependent old age (Uhlenberg, 1979). Even if kin are available, several changes converge to reduce the potential efficacy of kin: The employment of women in full-time careers limits the pool of available traditional caregivers, and the extension of life has brought about the "life cycle squeeze," where the children of the "old old" are old themselves and, therefore, unable to provide the necessary supports to their parents (Brody, 1981; Hogan, Eggebeen, & Snaith, 1993). The only way in which kin could be utilized to aid aging relatives would be by providing them with public supports to carry out these tasks.

Alternatively, new, complex, and more flexible kinship and surrogate kinship configurations are emerging as a result of divorce, remarriage, the formation of blended families, and cohabitation. These new kinship ties could be strengthened and utilized in a constructive way for the care of aging relatives. As Riley and Riley (1994) point out, these new networks, including "step-kin and in-laws and also adopted and other surrogate relatives chosen from outside the family," form "a latent web of continually shifting linkages that provide the potential for activating and intensifying close kin relationships as they are needed" (p. 173). Such networks could make it possible to form new configurations of assistance at various stages of the life course.

PRIVACY AND THE FAMILY'S RETREAT FROM THE COMMUNITY

The emergence of privacy as one of the central values governing family life has handicapped the family's effective interaction with other social institutions. Originating at first with the urban middle class in the 19th century, privacy has become an ideal of family life and of individual comportment in the larger society (Ariés, 1962; Lasch, 1977). Privacy gradually became pervasive with the triumph of middle-class values and their acceptance by working-class families and by the older waves of immigrants as they became Americanized.

The triumph of the values of privacy has led to an increasing separation of the nuclear family from extended kin and to the closing of the household to nonrelatives. The idealization of the family's role as a private retreat and as an emotional haven is misguided in light of our knowledge of the past. The loss of the family's sociability as a result of its function as a refuge from the outside world has rendered it less flexible and less capable of handling internal, as well as external, crises. According to Ariés (1962), family life in the past exposed children to a diversity of role models—friends, clients, relatives, and protégés—equipping them to function in a complex society. Paradoxically, as the society and the economy have become more diversified over time, the family has become more streamlined and segregated from the outside world. The tendency of the family to shelter its members from other social institutions may well have weakened its ability to affect social change or to influence the programs and legislation that public agencies have directed toward the family.

Closely related to the ideals of privacy in the family has been an excessive emphasis on individual rather than collective needs and on sentiment as the core of family relations. Over the past several decades, American families have been experiencing their members' increasing preference to follow individual priorities and preferences over collective family needs. This major historical change from a view of the family collectivity to one of individualization and sentiment has caused a further lag in the family's adaptability.

The individualization of family relations has combined with an exaggerated emphasis on emotional nurture and sentiment as the crucible of the family's role. On the one hand, it has contributed considerably to the liberation of individuals from familial pressures; on the other hand, it has eroded the resilience of the family and its malleability in weathering crises and coping with change. Moreover, it has led to a greater separation among the generations and especially to the isolation of older people. One of the major sources of the crisis of the private nuclear family today may be its difficulty in adapting to the emotional responsibilities thrust on it. Concentration on the nurturing and sentimental functions of the family has grown at the expense of another of the family's much-needed roles: to prepare members to function in a complex bureaucratic society.

In the past, instrumental relations in the family and in the wider kinship group provided important supports to individuals and families, particularly during social and economic crises and critical life situations. Family members were valued not merely for providing emotional satisfaction to each other, but for a wide array of services on their part for the family. A collective view of familial obligations was at the very basis of survival. From such a perspective, marriage and parenthood were not merely love relationships but partnerships directed to serve the family's goals and needs (Hareven, 1982). The relationships between husbands and wives, parents and children, and other kin were based on reciprocal assistance and supports. Such "instrumental" relations drew their strength from the assumption that family members had mutual obligations and engaged in reciprocity. Although obligations were not specifically defined by contract, they rested on the accepted social expectation of what family members owed to each other (Anderson, 1971; Hareven, 1982).

The experience of working-class families in the 19th century and of ethnic families in the more recent past was drastically different from that of middle-class families, among whom sentimentality emerged as the dominant base of family relationships. Among the former, sentiment was secondary to family needs and survival strategies. Hence, the timing of children's leaving home and of marriage and the commencement of work careers were regulated in accordance with collective family considerations rather than guided by individual preferences. For example, parents tried to delay the marriage of the last child in the household, commonly a daughter, to secure continued supports in later life when they were withdrawing from the labor force. Certain working-class and ethnic families have continued to adhere to earlier ways of life by maintaining a collective view of the family and its economy (Hareven, 1982). In contrast to the values of individualism that govern much of family life today, traditional values of family collectivity have persisted among certain ethnic groups.

In the preindustrial period, the family interacted closely with the community in discharging responsibilities of welfare and social control for family members as well as for unattached members of the community. The family not only reared children but also served as a workshop, a school, a church, and a welfare agency. Preindustrial families meshed closely with the community and carried a variety of public responsibilities within the larger society (Demos, 1970). Over the 19th century, however, the family surrendered many of the functions previously concentrated within it to other social, economic, and welfare institutions. The family's retreat from public life and the commitment to the privacy of initially the modern middle-class family have drawn sharper boundaries between family and community at the very time in historical development when families could have benefited from various forms of interaction with the larger society in areas such as care for family members during critical life situations, as well as for children and for aged relatives. The community has ceased to rely on the family as the major agency of welfare and social control, and the family has ceased to be the primary source of support for its dependent members. Nevertheless, no adequate substitute agencies for the care of elderly dependent people have been developed.

THE IDEOLOGY OF DOMESTICITY AND WOMEN'S WORK

Married women's entry into the labor force and their pursuit of a career have been handicapped by the structural and cultural lags between women's changing roles and the tenacity of older institutional and ideological practices. While married women, especially mothers, have been assuming full-time careers, institutional adjustments have not kept apace with these developments. First, child-care facilities in contemporary society have not fully met the needs of working mothers, especially in low-income groups (see Chapter 7). Second, mothers have had to carry out their work in a climate where vestiges of the ideology of domesticity still prevail. Appearing first in the early 19th century in middle-class families, this ideology has idealized motherhood and homemaking as women's full-time occupations and consequently, it has constrained the opportunities for mothers to develop careers in paid work outside the home.

Women's labor force participation has also been at odds with the increasing need to provide care in the home for the dependent and chronically ill elderly. Because the major responsibilities for the care of children and older people and various other aspects of kin assistance have been historically in the women's domain, it is not surprising that women have emerged as the main caretakers of elderly relatives today. The "generation in the middle," consisting of stressed-out, caregiving women, usually daughters of dependent, frail, or chronically ill elderly, has become a well-known phenomenon of the aging society

(Brody, 1981). Ironically, the burden of care for aging relatives has been thrust on certain cohorts of women just at the time when they were trying to pursue individual work careers, after launching their children into adulthood.

In preindustrial society, even though families contained large numbers of children, women invested relatively less time fulfilling the duties of motherhood than did their successors in the 19th century, as well as in our time. Child care was part of a collective family effort, rather than a woman's exclusive preoccupation. From an early age on, children were viewed not merely as tender objects of nurture but as productive members of the family and society. Responsibility for the tasks of child rearing did not fall exclusively on mothers; older siblings and other relatives living nearby also participated in this process. The integration of family and work allowed for an intensive sharing of labor between husbands and wives, and between parents and children, that was later diminished in industrial society. Housework was inseparable from domestic industries or agricultural work, and it was valued, therefore, as an economic asset.

Under the impact of industrialization, the family's functions of production were transferred to agencies and institutions outside the family. The workplace was separated from the home, and asylums and reformatories assumed many of the functions of social welfare and social control previously held by the family. "The family has become *a more specialized agency than before*," wrote Talcott Parsons (1955), ". . . but not in any general sense less important, because the society is dependent *more* exclusively on it for the performance of *certain* of its vital functions" (pp. 9–10). These include childbearing, child rearing, and socialization. The family has ceased to be a work unit and has limited its economic activities primarily to consumption and child care.

These changes in family life that accompanied industrialization were gradual, however, and varied significantly from class to class as well as among different ethnic groups. Preindustrial family patterns persisted over longer time periods among rural and urban working-class families. Most working-class families still considered their members' work a family enterprise, even when they were employed outside the home. The labor of wives, sons, and daughters was carefully regulated by the collective strategies of the family unit. Much of what we perceive today as individual work careers was actually considered part of a collective family effort. Women continued to function as integral partners in the family's productive effort, even when they worked in factories. Daughters were considered assets, both for their contribution to the family's economy during their youth and for the prospect of their support during their parents' old age (Hareven, 1982; Tilly & Scott, 1978).

This continuity in the family's function as a collective economic unit is significant for understanding the changes in the roles of women that industrialization introduced into working-class life. Industrialization offered women the opportunity to become wage earners outside the home. In the working class, however, it did not bring about immediate changes in the family's collective identity—at least not during the early stages of industrialization.

Among middle-class families, on the other hand, industrialization initially had a more dramatic impact on gender roles. The transformation of the household from a busy workplace and social center to the family's private abode involved the exclusion of nonrelatives, such as business associates, partners, journeymen, apprentices, and boarders, from the household. It led to a more rigorous separation of husbands from wives and fathers from children in the course of the workday. Men worked outside the home while women stayed at home and children went to school. The separation of the home from the workplace that followed in the wake of industrialization led to the enshrinement of the home as a domestic retreat from the outside world, and to the development of the child-centered family (Demos, 1970; Welter, 1966; Wishy, 1968).

The ideology of domesticity and the new view of childhood as a tender stage of life requiring nurture, combined to revise expectations of parenthood. The roles of husbands and wives became gradually more separate. A clear division of labor replaced the old economic cooperation. The wives' efforts concentrated on homemaking and child rearing, while men worked outside the home. Time invested in fatherhood was concentrated primarily on leisure. As custodians of this retreat, women were expected to concentrate on perfect homemaking, and on child rearing, rather than on serving as economic partners in the family. Tenderness, gentleness, affection, sweetness, and a comforting demeanor began to emerge as the crucible of family relationships. Stripped of the multiplicity of functions that had been previously concentrated in the family, urban middle-class families developed into private, domestic, and child-centered retreats from the world of work and politics (Degler, 1980; Welter, 1966).

These patterns, which emerged in the early 19th century, formed the base of relations characteristic of the contemporary middle-class American family. Some of them have persisted to the present day and are the root of certain problems in the family and in the contemporary gendered division of labor. Because the prejudices against mothers' labor force participation persevered at least until the 1960s and handicapped women's pursuits of occupations outside the home, it is important to understand their origin in the 19th-century cult of domesticity (Degler, 1980; Welter, 1966).

The ideology of domesticity and of full-time motherhood that developed in the first half of the 19th century relegated women to the home and glorified their role as homemakers and mothers. Ironically, this ideology was closely connected to the decline in the average number of children a woman had and to the new attitudes toward childhood that were emerging in the 19th century. The recognition of childhood as a distinct stage of life among urban middle-class families led to the treatment of children as objects of nurture, rather than as contributing members to the family economy (Wishy, 1968).

Over the late 19th century and the early part of the 20th century, the ideology of domesticity was gradually adopted as the dominant model for family life in the entire society. Second- and third-generation immigrant families, who originally held a view of the family as an integrated corporate unit, and who had earlier accepted the wife's work outside the home, began to embrace the ideology of domesticity as part of the process of "Americanization" (Hareven & Modell, 1980). In the early part of the 20th century, after internalizing the values of domesticity, ethnic and working-class families also began to view women's labor force participation as demeaning, compromising for the husband, and harmful for the children. Consequently, married women entered the labor force only when driven by economic necessity.

Until very recently, the ideology of domesticity has dominated perceptions of women's roles and has shaped prevailing assumptions governing family life. The consequences of this ideology have been the insistence on confining women's main activities to the domestic sphere, and the misguided assumption that mothers' work outside the home would be harmful to family and society. Only over the past few decades, as a result of the women's movement, have these values been criticized and partly rejected. But the cultural lag from the 19th century is still reflected in the censure of mothers' labor force participation.

CHANGES IN THE TIMING OF LIFE TRANSITIONS

Paradoxically, while demographic and social changes over the past two decades have propelled families and individuals into more complex family configurations and into the erratic timing of life course transitions, the normative and institutional ideal of a streamlined, uniform life course still prevails. One widely held myth about the distant past is that the timing of life transitions was more orderly and stable than it is today. The complexity that governs family life today, as well as the variations in family roles and in transitions into them, are frequently contrasted with this more placid past.

The historical experience, however, reveals a very different condition: Patterns of family timing in the past were often as complex, diverse, and erratic as they are today (Uhlenberg, 1978). From the late 19th to the mid 20th century, however, the timing of life course transitions in American society did become more streamlined, more uniform, and more closely articulated to age grading and age norms. Voluntary and involuntary demographic changes that started in the late 19th century resulted in a period of greater uniformity in the timing of transitions. Yet, the developments of the past two decades have led to the reemergence of erratic timing of life transitions. As will be explained, however, the reasons for these contemporary patterns of timing differ from those in the past.

In the 19th century, the timing of life transitions to adulthood (leaving school, starting to work, leaving home, setting up a separate household, and getting married) was erratic, did not follow an established sequence, and took a long time to accomplish. Young people shuttled back and forth from school to work, moved in and out of the parental home, and did not set up a separate household until their marriage. Even after marriage, young couples returned to live temporarily with their parents if the parents needed assistance, or during housing shortages (Modell, Furstenberg, & Hershberg, 1976). The timing of early life transitions was bound up with later ones in a continuum of familial obligations. Aging parents' needs for support from their children affected the latter's transitions into independent adulthood (Modell & Hareven, 1978).

In the 19th century, later life transitions were timed even more erratically than earlier ones. In the absence of mandatory retirement, people worked as long as they could. When older men were not able to work any longer on their regular occupations, they alternated between periods of work and unemployment and took on downwardly mobile but physically less demanding jobs (Hareven, 1982; see also Chapters 3 and 11). Women's work lives were erratic over their entire life course, in relation to marriage, childbearing, and child rearing. Older women experienced more marked life transitions than men because losing a spouse was more commonly the experience of women. The continuing presence of adult children in the household, however, meant that widowhood did not necessarily represent a dramatic transition into an empty nest (Chudacoff & Hareven, 1979).

Timing of early life transitions was erratic in the 19th century, because it followed family needs and obligations rather than specific age norms. During the 1970s and 1980s, by contrast, age norms and individual preferences emerged as more important determinants of timing than familial obligations. As Modell et al. (1976) characterized this difference: "'Timely' action to 19th-century families consisted of helpful response in times of trouble; in the 20th century, timeliness connotes adherence to a socially-sanctioned schedule." A rigid, age-related timing of family transitions is mainly a mid-20th-century phenomenon (p. 30).

Over the past two decades or so, however, the erratic, more flexible patterns of timing of life course transitions have emerged again. These new patterns depart from the earlier age-related rigidities in timing to reflect changes in family arrangements, values governing generational relations, a greater individualization, and new policies regulating the work life. For example, over the past decade, the age of first marriage has risen. Remarriage following divorce has resulted in a wide spread in the age at marriage, in greater age differences between spouses, and in later commencement of childbearing. There has also been an erratic movement of young adult children in and out of the parental home (Goldscheider & Waite, 1991). The continued residence of young adult children in the parental home, or their return after having left home, however, differs from this practice in the past in a fundamental way: In the late 19th century, children continued to stay at home, or returned after they had left, to meet the needs of their family of orientation—to take care of aging parents in some cases and of young siblings in others. In contemporary society, young adult children (including divorced or unmarried daughters with their own young children) return home to meet their own needs: because of their inability to develop an independent work career or to find afford-able housing or because they need help in child care (Cherlin, 1992).

The contemporary erratic style of family transitions coincides with changing patterns of retirement (as discussed in Chapters 3 and 11). The rigid end to a work career is becoming erratic once again, but for very different reasons than those in the past. The "golden handshake" to encourage or force early retirement does not solve the dilemma of the lag described in the Introduction: "Today by con-trast [to the 19th century], survival into old age is commonplace and many years of vigorous postretirement life are the realistic expecta-tion . . . . Nevertheless, the major responsibilities for work and family are still crowded into what are now the middle years of long life. . . . Despite the 20th-century metamorphosis in human lives . . . the social structures and norms that define opportunities and expectations throughout the life course carry the vestigial marks of the 19th century."

REDUCING THE MISFIT

Currently, there are two sources of misfit between family and society: (1) some societal institutions lag behind the changing needs of the family unit and of individual family members; and (2) the family has not always adapted to contemporary social and cultural changes. To achieve a balance that serves well the family as well as individuals will require adaptive changes in the family, in other societal institutions, and in cultural attitudes governing family comportment. In this re-gard, it is helpful to call on some of the historical patterns of family behavior in the past outlined in this chapter. This is not to suggest that we turn the clock backward or revive older patterns that are incompat-ible with the present. Rather, certain models from the past could be adapted to contemporary needs to overcome the structural and cul-tural lag between the family and other social structures. This task is rendered easier because some of these historic patterns are still surviv-ing in the experience of certain ethnic groups.

American society is multilayered, containing significant differences in values and attitudes toward the family based on differences in class and ethnicity. Because of differences in the timing of the influx of various ethnic groups into American society, some of the historic family patterns that would be compatible with contemporary needs still survive. Such patterns were often denigrated because they did not conform to the stereotype of the nuclear, WASP family ideal (Hareven & Modell, 1980). Over the past two decades, however, these varieties of family and kin configurations and patterns of mutual assistance have gained increasing recognition and appreciation for their ability to negotiate the complexity of institutional change—to aid the family as broker between individuals and other structures.

Now is the time to recognize these family forms and to foster their adaptation to contemporary needs. At the same time, institutions and cultural stereotypes upholding the "ideal" family and women's roles must be modified to meet the pressing needs resulting from changes in the family, in women's work patterns, and in the life course. Now is the time to reduce both the structural and the cultural lag.

REFERENCES

Anderson, M. (1971). *Family structure in nineteenth-century Lancashire*. Cambridge: Cambridge University Press.

Ariés, P. (1962). In R. Baldick (Trans.), *Centuries of childhood*. New York: Knopf.

Brody, E. (1981). Women in the middle and family help to older people. *The Gerontologist, 21*(5), 471–480.

Cherlin, A. J. (1992). *Marriage, divorce, remarriage*. Cambridge: Harvard University Press.

Chudacoff, H. (1978). Newlyweds and Family Extension: The First Stage of the Family Cycle in Providence, Rhode Island, 1864–1865 and 1879–1880. In T. K. Hareven & M. A. Vinovskis (Eds.), *Family and Population in Nineteenth-Century America*. Princeton, NJ: Princeton University Press.

Chudacoff, H., & Hareven, T. K. (1978). Family transitions and household structure in the later years of life. In T. K. Hareven (Ed.), *Transitions: The family life and the life course in historical perspective*. New York: Academic Press.

Chudacoff, H., & Hareven, T. K. (1979). From the empty nest to family dissolution. *Journal of Family History, 4,* 59–63.

Degler, C. N. (1980). *At odds: Women and the family in America from the Revolution to the present*. New York: Oxford University Press.

Demos, J. (1970). *A little commonwealth: Family life in Plymouth Colony*. New York: Oxford University Press.

Glasco, L. A. (1977). The life cycles and household structure of American ethnic groups: Irish, Germans and native-born whites in Buffalo, NY, 1885. In T. K.

Hareven (Ed.), *Family and kin in American urban communities, 1700–1930*. New York: Franklin Watts, New Viewpoints.

Goldscheider, F. K., & Waite, L. J. (1991). *New families, no families?* Berkeley, CA: University of California Press.

Goode, W. (1963). *World revolution and family patterns.* New York: Macmillan, Free Press.

Greven, P. J. (1970). *Four generations: Population, land, and family in Colonial Andover, MA.* Ithaca, NY: Cornell University Press.

Hareven, T. K. (1977a). The historical study of the family in urban society. In T. K. Hareven (Ed.), *Family and kin in urban communities, 1700–1930.* New York: Franklin Watts, New Viewpoints.

Hareven, T. K. (1977b). Family time and historical time. *Daedalus, 106,* 57–70.

Hareven, T. K. (1978). The dynamics of kin in an industrial community. In J. Demos & S. Boocock (Eds.), *Turning points: Historical and sociological essays on the family.* Chicago, IL: American Journal of Sociology, Supp., *84,* S151–S182.

Hareven, T. K. (1981). American families in transition: Historical perspectives on change. In F. Walsh (Ed.), *Normal families in social cultural context.* New York: Guilford Press.

Hareven, T. K. (1982). *Family time and industrial time.* New York: Cambridge University Press.

Hareven, T. K. (1990). A Complex Relationship: Family Strategies and the Processes of Economic and Social Change. In R. Friedland and A. F. Robertson (Ed.) *Beyond the Marketplace.* New York: Aldine de Gruyter.

Hareven, T. K. (1992). Continuity and Change in American Family Life. In L. S. Luedtke (Ed.), *Making America: The Society & Culture of the United States.* Chapel Hill, NC: The University of North Carolina Press.

Hareven, T. K., & Adams, K. (1994, Forthcoming). The generation in the middle: Cohort comparisons in assistance to aging parents in an American community. In T. K. Hareven (Ed.), *Aging and generational relations over the life course: A historical and cross-cultural perspective.* Berlin: De Gruyter.

Hareven, T. K., & Modell, J. (1980). Family patterns. In S. Thernstrom (Ed.), *Harvard encyclopedia of American ethnic groups.* Cambridge: Harvard University Press, Belknap Press.

Hogan, D., Eggebeen, D., & Snaith, S. (1993, Forthcoming). The well-being of aging Americans with very old parents. In T. K. Hareven (Ed.), *Aging and generational relations over the life course: A historical and cross-cultural perspective.* Berlin: De Gruyter.

Lasch, C. (1977). *Haven in a heartless world.* New York: Basic Books.

Laslett, P., & Wall, R. (Eds.). (1972). *Household and family in past time.* Cambridge: Cambridge University Press.

Litwak, E. (1960). Geographical mobility and extended family cohesion. *American Sociological Review, 25,* 385–394.

Modell, J., Furstenberg, F., & Hershberg, T. (1976). Social change and transition to adulthood in historical perspective. *Journal of Family History, 1,* 7–32.

Modell, J., & Hareven, T. K. (1973). Urbanization and the malleable household: An examination of boarding and lodging in American families. *Journal of Marriage and the Family, 35,* 467–479.

Modell, J., & Hareven, T. K. (1978). Patterns of timing. In T. K. Hareven (Ed.), *Transitions: The family and the life course in historical perspective.* New York: Academic Press.

Parsons, T. (1955). The American family: Its relations to personality and to the social structure. In R. Parsons & R. Bales (Eds.), *Family, socialization, and interaction process.* Glencoe, IL: Free Press.

Riley, M. W., & Riley, J. W. (1994). Generational relations: A future perspective. In T. K. Hareven (Ed.), *Aging and generational relations over the life course: A historical and cross-cultural perspective.* Berlin: De Gruyter.

Ruggles, S. (1987). *Prolonged connections: The rise of the extended family in nineteenth-century England and America.* Madison, WI: University of Wisconsin Press.

Shanas, E. et al. (1968). *Old People in Three Industrial Societies.* New York: Atherton Press.

Sussman, M., & Burchinal, L. (1962). Kin family network: Unheralded structure in current conceptualization of family functioning. *Marriage and Family Living, 24,* 231–240.

Tilly, L. A., & Scott, J. W. (1978). *Women, work & family.* New York: Holt, Rinehart and Winston.

Uhlenberg, P. (1978). Changing configurations of the life course. In T. K. Hareven (Ed.), *Transitions: The family and the life course in historical perspective.* New York: Academic Press.

Uhlenberg, P. (1979). Demographic change and problems of the aged. In M. W. Riley (Ed.), *Aging from birth to death.* Boulder, CO: Westview.

U.S. Congress. Senate. *Family Protection Act.* 96th Cong., 1st sess., 1979. S. Bill 1808.

U.S. Congress. Senate. *Family Protection Act.* 97th Cong., 1st sess., 1981. S. Bill 1378.

Welter, B. (1966). The cult of true womanhood: 1820–1860. *American Quarterly, 18,* 151–174.

Wishy, B. (1968). *The child and the republic: The dawn of modern American child nurture.* Philadelphia, PA: University of Pennsylvania Press.

CHAPTER 7

Women, Work, and Family: A Sociological Perspective on Changing Roles[1]

Phyllis Moen

TWO REVOLUTIONS

T he United States, in approaching the 21st century, is undergoing dramatic life course changes, due principally to increased longevity and to changing gender roles. Two revolutions are transforming American society: the revolution in longevity, so that most people now live to be old; and the revolution in gender, resulting in the increasing labor force participation of women of all ages—even mothers of infants. In the face of these momentous changes, however, the nation is hampered by structural lag because societal norms, institutions, and practices have not kept pace with the shifting realities of contemporary life. For example:

[1] Support for the preparation of this chapter was provided by the U.S. Dept. of Agriculture (Hatch 321420), Phyllis Moen, Principal Investigator; and from the National Institute on Aging (#IT50 AG11711-01), Karl Pillemer and Phyllis Moen, Co-Principal Investigators.

- We have extended the average length of life to an impressive degree, but public and private sector retirement policies encourage workers to leave the labor force at progressively earlier ages.
- Women who are mothers of infants and preschoolers are entering, remaining, and reentering the labor force at unprecedented rates, but jobs remain designed as if workers had no family responsibilities, and society continues to assign women the primary responsibility for child care.

We live in an era of rapid and profound transitions, but our governments, industries, and families are not keeping pace with the tide of changes enveloping them. And, as in other times of rapid social change, we in the United States must devise new strategies that will enable us and our children to accommodate to today's and tomorrow's realities. We must design new institutional arrangements more appropriate to the demographic and social changes that are virtually revolutionizing American society and promote new public and private policy initiatives toward that end.

One such new social invention could be a transformation offering greater flexibility and options in the time and timing of work. Our society currently prescribes a lockstep pattern of roles, a sequence beginning with education during the early years, followed by employment, and culminating in the "leisure" of retirement. The typical life pattern for American men has consisted of early years of schooling, 40 or more years of employment, and the remaining years of life spent in retirement leisure. For American women, by contrast, the prime working years have been a combination and sequencing of homemaking and paid labor. As women have moved into and now remain in the labor force they have been adopting a modified version of the traditional male life course, but have *combined* it with their continuing family responsibilities. This means that the years of heaviest family responsibilities are also the years most heavily invested in building a career, and the years of the least family responsibilities are also the years of retirement. These contradictions obviously point to a redesign in the configuration of the life course and the surrounding social structures.

Rethinking this traditional lockstep pattern of education, employment, and retirement could suggest a variety of arrangements, including returning to school at various ages and engaging in paid work both during late adolescence (but prior to the completion of education) and beyond the typical age of retirement. It could also encourage both men and women to reduce their working hours or even take extended sabbaticals while their children are young. And it could encourage those beyond the "normal" years of retirement to begin second, third, or fourth careers, in jobs that could be part-year or part-time as well as full-time. The changes our society is undergoing call forcefully for a thoughtful reexamination of existing—and increasingly inappropriate—life patterns.

In this chapter, I examine the circumstances in the United States that are extending or curtailing the work options of women—and men—who combine employment with parenting responsibilities. Because of the complex and unequal pace of social change, there are built-in contradictions and inconsistencies in what men and women raising families expect of themselves and each other, in what employers expect of workers, and in what society expects of men and women generally, and at various ages. Clarifying the process by which traditional arrangements at work are being modified—albeit at a glacial pace—to accommodate mothers of young children can provide insights into possible structural modifications that broaden the options at the opposite end of the age spectrum as well. Flexibility in working hours and in the sequencing of work and "leisure" (nonwork time) can be beneficial in maximizing choice and opportunity not only for women and men raising young children, but also for those beyond the modal age of retirement, and, indeed, at all stages of the life course.

THE REVOLUTION IN WOMEN'S ROLES[2]

Throughout history, women have been workers as well as wives and mothers—but not necessarily at the *same time*. In the aftermath of the industrial revolution, marked by the separation of paid work from home life, women held work and family roles *sequentially*.[3]

---

[2] Much of this material is drawn from Moen (1992).

[3] In the early phases of the industrial revolution, women were not excluded from employment. However, a combination of forces culminated in their relegation to the domestic sphere. See the discussions by Cohn, 1985; Hartmann, 1976; Tentler, 1979; Walby, 1986. Throughout this chapter, I use the words "working" and "employed" interchangeably, as is common

Young unmarried girls during this era commonly worked in factories or as domestics. When they married, they left their jobs if it were financially possible to do so. As wives and mothers, women also contributed to the family economy when necessary, but at times and in ways that did not seriously conflict with their principal homemaking responsibilities—by doing "piecework" at home, washing other people's laundry, or taking in boarders (Banner, 1974; Degler, 1980; Evans, 1989; Katzman, 1977; Mintz & Kellogg, 1988; Modell & Hareven, 1973; Tilly & Scott, 1978). For most women, sequencing work and family roles meant working outside the home before marriage and motherhood, and then permanently withdrawing from the labor force to tend to household and child-care obligations.

The first half of the 20th century added another form of sequencing: Women gradually began returning to employment once their children were grown. In fact, by 1945, the average female worker in the United States was married and over 35. In the mid-1950s, Alva Myrdal and Viola Klein's book (1956) on women's two roles argued that women could successfully mesh their home and work roles and need not "forgo the pleasures of one sphere in order to enjoy the satisfactions of the other" (p. xiii). The optimal arrangement, as they saw it, was precisely through role sequencing, with family and work roles each "given its own place in a chronological sequence" (p. 155). Their proposed solution was for women to continue the practice of leaving the labor force to bear and raise children but to reenter it once their children reached school age.

From the 1950s on, women in fact have spent increasingly larger portions of their adulthood in employment, typically in the sequential fashion recommended by Myrdal and Klein. But unlike earlier generations, American mothers in the 1970s, 1980s, and now in the 1990s have returned to employment even more quickly—or have never left it at all. By 1990, over half (59.4%) the married mothers of preschoolers and, even more strikingly, over half (51.3%) the mothers of *infants* (children under age one) were in the labor force.

Women are now caught up in a tide of change that makes paid work both more attractive and more financially essential, even while their children are young. By the 1990s, *not* being employed, for any

---

usage. I am nonetheless cognizant that homemakers indeed "work," though they are not paid for their labor. Here, however, I am concentrating on paid labor force participation.

extended period of time, has become less of a realistic option for most American mothers (see Bianchi & Spain, 1986; McLaughlin et al., 1988).[4]

Employment is becoming increasingly central in women's lives, as it has always been in men's. And it is the *combination* of employment with the mothering of babies and toddlers that is especially demanding—and increasingly controversial. Women's changing roles are now being widely and often emotionally discussed and debated in the media, in the classroom, and in government, as well as at work and at home. By no means is this a new issue; social scientists have studied and written about women's employment throughout much of the 20th century. What *is* new, however, is the urgency with which these discussions and debates are voiced as working mothers of infants and preschoolers become an established fact of life. Social observers have concluded that women's lives will never again resemble what we think of as traditional, and this transformation penetrates to the heart of two of our most fundamental institutions: the family and the economy.

CIRCUMSTANCES RELATED TO STRUCTURAL LAG

My focus in this chapter is on the conditions accounting for the complexity and unevenness of this social change that implicate both American society in general and individuals and their families. Ambivalence, discomfort, and apprehension pervade social attitudes, actions, and institutional arrangements. I shall discuss seven major conditions that underly the restructuring of women's work and family roles: the emergence of economic and social crises, the adoption of federal government initiatives, the leverage of government as employer, new state-level policy initiatives, the influence of labor unions, the continuing demand for women workers, and the rigidity of ideological traditions. These occurrences are key to the narrowing—or, conversely, the widening—of the structural and cultural gaps between the reality of women's labor force involvement and society's response to that reality.

---

[4] For information on the women's movement, see Chafetz and Dworkin (1986), and Wandersee (1988).

The Emergence of Economic and Social Crises

Economic and military crises have been especially consequential in affecting social norms and policies regarding women's employment. This is perhaps best illustrated by the Great Depression of the 1930s. During that period, 26 states enacted laws prohibiting the hiring of married women. In fact, a national poll in 1938 found that four-fifths (82%) of the men and three-fourths (75%) of the women interviewed believed that "wives should *not* work if their husband is employed" (Banner, 1974).

But World War II and the accompanying civilian labor shortage encouraged quite different sentiments. Opinion polls in 1942 found that 60% of those surveyed agreed that married women *should* work in war industries. The Office of War Information challenged married women to do so by asking, "Are you being old-fashioned and getting by just being a 'good wife and mother'?" (Margolis, 1984, p. 215). The Women's Bureau, in a publication on standards for maternity care, suggested, "Some women who are pregnant or who have young children may find it necessary to work" (U.S. Dept of Labor, 1942, cited in Gladstone, Williams, & Belous, 1985). The World War II period also witnessed the passage of the Lanham Act of 1942, which provided matching grants to states for day-care centers to facilitate the employment of women in war-production industries (see Campbell, 1984; Kaledin, 1984; Margolis, 1984; Milkman, 1987; Tobias & Anderson, 1974).

World War II marked a pivotal point in *wives'* labor force participation. In 1940, only 14.7% of married women were employed; by 1944, 21.7% were working. In fact, fully 75% of the new female entrants during the war were wives. For the first time in history, over half the female labor force in the United States was married, and by 1945 the majority of women workers were over age 35.

Historians and other social observers generally pinpoint World War II, with its civilian labor shortage, as the period when *first* women's behavior and *then* social attitudes, changed. According to William Chafe (1972):

> If the nation—including women—had been asked in 1939 whether it desired, or would tolerate such a far-reaching change, the answer would undoubtedly have been an overwhelming no.

But events bypassed public opinion, and made the change an accomplished fact. The war, in short, was a catalyst which broke up old modes of behavior and helped to forge new ones. (p. 247)

Surprisingly, there was no mass exodus back to the kitchen at the war's end. To be sure, there was a brief turnaround; women's labor force participation rate fell 5 percentage points from 1944 to 1947 (dropping from 35% to 30%). But after the war, married women continued to move into employment, especially those in midlife (ages 45–59) whose years of child rearing were ending. The postwar period marked a dramatic reversal in public objections to married women's employment (see Duncan & Duncan, 1978; Mason, Czajka, & Arber, 1976; Spitze & Huber, 1980).

The Adoption of Federal Government Initiatives

The expansion of the service sector, the civil rights movement of the 1960s, and the beginning of the women's movement in the early 1970s led to landmark pieces of legislation with wide-ranging consequences for women's employment. The Equal Pay Act of 1963, the Civil Rights Act of 1964, and Executive Order 11246 on affirmative action all represented a push toward gender equality. Changes in higher education legislation also had broad repercussions. For example, Title IX of the Education Amendments of 1972 and the Women's Educational Equity Act of 1974 prohibited sex discrimination in any program receiving federal money.

The decade of the 1970s saw the flowering of the women's movement, encompassing a range of individuals, ideologies, and collective efforts aimed at promoting women's rights in all facets of society. This movement not only inspired legislation but gave legitimacy to women's quest for equality and engendered a new consciousness and self-concept among women. This decade was marked by a notable transformation of public attitudes toward women's roles. The majority of American men and women came to accept and even endorse the labor force participation of married women. And concurrently, the traditional housewife role became even more devalued, even though half of all married women still functioned as full-time homemakers in 1980 (Andre, 1981).

Legislators in the 1960s and early 1970s concentrated principally on the enactment of nondiscrimination and affirmative action laws. One such law, having wide repercussions, is the Pregnancy Discrimination Act of 1978 (Public Law 95-555). It mandates:

> Women affected by pregnancy, childbirth, or related medical conditions shall be treated the same for all employment-related purposes, including receipt of benefits under fringe benefit programs, as other persons not so affected but similar in their inability to work.

If an employer generally provides disability benefits, such benefits must also be available to pregnant women. As of 1992, five states (California, Hawaii, New Jersey, New York, and Rhode Island) and Puerto Rico mandate the provision of temporary disability benefits to workers. This means that approximately 40% of employed women in the United States have the right to a maternity leave with partial wage replacement—usually for six weeks—at the time of childbirth. Prior to the passage and signing into law of the Family and Medical Leave Act in February 1993, the Pregnancy Discrimination Act established the only federal policy adopted expressly to provide maternity or parental leave-related benefits.

Historically, both federal and state governments have taken a largely "hands off" position concerning policies for working mothers and their children. Indeed, there is still no consensus among public officials—or throughout society generally—about the desirability of mothers of young children even being in the labor force. The fact that there is still no major national policy on either child care or maternity-related benefits underscores the uncertainty and often deep ambivalence of Americans regarding maternal employment. Indeed, this ambivalence helps explain why the United States is the only industrialized nation without such family supports (Gladstone, Williams, & Belous, 1985; Kamerman & Kahn, 1988; Kamerman, Kahn, & Kingston, 1983; Moen, 1989). The adoption of the Family and Medical Leave Act by President Clinton in 1993 was an event of major import. Though many workers are not covered (businesses with fewer than 50 employees are exempt), it nevertheless represents a formal recognition of the dilemmas of working parents. It is a step in the direction of structural change.

The Leverage of Government as Employer

As the nation's largest employer, the federal government can serve as both an innovator of enlightened personnel policies and a model for the private as well as the public sector. Two pieces of legislation enacted in 1978 granted to federal employees greater discretion in fashioning their working hours. Public Law 95-347 encourages part-time employment, especially "career" part-time employment, for workers who desire less than full-time hours on the job. Following a favorable evaluation of a 3-year experiment with flexible work schedules by the Office of Personnel Management, Congress enacted Public Law 95-390, providing the option of flextime in all federal agencies. With this encouragement, almost a fourth of all federal workers opted to work on flexible schedules. Overall in the public sector, a 1987 survey found that almost two in five (38%) federal, state, and local government agencies reported having flextime policies. While this proportion was lower than that of private industry establishments with flextime (44%), these government agencies were far more likely (26% versus 10%) to have employer-sponsored day care than were private-sector establishments (Bureau of Labor Statistics, 1988).

But government policies may inhibit as well as promote changes in employment conditions that would help workers with young children reduce their time pressures. For example, certain fixed labor costs, such as premiums for unemployment and disability insurance, make two part-time workers more expensive to employ than one full-time worker. And wage-and-hour laws require the payment of overtime rates beyond the 8-hour day, discouraging flexibility in arranging work time. Federal laws, then, sometimes work at cross-purposes, inadvertently impeding innovations in the way work—and the life course—is structured.

New State-Level Policy Initiatives

States have been more likely than the federal government to acknowledge and seek remedies for the structural gaps resulting from the revolution in gender roles. In the 1970s, Montana, Connecticut, and Massachusetts, and in 1980 California passed maternity leave legislation. In 1987, Minnesota enacted the first parental leave law in the nation, enabling each parent to take up to six weeks of unpaid leave following the birth or adoption of a child. Subsequently, a number of other states passed similar maternity or parental leave laws.[5] Work-family concerns have become firmly established as public issues in a growing number of states.

The Influence of Labor Unions

Historically, unions have fought for improvements in wages and job security as their top priorities before turning to such "peripheral" issues as child care and maternity leave. However, with benefits a progressively larger portion of the total compensation package, family-related concerns are becoming an increasingly important bargaining issue (see Foner, 1980, 1987; Needleman & Tanner, 1987).[6]

But being represented by a union does not necessarily increase the likelihood of receiving family benefits. For example, a study by labor economists Freeman and Medoff (1984) found that—given similar companies, work forces, and economic and social conditions—union members were *less* likely than unrepresented workers to be eligible for maternity leave with pay. On the other hand, they were *more* likely to have maternity leave with full return rights and *more* likely to have day care as a fringe benefit (see also Freeman & Leonard, 1987).

Given the major influx of women into labor unions, as well as the general decline in the organized segment of the workforce, family support issues are likely to become more prominent at the bargaining table and in organizing campaigns. Moreover, the provision of greater flexibilities in the time structure of work may be more negotiable

---

[5] For a discussion of the effects of state maternity leave statutes, see Trzcinski (1989; 1991). States having maternity or parental leave law legislation as of 1990 are Connecticut, Iowa, Louisiana, Maine, Minnesota, Oregon, Rhode Island, Tennessee, Washington, West Virginia, and Wisconsin (Dinn-Stevenson & Trzcinski, 1990). A few local governments also have addressed the work–family predicament. In California, for example, the cities of Concord and San Francisco imposed in 1985 a small fee on commercial developments within the city, earmarking these funds for child care (Lydenberg, 1986).

[6] In 1951, fringe benefits accounted for less than 19% of total payroll costs; by 1982, this had risen to almost 37%. By 1983, maternity leave provisions were included in over a third (36%) of the collective bargaining agreements. By comparison, more than three-fourths of the contracts provided for military leave (76%) and personal leave (75%) (Gladstone, Williams, & Belous, 1985).

than the size of the total wage package, in an era of economic adversity marked by wage cutbacks and layoffs.[7]

The Continuing Demand for Women Workers

The forces shaping the American economy suggest that the demand for women workers will continue unabated. The Bureau of Labor Statistics (Johnston & Packer, 1987) estimated that 90% of the 16 million new jobs created from 1987 through 1995 would be in service industries. That, coupled with possible labor force shortages in some areas, undoubtedly will draw even more mothers of young children into paid employment.

Concomitant with the expansion of the service sector has been the growth of part-time and temporary jobs. Service industries seldom require the scheduling rigidities endemic to assembly-line work or continuous production, making service jobs more suitable for part-time or short-term employment. In 1955, only about 1 in 10 United States workers was putting in less than 35 hours a week; by 1988, about 1 in 6 was a part-time employee. In fact, in the 1980s, the part-time workforce grew about twice as fast as total employment in the U.S. economy, increasing from 16.3 million workers in 1980 to 19.8 million in 1988. The growth of temporary jobs is even more striking, moving from a minuscule 0.4 million in 1980 to 1.1 million in 1988, a 175% increase (Belous, 1989; Nine to Five, 1986).

Not surprisingly, given their child-care and other domestic responsibilities, women hold the majority of part-time and temporary jobs. In 1985, over two-thirds (67.6%) of the part-timers were women, as were almost two-thirds (64.2%) of the temporary workers. But the proliferation of these jobs is far more a result of the changing economy than a response to the needs of women balancing work and family roles. Employers recruit such a "contingent workforce" because it is flexible and encumbers significantly lower labor costs. These working

---

[7] The innovative policies on flexible schedules, voluntary furloughs, and on-site day care adopted through negotiations between New York State and the unions representing its employees stand as an exemplary case of what can be accomplished through the collaborative efforts of management and labor, and point to the leadership role that can be assumed by unions in easing the burdens of working parents (Bureau of National Affairs, 1984, 1986).

arrangements offer women more flexibility and discretionary time in reconciling their work and family obligations. But they also exact a heavy price: Part-time and temporary jobs tend to be low-wage jobs with few benefits, typically without security and providing little opportunity for advancement.[8]

The Rigidity of Ideological Traditions

Deeply entrenched ideologies in the United States about families, individuals, and government have hampered the recognition of, much less an adequate response to, the gender-role revolution. We have long upheld a "doctrine of two spheres" that designates the home and family as a private arena, the place where children should be taught values and belief systems, and very much the special province of wives and mothers. The sanctity of the family means that it typically has been put off limits to government intrusion. Moreover, the traditional emphasis in the United States on free enterprise and on the supremacy of the individual, along with the pluralistic nature of our society, has long delayed the inclusion of family goals in the political agenda. The laissez-faire orientation has underscored the preeminence of economic interests. One must ask whether President Bush's 1990 and 1992 vetoes of the Family and Medical Leave Act, because he felt that it established government mandates presumed injurious to the business community, presages an attitude that will continue into the future. The importance assigned to individualism militates against government intervention into family life and has given birth to policies that are often antithetical to the best interests of families and children. (The Clinton administration's endorsement of the Family and Medical Leave Act may represent a real turning point toward the enactment of more "profamily" policies and may galvanize structural change, or it may prove an exception to the ongoing concern about government "interference.")

Regional, ethnic, and religious differences in values have precluded a consensus on the meaning of family well-being, much less a common understanding of the "proper" roles of women and men within

---

[8] For a discussion of part-time workers, see Belous (1989), International Labour Organization (1989), and Kahne (1985).

society. Similarly, the layers of government—city, county, state, federal, as well as their executive, legislative, and judicial structure—encourage a patchwork of often incompatible laws and regulations in lieu of a coherent national policy addressing the quandaries growing out of maternal employment.

Even the changes in women's employment during and following World War II did not significantly alter the primacy of women's family role. The family work—of child care, husband care, housework, and emotional nurturance—still preoccupied and restricted women's lives. Most women reentered the labor force only after their children were in school or launched from the home. So long as their children were young, women's principal functions remained caretaking and homemaking. And by the 1950s, wives were again encouraged to be full-time homemakers. As Agnes E. Mayer said in a 1950 *Atlantic Monthly* article, "Women have many careers but only one vocation—motherhood" (Evans, 1989, p. 245). In fact, many women went to work in the 1950s *because* of their families—to improve their standard of living. Following the war, women found themselves caught between "the promise of change and the restoration of tradition" (Berkin & Lovett, 1980, p. 3).

We in the United States confront a true cultural dilemma, with the employment of mothers at odds with ingrained values concerning the family. Although Americans of all ages increasingly endorse the notion of *wives'* employment, many remain uneasy about the employment of *mothers of young children*. There are inherent cultural contradictions in having mothers of young children employed because women still have the principal responsibility for child care. While the federal government has been notably reluctant to intervene in providing supports for working mothers (or parents), it promotes equality of opportunity for women. American society thus conveys a mixed message that reinforces the primacy of domesticity in women's lives but stresses the increasing significance of their employment.[9]

---

[9] For a discussion of the doctrine of two spheres, see Cott and Pleck (1979), and Degler (1980). A fuller discussion of the ambivalence concerning policies affecting family life is in Moen and Schorr (1987) and Klatch (1987). The Civil Rights Act of 1964 was an important ingredient in the drive toward equality of employment opportunity for women. And an example of societal ambivalence about maternal employment is the Family Support Act of 1988, which requires certain mothers receiving welfare (AFDC) to enroll in work programs.

IMPLICATIONS OF THE GENDER ROLE REVOLUTION FOR THE LONGEVITY REVOLUTION

The structural lag resulting from the gender role revolution—the mismatch between prevailing institutional conditions and the spiraling numbers of mothers in the workforce—has implications for the revolution in longevity and the aging of American society as well. We have traditionally operated on the premise that wives and mothers would do the domestic labor of society to free husbands and fathers to work in the paid economy; and that all workers, male and female, would spend their last years in the leisure of retirement. Almost half the labor force is now female challenging well-entrenched employment policies and practices designed for an essentially male workforce without child-care responsibilities. Similar challenges are posed by the growth of an educated, vigorous, more active population that can anticipate several decades of life beyond the normal retirement age. The seven circumstances related to the restructuring of women's work and parenting roles discussed in this chapter provide clues to the *processes of modifying established structures.* How might these occurrences affecting women's roles relate more generally to other innovations affecting people of all ages?

The revolution in gender roles is a revolution in progress, but it does suggest the beginnings of structural and cultural transformations. Like all institutions, the world of work is resistant to change. New and more appropriate policies and practices will come about only when the economic and social costs of doing nothing outweigh the costs of change. And outmoded conventions and stereotypes operate as a real impediment. The circumstances encouraging or impeding the transformation in women's roles suggest that what is troublesome is *not* how to alter existing structures, but the *recognition that we need to do so.*

CHALLENGING OLD STEREOTYPES AND DESIGNING NEW STRATEGIES

We in the United States, individually and collectively, remain uncertain and often divided as to what men's and women's roles should be, and what it means to grow old in a society where increasing numbers of people are in and beyond their sixth decade. Prevailing attitudes about gender and age remain ambivalent and contradictory. This is a matter of pivotal importance in seeking to understand the absence of coherent political and private sector response to the gender and longevity revolutions in this country. Because of the absence of consensus about women's roles or what it means to grow old in our society, we are seriously constrained from adopting social policies and institutional arrangements to reduce the structural lags that are becoming so prominent.

A major issue underlying the absence of response to both the gender-role and the longevity revolutions concerns the typical career trajectory of most jobs. If workers take time out of the labor force or even work a reduced schedule while their children are young, it can wreak havoc on seniority and upward occupational mobility. For example, a job sharer at Michigan State University speaks of her career as being "on hold" and concedes, "I'm not going to go anywhere in a half-time job and I know that" (Apgar, 1985). Similarly, remaining in jobs beyond the usual age of retirement creates a bottleneck in the opportunity structure for younger workers. What is required are life-course solutions offering greater flexibility in the scheduling of working hours and greater variability in the paths leading to long-term occupational goals. Everyone need not march in lockstep through life, progressing from education to employment and ultimately to retirement in a fixed order and schedule. Rather, innovative policies permitting time off and/or reduced work time in the child-rearing years and full-time, part-year, or part-time jobs in the "retirement" years could introduce greater flexibility and creativity in structuring education, work, and free time throughout the life course. These arrangements not only could help meet the needs of working parents and older individuals but also could contribute to the creation of the more flexible and adaptable workforce required by the economy.

FLEXIBILITY AS A GOAL

Three interrelated concerns are central to contemporary discussions of the economic scene in the United States: flexibility, productivity, and competitiveness. Social scientists generally acknowledge that greater flexibility in the organization of work can enhance productivity, and that productivity is the key to improving this nation's competitive position in the world market. This premise may be good news for women trying to combine work and family roles and for older people seeking employment, since "flexibility" is their goal as well. And, to be sure, a number of employers in the 1980s adopted policies permitting much greater flexibility in the allocation of time, thereby easing the strains on working parents and opening up jobs to older workers.

However, the reality is that most firms, rather than initiating innovations, tend to react to government exhortations or the prospect of legislative mandates. For example, in a 1984 survey, over half a sample of the largest U.S. corporations reported changing their parental leave policies within the past five years, largely in response to the Pregnancy Discrimination Act (Catalyst, 1986). But in the absence of government encouragement and regulation, private sector supports for working parents seem destined to remain uneven, offering only minimal assistance to the majority of workers.

The lockstep sequence of education, employment, and retirement is obsolete, a relic of a society that no longer exists. This typical life course renders older women especially economically vulnerable. Taking time out for child rearing or taking temporary or part-time jobs means that women are less likely than men to have economic security in the form of pensions. What is required is a thoughtful reappraisal of existing life patterns. This could lead to a reconfiguration of the life course in ways that create more options and more variety for both men and women in youth, early adulthood, midlife, and the later years[10] (Best, 1980; Harriman, 1982; Kahne, 1985).

We in the United States now stand at something of a crossroads. Customary institutional patterns, at home and at work, make combining the successful mothering of young children with successful employment both frustrating and exhausting, if not impossible. Traditional institutional arrangements also foreclose employment (and other role) options in the later years of adulthood, making growing old in the United States a time of serious role loss. And yet, as in the

---

[10] Sweden is trying to offer such flexibilities of working parents (see Moen, 1989). The flexibility that new technologies are requiring of the workforce—to change jobs, to be continually trained and retrained—is comparable to that needed by workers in the early years of childbearing. And see Riley and Riley, (1989) for a discussion of the need to refashion the age structure in light of shifts in the age composition.

case of women's roles during World War II, these traditional institutional arrangements are alterable. What is difficult is coming to terms with the need to do so.

To deal with the new realities of the gender-role and longevity revolutions, powerful forces for change must be mustered, leading to new social inventions in the policy arena. What we need are modern-day counterparts to such successful social inventions of the past as Social Security and Head Start, and the willingness to be open to their possibilities. What may push us toward such structural change is that we are, once more, in a time of social and economic crisis. The nation stands at a critical juncture, with the forces shaping families and individual lives challenging traditional ways of thinking and conventional policy solutions.

What we see are more discontinuities than continuities in families, across the generations, and in personal experience and development. Men and women are not only living longer but they are also moving in and out of roles—in families, in the workplace, and in educational institutions—at an unprecedented rate. Americans are increasingly likely at some stage of their lives to experience the dislocations of divorce, single parenthood, and geographic mobility; the specter of poverty; the time and psychic strains of two-job families and/or the providing of care for aged or infirm relatives; and the isolation of living alone. Given these experiences, a "successful" or even predictable life course, from early infancy to old age, is increasingly problematic. We need new policies and practices more in keeping with these new realities of the American experience, borne of a new frame of reference that incorporates greater flexibilities in work and other roles throughout the life course.

We as a nation have not been responsive to these dramatic alterations in the social fabric of our society. We have been much more adept in responding to *technological* challenges than to *social* challenges. Yet questions involving the human condition are both more perplexing and more critical to the nation's future than ever before.

REFERENCES

Andre, R. (1981). *Homemakers: The forgotten workers.* Chicago, IL: University of Chicago Press.

Apgar, L. (1985). Labor letter. *The Wall Street Journal, July 30.*

Banner, L. (1974). *Women in modern America: Brief history.* New York: Harcourt Brace Javanovich.

Belous, R. (1989). *The contingent economy: The growth of the temporary, part-time and subcontracted workforce.* Washington, DC: National Planning Association.

Berkin, C., & Lovett, C. (Eds.). (1980). *Women, war, and revolution.* New York: Holmes & Meier.

Best, F. (1980). *Flexible life scheduling: Breaking the education-work-retirement lockstep.* New York: Praeger.

Bianchi, S. M., & Spain, D. (1986). *American women in transition.* New York: Sage.

Bureau of Labor Statistics, U.S. Dept. of Labor. (1988). *BLS Reports on employer child-care practices.* News, USDL 88-7.

Bureau of National Affairs. (1984). *Employers and child care: Development of a new employee benefit.* Washington, DC: The Bureau of National Affairs, Inc.

Bureau of National Affairs. (1986). *Work and family: A changing dynamic.* Washington, DC: The Bureau of National Affairs, Inc.

Campbell, D. (1984). *Women at war with America: Private lives in a patriotic era.* Cambridge, MA: Harvard University Press.

Catalyst. (1986). *Report on a national study of parental leaves.* New York: Catalyst.

Chafe, W. (1972). *The American woman: Her changing social, economic, and political roles, 1920–1970.* New York: Oxford University Press.

Chafetz, J., & Dworkin, A. (1986). *Female revolt: Women's movements in world and historical perspective.* Totowa, NJ: Rowman & Allanheld.

Cohn, S. (1985). *The process of occupational sex-typing.* Philadelphia, PA: Temple University Press.

Cott, N., & Pleck, E. (1979). *A heritage of her own: Toward a new social history of American women.* New York: Simon & Schuster.

Degler, C. (1980). *At odds: Women and the family in America from the revolution to the present.* New York: Oxford University Press.

Dinn-Stevenson, M., & Trzcinski, E. (1990). *Public policy issues surrounding parental leave: A state-by-state analysis of parental leave legislation.* Unpublished draft.

Duncan, B., & Duncan, O. D. (1978). *Sex-typing and social roles: A research report.* New York: Academic Press.

Evans, S. (1989). *Born for liberty: A history of women in America.* New York: Free Press.

Foner, P. (1980). *Women and the American labor movement: From World War I to the present.* New York: Free Press.

Foner, P. (1987). Women and the American labor movement: A historical perspective. In K. S. Koziara, M. H. Moskow, & L. D. Tanner (Eds.), *Working women: Past, present, future* (pp. 154–186). Washington, DC: Bureau of National Affairs.

Freeman, R., & Leonard, J. (1987). Union maids: Unions and the female work force. In C. Brown & J. Pechman (Eds.), *Gender in the workplace* (pp. 189–216). Washington, DC: Brookings Institution.

Freeman, R., & Medoff, J. (1984). *What do unions do?* New York: Basic Books.

Gladstone, L., Williams, J., & Belous, R. (1985). *Maternity and parental leave policies: A comparative analysis.* Congressional Research Service Rep. No. 85-148 G Gov., July 16.

Harriman, A. (1982). *The work/leisure trade off.* New York: Praeger.

Hartmann, H. (1976). Capitalism, patriarchy and job segregation by sex. *Signs, 1-3,* 187–171.

International Labour Organization. (1989). Part-time work. *Conditions of Work Digest,* Vol. 8.N.1. Geneva: ILO.

Johnston, W., & Packer, A. (1987). *Workforce 2000: Work and workers for the 21st-century.* Indianapolis, IN: Hudson Institute.

Kahne, H. (1985). *Reconceiving part-time work: New perspectives for older workers and women.* Totowa, NJ: Rowman & Allanheld.

Kaledin, E. (1984). *Mothers and more: American women in the 1950s.* Boston, MA: Twayne.

Kamerman, S., & Kahn, A. (1988). Social policy and children in the United States and Europe. In J. L. Palmer, T. Smeeding, & B. B. Torrey (Eds.), *The vulnerable* (pp. 351–380). Washington, DC: Urban Institute Press.

Kamerman, S., Kahn, A., & Kingston, P. (1983). *Maternity policies and working women.* New York: Columbia University Press.

Katzman, D. (1977). *Seven days a week: Women and domestic service in industrializing America.* New York: Oxford University Press.

Klatch, R. (1987). *Women of the new right.* Philadelphia, PA: Temple University Press.

Lydenberg, S. (1986). Child care update: Business takes first real steps. *Newsletter, Council on Economic Priorities, N86-11* (Nov.): 1–6.

Margolis, M. (1984). *Mothers and such: Views of American women and why they changed.* Berkeley, CA: University of California.

Mason, K., Czajka, J., & Arber, S. (1976). Change in U.S. women's sex-role attitudes, 1964–1974. *American Sociological Review, 41,* 573–596.

McLaughlin, S., Melber, B., Billy, J., Zimmerle, D., Winges, L., & Johnson, T. (1988). *The changing lives of American women.* Chapel Hill, NC: University of North Carolina Press.

Milkman, R. (1987). *Gender at work: The dynamics of job segregation by sex during World War II.* Chicago, IL: University of Illinois Press.

Mintz, S., & Kellogg, S. (1988). *Domestic revolutions: A social history of American family life.* New York: Free Press.

Modell, J., & Hareven, T. (1973). Urbanization and the malleable household: An examination of boarding and lodging in American families. *Journal of Marriage and the Family, 35,* 467–479.

Moen, P. (1989). *Working parents: Transformations in gender roles and public policies in Sweden.* Madison, WI: University of Wisconsin Press.

Moen, P. (1992). *Women's two roles: A contemporary dilemma.* New York: Auburn House (Greenwood Press).

Moen, P., & Schorr, A. (1987). Families and social policy. In M. B. Sussman & S. K. Steinmetz (Eds.), *Handbook of marriage and the family* (pp. 795–813). New York: Plenum Press.

Myrdal, A., & Klein, V. (1956). *Women's two roles: Home and work.* London: Routledge & Kegan Paul.

Needleman, R., & Tanner, L. D. (1987). Women in unions: Current issues. In K. S. Koziara, M. H. Moskow, & L. D. Tanner (Eds.), *Working women: Past, present, future* (pp. 187–224). Washington, DC: Bureau of National Affairs.

Nine to Five, National Association of Working Women. (1986, Sept.). *Working at the margins: Part-time and temporary workers in the United States.* Cleveland, OH: 9 to 5, National Association of Working Women.

Riley, M. W., & Riley, J. W., Jr. (1989). The lives of older people and changing social roles. *The Annals of the American Academy of Political and Social Science, 503,* 14–28.

Spitze, G., & Huber, J. (1980). Changing attitudes toward women's non-family roles: 1938–1978. *Sociology of Work and Occupations, 7,* 317–335.

Tentler, L. (1979). *Wage-earning women: Industrial work and family life in the United States, 1900–1930.* New York: Oxford University Press.

Tilly, L. A., & Scott, J. (1978). *Women, work, and family.* New York: Holt, Rinehart and Winston.

Tobias, S., & Anderson, L. (1974). *What really happened to Rosie the Riveter? Demobilization and the female labor force 1944–1947.* New York: MMS Moduler Publications, Inc., Module 9.

Trzcinski, E. (1989). Employer's parental leave policies: Does the labor market provide parental leave via market forces of supply and demand? In J. Hyde (Ed.), *Parental leave and childcare: Setting a research and policy agenda.* Philadelphia, PA: Temple University Press.

Trzcinski, E. (1991). Separate versus equal treatment approaches to parental leave: Theoretical issues and empirical evidence. *Law and Policy, 13,* 1–33.

Walby, S. (1986). *Patriarchy at work.* Minneapolis, MN: University of Minnesota Press.

Wandersee, W. (1988). *On the move: American women in the 1970s.* Boston, MA: Twayne.

CHAPTER 8

Education and the Economic Transformation of Nineteenth-Century America[1]

Maris A. Vinovskis

T his chapter focuses on the relationship between economic and educational developments in American history. At first glance, this historical examination of the development of mass education may seem far removed from the central concept around which this book is organized: structural lag, or the proposition that changes in societal institutions and structures lag

[1] The preparation of an earlier version of this chapter was funded by the National Center on Education and Employment, of the Institute on Education and the Economy, Teachers College, Columbia University, as a background paper for a 1989 conference on "Education and the Economy: Hard Questions, Hard Answers." The National Center on Education and Employment was funded by a grant from the Office of Research, Office of Educational Research and Improvement, U.S. Department of Education.

Robert Kahn provided valuable assistance in revising this chapter. Susan Carter, Raymond Grew, Kenneth Lockridge, Terrence McDonald, Jeffrey Mirel, Jacob Price, and Diane Ravitch provided very helpful comments on an earlier draft.

behind the changing capacities and needs of individuals over the life course. Yet the three main issues discussed in this chapter raise questions highly pertinent to structural lag, and to broader questions about the nature of structural change.

The following issues are addressed here:

1. The relationship of early industrialization to the development of mass schooling.
2. The economic productivity of education.
3. The relationship of education to social mobility and people's life chances.

In analyzing the historical evidence on these issues, such critical questions arise as the following:

- Were 19th-century educational institutions lagging behind the needs of individuals in a changing society?
- What was the impact of educational reform and expansion on individual lives?
- In turn, how did changes in individuals' abilities, as brought about by educational reforms, affect the productivity of other societal institutions?

In pursuing such questions, the chapter shows that the detailed studies provided by educational historians can help shed light on these questions (e.g., Cohen, 1977; Cremin, 1977; Katz, 1976); and economic historians have covered a wide range of related topics. Nevertheless, little effort has been made to pay direct attention to the economic aspects of 19th-century educational development in the United States. To stimulate further research and thinking about the relationship between economic and educational development in the past, and the possible implications for the future, this chapter focuses on the period before the Civil War; a time of great change in both economic and educational spheres. Early industrialization began in the United States during the first half of the 19th century and seems to have coincided with school expansion and reforms. An examination of educational changes in the decades prior to the Civil War from an economic perspective may provide us with a better sense of the relationship between broad socioeconomic change and schooling. It will also offer insights about how changes in schooling may have affected individuals over their life course.

EARLY INDUSTRIALIZATION AND THE DEVELOPMENT OF MASS EDUCATION

Overemphasis on Economic Sources of Change

Only a few historians have approached the study of educational development in the United States from an economic perspective. Two economists, however, Samuel Bowles and Herbert Gintis (1976), have produced a comprehensive neo-Marxist theory of the relationship between American educational and economic development. They applied their theoretical framework to explain the origins of mass public education in the two decades before the Civil War, the relationship between corporate capital and progressive education in the early 20th century, and the transformation of higher education in the 1960s and 1970s as a response to the emergence of a white-collar proletariat. Although their theoretical and empirical work has been challenged, it remains one of the few major theoretical and empirical attempts to link educational developments to the changes in the structure of the American economy.

For Bowles and Gintis, there is a causal correspondence between the social relations of production and the characteristics of the educational system at that particular time. They locate the origins and reform of American mass education prior to the Civil War and associate it with the industrialization of the economy. They note also a recurring pattern of political and financial support for educational change. Although the impetus for educational reform sometimes came from disgruntled farmers or workers, the leadership of the movement—which succeeded in stamping its unmistakable imprint on the form and direction of the educational innovation—was without exception in the hands of a coalition of professionals and capitalists from the leading sectors of the economy (Bowles & Gintis, 1976, pp. 178–179).

A fundamental problem with many studies of antebellum education is that they use the terms educational "expansion" and "reform" interchangeably without ever considering whether or not these two developments occurred simultaneously or in the same geographic areas. Nor is it clear what is meant by each of these terms. Should educational expansion be measured by looking at increasing rates of adult literacy, the shift from educating children in the home to educating them in schools, or the replacement of private schools by public schools? Similarly, given the wide variety of educational reforms proposed during the antebellum period, should we consider them equally important or were some innovations more central to educational development in the United States?

Such broad questions do not distinguish between expansion and reform. There are major differences in where and when educational expansion occurred in the United States during the 19th century, and increases in education did not always coincide with attempts to improve existing schools.

An often used benchmark for the origins of mass education and school reforms is the appointment of Horace Mann as the Secretary of the Massachusetts Board of Education. Bowles and Gintis adopt this strategy because it allows them to link educational changes directly to the increasing industrialization of that state in the two decades prior to the Civil War, and they imply that their analysis is valid for the entire country. It is appropriate to ask, therefore, whether Mann's appointment really marked a major turning point in educational expansion.

If we focus on adult literacy, the period of change is the 17th and 18th centuries rather than the two decades prior to the Civil War—a change that could be enormously instructive for literacy problems in the United States today. Only about 60% of the men and 30% of the women among the first settlers of New England could sign their wills. By 1790, however, about 90% of New England males and 50% of New England females could sign their wills (Lockridge, 1974). Indeed, by 1840, only 1.1% of the white population in Massachusetts ages 20 and above could not read and write (Sixth Census, 1841). Thus, if educational attainment is measured in terms of adult literacy, especially adult male literacy, most of it occurred well before the Commonwealth even began to industrialize (Moran & Vinovskis, 1985).

A different measure of educational expansion, perhaps more appropriate from the perspective of Bowles and Gintis, is the replacement of parents by teachers as the primary educators of children. Bowles and Gintis (1976, pp. 157–158) argue that as households ceased to be sites for production in the early 19th century, it became necessary to shift the training of children to schools that not only provided cognitive skills but accustomed students to accept the same type of social hierarchy and discipline they would encounter in the newly established factories.

Was Mann's tenure as Secretary of the Massachusetts Board of Education associated with a dramatic increase in school enrollments? Although it is difficult to obtain detailed records on school attendance prior to 1840, the available evidence suggests that Massachusetts school attendance was already high by 1800 and that it increased gradually during the next four decades. During the period 1840 to 1860, however, school attendance in Massachusetts actually declined. The percentage of children under age 20 enrolled in any school dropped from 67.4 in 1840 to 56.8 in 1860—in large part due to the elimination of the infant schools that 3- and 4-year-olds had been attending earlier—a change of considerable relevance to programs like Head Start in the United States today (Kaestle & Vinovskis, 1980).

With the lengthening of the school year and the increasing regularity of attendance, the average annual number of days of school per child under age 20 did increase slightly from 60.6 days in 1840 to 62.3 days in 1860. Furthermore, there was a sizable shift from private to public schooling. In 1840, 18.7% of all those enrolled received at least some private schooling, whereas in 1860 that proportion had dropped to 8.0% (Kaestle & Vinovskis, 1980). Nevertheless, it is important to remember that by the time Mann first came to power, more than four out of five students were already going exclusively to a public school. Thus, in terms of the changes in the overall rate of school attendance, the annual number of days of schooling received, or the proportion of students attending public schools in Massachusetts, the two decades prior to the Civil War did not witness a dramatic turning point.

If the percentage of Massachusetts children attending school did not increase prior to the Civil War, what about trends in the rest of the United States? New England, which was one of the most industrialized areas, declined in enrollment from 81.8% of whites under age 20 attending school in 1840 to 73.8% in 1860. But in the United States as a whole, there was a substantial increase in the percentage of whites ages 0 to 19 attending schools between 1840 and 1860 (Fishlow, 1966). The largest increases occurred in the largely agricultural

North Central states, where the percentage of attendance rose from 29.0 percent in 1840 to 70.3 percent in 1860 (Vinovskis, 1985).

A similar picture emerges if we estimate the distribution of the total number of new students between 1840 and 1860 by region. Whereas the more industrialized regions of New England and the Middle Atlantic contributed only 2.7% and 21.7% respectively of new students, the North Central region accounted for 55.7% of the additional students during those two decades (Vinovskis, 1985).

Whether we look at the state of Massachusetts specifically or at all regions of the country, there is little evidence to support the notion that industrialization immediately preceded or caused the growth of mass public education in the United States. Mass public schooling preceded industrialization in Massachusetts and the greatest increases in school attendance occurred in the largely agricultural North Central region.

Bowles and Gintis are correct, however, to point to the increased reform activity that focused on schools during the 1830s, 1840s, and 1850s—much of it directed to the urban and industrializing communities of the Northeast. Educators such as Henry Barnard and Mann emphasized the need for better trained teachers, more public funds for schools, more regular school attendance, and a consolidation and centralization of existing public schools. Whereas in the Midwest or the South, school promoters were concerned about the quantity as well as the quality of schooling being offered, in the Northeast the main emphasis was on the quality of that education.

"Revisionist" historians of education emphasize the importance of manufacturers, aided by professionals, in initiating these common school reforms. Rejecting the more traditional interpretation of educational reformers as benign humanitarians, scholars such as Field (1974), Katz (1987), and Bowles and Gintis (1976) stress the role of manufacturers in the school reform movement and attribute it to their fear of the social unrest caused by the industrialization of the economy. Katz argues even that schooling was imposed on the workers by the capitalists.

Several observations can be made about the relationship between early industrialization and antebellum school reforms. First, educators did devote much of their attention and energy to improving urban schools. But they were also concerned with rural schools, which faced somewhat different problems than their urban counterparts. For example, while urban schools struggled to provide enough classroom seats for everyone and to get immigrant children to attend public schools on a regular basis, rural schools were more concerned about extending the length of the public school year. The educational reform impetus was not confined to areas that were rapidly becoming urbanized and industrialized but was felt throughout the entire society.

Second, reform efforts were not restricted to the Northeast. The educational reform efforts of John Pierce in Michigan, Calvin Stowe in Ohio, and Calvin Wiley in North Carolina occurred at the same time as the activities of Mann. The suggestion that antebellum educational reforms arose mainly as a response to the social tensions generated by industrialization ignores the parallel movements in states that were still largely rural and agricultural (Kaestle, 1987).

Third, the leadership of educational expansion and reform included clergymen and others, not just manufacturers and capitalists (Vinovskis, 1985). For example, the most influential and vocal proponents of the public high school in Beverly, Massachusetts, when it was threatened with abolition, were the Protestant ministers.

Fourth, although the revisionists often portray public education as being imposed on an indifferent if not hostile working class, there are strong indications that many, if not most, workers welcomed the creation and maintenance of public schools. Although the workers were sometimes divided among themselves on certain aspects of educational strategy, such as the trade-off between the creation of public high schools and further funding for common schools, they recognized the importance of providing at least some common school training for all children (Katznelson & Weir, 1985; Vinovskis, 1985).

Finally, the school curriculum was not an unadulterated lesson in hierarchy. Scholars such as Bowles and Gintis portray schools as only preparing students for the social relations of production by alienating them from each other through intense individualistic competition and by accustoming them to bureaucratic hierarchical structures in schools that paralleled those they would encounter in the workplace. Such statements ignore contradictory tendencies within schools such as the emphasis on democracy and equality, and they deny any autonomy to the school system.

Complexity of Sources of Change

By now it should be apparent that the close, causal relationship between early industrialization and the rise of mass public schooling proposed by Bowles and Gintis is not an accurate or adequate portrayal of educational development in the United States. There is no single, simple explanation for the growth of mass public schooling; it is a complex phenomenon whose origins vary regionally. In New England, for which we have the most detailed studies, much of the impetus behind educating children came from the Puritan religion, which emphasized the necessity for everyone being able to read the Bible. This religious motive was supplemented by the growing recognition that sons who planned to enter a profession or pursue a commercial career needed additional schooling (Soltow & Stevens, 1981).

The religious emphasis on the importance of education persisted throughout the antebellum period and was reinforced after the American Revolution by the need for an educated electorate. As barriers to white male suffrage were lowered and as political participation increased with the unanticipated rise of political parties, schooling was seen as a means of educating the electorate and preserving the Republic (Cremin, 1970). The role of mothers as the educators of the next generation of leaders and voters provided a convenient and important rationale for giving women more access to formal schooling as well (Kerber, 1980; Norton, 1980).

Thus, the ideological justifications for providing schooling for almost everyone as well as the institutions designed to deliver these services were already well in place in areas like New England before the increasing urbanization and industrialization of that region occurred in the 1820s and 1830s.

Nevertheless, industrialization in New England certainly contributed to providing an environment in which the already high levels of education could be sustained and improved in quality. Nineteenth-century anxiety about unrest in urban and industrial settings, particularly where large numbers of immigrants were living, reinforced the belief that public education was necessary not only to enhance the lives of individuals but also to preserve and protect society (Carnoy & Levin, 1985; Graff, 1979). Furthermore, the increase in population concentration and growth of aggregate wealth caused in part by manufacturing made it easier to implement improvements in public common schools (Soltow & Stevens, 1981). Although education expenditures as a percentage of the gross national product increased only slightly during the antebellum period, total expenditures for public and private schooling increased substantially (Fishlow, 1971).

As a result, early industrialization as well as other socioeconomic changes contributed to improvements in the quality of education provided in New England communities, but industrialization was only one of a complex set of causal factors. Industrialization played an even smaller role in the rapid expansion of public education in other regions, but the general social and economic transformation of society in those areas also created a setting in which educational growth and improvement could occur.

There is another implication of the beginnings of the rise of mass, formal schooling in the late 18th- and early 19th-century United States. Whereas earlier families had been expected to teach their own children how to read or write, parents now relied more on private or public schools to handle those functions. Moreover, prior to the 19th century, the institution of early apprenticeship had been supplemented by informal and intermittent training throughout the life course; education now became more narrowly identified with formal schooling, and (of special interest for this book) increasingly it became age-graded (Angus, Mirel, & Vinovskis, 1988).

In regard to structural lag, then, the overall pattern of American educational reform and expansion in the 19th century can be seen in part as a response to the needs and goals of people: workers' beliefs that all children should receive some common schooling, the need for an educated electorate, the requirement that people of all ages be able to read the Bible, and the necessity to replace parents in socialization and apprenticeships.

THE ECONOMIC PRODUCTIVITY OF EDUCATION

If 19th-century educational development was traceable only in part to changes in economic structures, did it contribute to productivity throughout other social institutions, and hence to the economic productivity of people's lives? This is a question very much alive in the United States today. Education, as a form of investment in human capital, was recognized as an important component of economic development in the 1960s. Numerous articles and books were published extolling the necessity of providing more schooling in the developing countries as a means of stimulating national economic growth and individual well-being (Anderson & Bowman, 1965; Blaug, 1968).

Although the enthusiasm for a human capital approach diminished somewhat in the following decade, as many of the exaggerated claims of the previous studies were corrected, there is renewed interest in the topic today (Hornbeck & Salmon, 1991; Marshall & Tucker, 1992; Psacharopoulos & Woodhall, 1985; Schultz, 1981).

Early Views

In the wake of current studies that view schooling as a form of human investment, efforts have been made to investigate the economic productivity of education in the past. Scholars searched the writings of classical economists for awareness of human capital investment (Blitz, 1968; Johnson, 1964; Vaizey, 1962). Even during the period of mercantilism in the 17th and 18th centuries, some writers recognized the importance of learning and science in stimulating economic development. Some economists prior to Adam Smith, although they seldom mentioned education, considered it a goal of public policy to increase a nation's fund of knowledge and thus to make its citizens into more skillful producers (Johnson, 1964).

Education received more explicit treatment in the writings of the English classical economists such as Adam Smith and J. R. McCulloch. They sometimes mentioned education and a few even endorsed governmental support for schooling, but they did not attach much importance to the role of education in fostering economic growth (Blaug, 1986).

Adam Smith, for example, acknowledged that monetary rewards had to be provided to compensate workers for acquiring skills, but he did not develop the implications of those insights. Instead, he expressed concern that the increasing division of labor in a modern economy, which he strongly favored, might lead to social and political unrest that education could help to contain. Social control rather than economic improvement of the individual became his major rationale for state aid to education (Smith, 1937, pp. 739–740).

American economic writers, in comparison with their English counterparts, mentioned more frequently the value of education in improving the productivity of workers (Kaestle, 1976). Nevertheless, their emphasis was less on the beneficial aspects of schooling to the individual worker than on its benefit to the nation as a whole by fostering useful inventions or preserving social and political tranquility

(Phillips, 1828; Wayland, 1843). Education as an investment in human capital was mentioned by American economists, but not developed or stressed.

Perhaps one of the reasons many early American writers did not focus on the economic productivity of education is that much of the actual training of skilled workers had been provided through the institution of apprenticeship rather than formal schooling in colonial and early 19th-century America. As apprenticeships became more informal and less prevalent in the first quarter of the 19th century, alternative sources of training youth were sought (Rorabaugh, 1986).

If most 19th-century American economists saw in education a means of preserving the existing social and political order, some workers saw in education an escape from the domination of their employers. During the 1820s and 1830s, workers banded together and called for free public education. Although the attempts of workers to organize themselves into a separate political movement failed, both the Democrats and Whigs sought to accommodate their demands for more public schooling (though the two parties disagreed on how that education should be provided and controlled) (Carlton, 1908; Kaestle, 1983).

Yet even the leaders of the workers who advocated free public schooling for everyone did not emphasize the economic productivity of education for the employee or the employer. Instead, they saw in education a means for allowing workers to participate more equally and independently as employees and voters (Luther, 1832; Simpson, 1831).

After the economic value of schooling was stressed by educators in the two decades prior to the Civil War, working-class writers devoted more attention to the economic benefits of education to the individual. But their emphasis on the value of education was not always identical to that of the educators or the capitalists. As Harvey Graff (1979) noted in his analysis of Ontario workers:

> Labor deviated from the major premise of leading schoolmen who sought more education of the working class for greater productivity. Ambivalent about the proper role, form, and content of education, recognizing some contradictions, and often placing its benefits and application quite aside from their jobs, they sought to be free and independent, powerful in ways that would

not have pleased the men who desired to have the masses educated. (p. 215)

The Influence of Horace Mann

The American thinker of the mid-19th century who is most responsible for exploring and publicizing the idea of the economic productivity of education is Horace Mann. In his famous *Fifth Annual Report,* he made a serious, though ultimately flawed, estimate of the actual rate of return to education based on information about the earnings of textile workers (Mann, 1842).

Based on a few replies to a questionnaire he sent to leading manufacturers or their agents at the textile mills in Lowell, Mann (1842) argued that education was the most productive investment any individual or community could make:

> They [his evidence] seem to prove incontestably that education is not only a moral renovator, and a multiplier of intellectual power, but also that it is also the most prolific parent of material riches. It has a right, therefore, not only to be included in the grand inventory of a nation's resources, but to be placed at the very head of the inventory. It is not only the most honest and honorable, but the surest means of amassing property. (pp. 100–101)

He went on to compare industrialization in Massachusetts and England and concluded that the process was successful in the former because of the highly educated labor force in that state. For Mann, education made workers more industrious, reliable, and punctual. Education also made it possible for workers to tend the increasingly complex machinery and encouraged farmers to utilize chemical fertilizers and crop rotation to enhance the quality of their soil. Mann observed that educated workers were more apt to be content with their employment and less likely to join disruptive strikes. The major benefit of education for Mann, however, was the inventiveness of employees. Educated workers were more likely to discover and implement labor-saving ways of doing their jobs.

The businessmen who replied to Mann's questionnaires endorsed his views on the importance of education. Unlike Mann, however, these employers stressed better work discipline and loyalty to management rather than inventiveness as the most important advantages of educated workers.

Only two of the four businessmen replying to Mann's questionnaire provided specific estimates of the differential in wages for educated and uneducated workers. J. K. Mills observed that literate workers on the average earned 27% more than illiterate ones and J. Clark put that figure at 18.5%. The wage differential between the highest paid literate workers and the lowest paid illiterate workers was reported as 66% by Mills and 40% according to Clark (Mann, 1842).

Based on these replies, Mann claimed that educated workers earned about 50% more than uneducated ones. His estimate apparently was derived from reports of only two respondents, and in addition, there are several statistical and conceptual problems with his calculations. By using the extreme wage differentials of the literate and illiterate workers, Mann was looking at the unusual rather than the typical cases. He ignored the opportunity costs of attending school. Also, since nearly everyone in Massachusetts was already literate at that time, a more appropriate measure would have been the rate of return for an additional year of common school education rather than the advantage of literacy over illiteracy (Vinovskis, 1970).

If Mann's estimates of the rate of return for educated workers are limited and inadequate, however, his focus on this issue and his attempt to measure it were innovative and important. His contemporaries accepted his reasoning and calculations enthusiastically and without reservation. The *Fifth Annual Report* was widely cited and the New York legislature ordered a printing of 18,000 copies. A group of prominent Boston businessmen acknowledged his achievements in showing the economic benefits of public education. John D. Philbrick, another educational leader, said in 1863 that the *Fifth Annual Report* had "probably done more than all other publications written within the past twenty-five years to convince capitalists of the value of elementary instruction as a means of increasing the value of labor" (cited in Curti, 1965).

Was Mann correct in claiming that education was an important factor in enhancing the economic productivity of antebellum American workers? Scholars continue to be sharply divided on this issue.

Many analysts, such as Field (1976), question the overall contribution of education to workers from a human capital perspective. They point out that early industrialization did not require additionally skilled workers, but in fact permitted less skilled ones to replace better trained artisans. Others, like Douglass North (1971), argue that industrialization in the United States increased the demand not only for new laborsaving inventions but for a more educated and skilled labor force capable of adapting and modifying English manufacturing techniques to the American setting.

Analysts of 19th-century education as human capital often focus too narrowly on the manufacturing sector or concentrate mainly on the productivity of male workers. Schooling also provided opportunities for women to enter professions such as teaching (Clifford, 1982). Indeed, after the coming of the Irish to the textile mills, the pay of female schoolteachers exceeded that of female mill hands (Carter & Prus, 1982).

At this time, there is no way to decide definitively the impact of education on 19th-century American economic development. Everyone seems to be agreed that education helped to foster an environment in which conflicts between labor and capital were minimized and the regularity and the discipline of the workforce was enhanced. Similarly, most scholars, though not all, accept that education did improve the cognitive skills of workers and made them more adaptable to the technological changes taking place, but there is widespread disagreement on the importance of this contribution. Detailed microlevel studies necessary to resolve this debate are not available. A reasonable guess, however, would be that although the relatively high level of schooling among American workers in the Northeast was not caused by the skill demands of early industrialization, their education helped to speed the quick and efficient adoption of new laborsaving machinery and techniques in both the manufacturing and the agricultural sectors. While Mann's claims of a 50% rate of return to education are exaggerated, perhaps a more realistic guess would be a rate of return in the range of 10% to 20% for a common-school education (Vinovskis, 1970).

Like other institutional changes, the increasing emphasis on the formal schooling of young people and on the economic productivity of education may also have had unintended effects. For example, it may have contributed in part to a deemphasis of apprenticeship and lifelong learning in maintaining and enhancing the skills of older workers. Some policymakers and business leaders became increasingly persuaded that the key to economic growth and productivity rested more with early schooling than with adult training. This belief was reinforced by increasingly negative views of elderly workers in the second half of the 19th century, so that the education of the young in the schools seemed to be a more rational investment than retraining older workers (Achenbaum, 1978; Fischer, 1978; Graebner, 1980; Haber, 1983). Thus the current constraints on structural opportunities for productivity by workers at more advanced ages were already well established in the 19th century.

EDUCATION AND SOCIAL MOBILITY

The extent to which social mobility was real or imagined and the extent to which education was the major path to upward mobility over people's lives can be considered indicators of structural lag. They tell us whether educational institutions fulfilled the changing social needs and individual aspirations of the early industrial era. They tell us also whether other institutions, especially those that provided jobs, acknowledged and rewarded the changing educational credentials of their employees.

In the United States before the Civil War, the dominant ideology was that of social mobility. Inequities in wealth and power were often acknowledged, but it was said that everyone could improve their lives by being frugal, temperate, and hardworking (Cawelti, 1965; Wyllie, 1954). Books and newspapers celebrated individuals who overcame their disadvantages to become the next generation of business and political leaders.

Did social mobility really exist in that society? The answer depends in part on how social mobility is defined and measured. Historians, drawing on the work of earlier sociologists, concentrate on occupational mobility. Most of these studies subdivide the 19th-century occupational structure into five broad categories: (1) high white-collar, (2) low white-collar, (3) skilled, (4) semiskilled, and (5) unskilled. Social mobility is also often measured by whether someone is able to move from a manual occupation (skilled, semiskilled, or unskilled) to a nonmanual one (high white-collar or low white-collar). Furthermore, whereas some studies focus on the career mobility of individuals, others look at the intergenerational mobility between fathers and sons (Thernstrom, 1973).

The findings from the social mobility studies of Americans in the 19th century are somewhat mixed in terms of the opportunities available to the children of semiskilled or unskilled workers. The first case study, and perhaps still the most widely cited, is that of the lives of common laborers in the small urban community of Newburyport, Massachusetts, between 1850 and 1880. Thernstrom (1964) found that although many of the sons of the unskilled laborers who stayed in that community experienced a small increase in occupational status or were able to purchase their own homes, only about one out of six was able to move into a skilled or white-collar occupation. Similar results have been reported for Philadelphia in the four decades prior to the Civil War (Blumin, 1969).

Others have found higher rates of social mobility—particularly for the sons of the native-born population. Clyde Griffen's analysis of Poughkeepsie, New York, between 1850 and 1880 found that most immigrants and blacks did not fare well, but up to one-third of the sons of native-born fathers in manual trades moved up to nonmanual (white-collar) occupations—especially as owners of small craft and retail shops (Griffen, 1969).

A recent review of all the studies of 19th-century occupational mobility concluded that there was little difference between the United States and Europe in regard to overall career mobility, but that upward mobility among unskilled workers in the United States was slightly higher than in Europe. Compared with their European counterparts, Americans were also less likely to experience downward mobility into the working classes. In addition, there was great diversity in the rates of occupational mobility among American cities, with no simple explanations for the patterns. Furthermore, although upward mobility into skilled or nonmanual occupations was a distinct career possibility for some unskilled workers, the majority of them remained in the same occupational group or advanced only to semiskilled positions (Kaeble, 1985). Ravitch (1978, p. 88) concluded, "Pending further research, it does appear that upward social mobility trends have been established in certain American cities during the nineteenth and early twentieth centuries."

Was education a key to the social mobility that occurred in pre-Civil War America? Many educators, drawing on the work of Horace Mann, stressed the importance of education in enhancing the economic productivity of workers but did not focus on whether or not education promoted occupational mobility. Nevertheless, implicit in their discussions of the value of education for the individual and the society is the belief that through education children could advance into better paying and higher status occupations (Mayhew, 1850).

Other 19th-century writers, in discussing social mobility, did not place much emphasis on the importance of education. Instead, they stressed the value of good habits and hard work as the essential ingredients for advancement. While most of them assumed that a common-school education was essential, few pointed to the specific advantages of additional years of schooling (Cawelti, 1965; Wyllie, 1954).

Most studies of 19th-century careers have not tested for the role of education in promoting social mobility. The few historians who have commented on this issue are divided on the importance of literacy and education. Based on a detailed study of three Canadian cities, Graff (1979) concluded that even literacy was not an important factor in helping individuals succeed—at least among immigrants in unskilled or semiskilled occupations.

In a study using multiple classification analysis, Michael Katz and his colleagues tested whether school attendance in Hamilton, Ontario, in 1861 led to more social mobility 10 years later. They concluded that, with other factors held constant, school attendance exerted no influence on the occupation of young men from one decade to another (Katz, Doucet, & Stern, 1982).

Thernstrom, on the other hand, argues for the importance of education for fostering social mobility, but he also fails to establish that relationship statistically. In his study of Newburyport, he argues that a combination of misguided parental values toward education and the abject poverty of the family meant that lower-class children did not stay in school and therefore were severely handicapped in terms of their future social mobility.

Thernstrom documents the low rate of social mobility among children of unskilled workers, but he does not demonstrate that this was due to their lack of education—in part because he only studied the children of the common laborers in Newburyport and not the rest of the population. He simply assumed that because children of working-class fathers received little education and those of more affluent parents must have had more education, education must be a key factor in explaining their subsequent differential occupational mobility.

These studies of schooling and social mobility in the 19th century have a number of methodological limitations (May & Vinovskis, 1977; Vinovskis, 1983). Moreover, they focus on the impact of literacy or common-school education on occupational advancement. They do not address the role of a high-school education because it is usually assumed that few individuals attended such institutions, that those who did were almost always members of an already privileged middle or upper class, and that the few children of working-class families who attended high school were unable to compete effectively with those from more advantaged homes.

The first public high school was established in Boston in 1821, but it was only in the late 1840s and 1850s that these institutions spread rapidly into some other states (Grizzell, 1923). Most scholars believe that even by the 1880s, "It was a rare thing to go to high school" (Krug, 1969, p. 11). A closer look, however, at states such as Massachusetts, which led the way in establishing public high schools, suggests that a much higher percentage of children attended high school than had been suspected. In Newburyport in 1860, for example, almost one-third of the children received some high school education and in Essex County as a whole nearly one out of five children received some high school training, public or private (Vinovskis, 1988b).

Even if high schools were accessible in some areas, were they reserved mainly for members of the middle or upper classes and unavailable to those whose fathers were in manual occupations? Certainly children whose fathers were in white-collar occupations were overrepresented in 19th-century public high schools. But in some communities, a sizable minority of children from the working classes attended these institutions. In Newburyport in 1860, about 1 out of 6 children whose fathers were common laborers received some high-school education, compared with 4 out of 10 children whose fathers were in skilled occupations (Vinovskis, 1988a, 1988b). While these proportions may be high compared with those for other communities, by the end of the 19th century a substantial minority of high-school students were from blue-collar families (Angus, 1981; Ueda, 1987).

Some scholars argue that 19th-century public high schools discriminated against working-class families not only by excluding most of their children but by limiting the opportunities and rewards for those who were admitted. The few intensive studies of high-school education of that period suggest, however, that once someone entered high school, disadvantaged parental background was not an insurmountable barrier for success (Perlmann, 1985). For example, David Labaree's 1988 analysis of the Central High School of Philadelphia found that:

. . . students obtained admission to the school through a mixture of class background and academic ability. However, once admitted, they found themselves in a model meritocracy where academic performance was the only characteristic that determined who would receive the school's valuable diploma. (p. 37)

The remaining question is whether high-school attendance promoted social mobility or merely reinforced and legitimized the existing capitalist system? Scholars are divided on this question, and the empirical support for either interpretation is limited. But Ueda's analysis of intergenerational occupational mobility for Somerville, Massachusetts, grammar- and high-school students in the last quarter of the 19th century found, "Blue-collar sons who went to high school in Somerville achieved a higher and faster rate of entry into the white-collar field than blue-collar sons in Boston of all levels of schooling" (p. 179).

Similarly, Joel Perlmann's detailed, statistically sophisticated study of secondary schooling in Providence, Rhode Island, between 1880 and 1925 found that attending high school greatly improved a person's chances for upward occupational mobility—even after controlling for the effects of family background.

Despite these studies, the relationship between schooling and occupational mobility during the 19th century in the United States as a whole remains to be documented. Studies for the early 20th century, which are more comprehensive, suggest that schooling played a key role in fostering individual economic advancement (Jensen, 1987; Kett, 1977; Perlmann, 1988). Although comparable work for the antebellum years remains to be done, enough fragmentary evidence exists to suggest that education helped individuals to improve their economic well-being and occupational status, and thus had a significant impact on their lives.

CONCLUSION

Nineteenth-century educational development was related to and influenced by economic changes, but not as simply and directly as some have suggested. Mass public education in the United States was not caused or wholly preceded by antebellum industrialization. Rather, it began during the colonial period and early 19th century as a popular response to religious and political needs—particularly in New England. As a result, the United States was a relatively literate country when it first experienced industrialization.

But if industrialization did not cause the rise of mass education, it did help to create an environment in which schooling could flourish, expand, and improve. The potential and perceived turmoil associated with industrial development encouraged many Americans to support mass public education. Though industrial development was only one of many factors that caused 19th-century Americans to be anxious about their future life chances, that fear was important in mobilizing support for public schooling. In addition, industrialization contributed to the economic development of the United States and made additional public expenditures for education more tolerable.

Whereas some industrialists and other capitalists certainly participated actively in antebellum school reforms, they by no means dominated them. Educational reform efforts were broad-based coalitions that brought together individuals and groups from diverse backgrounds, including workers who had enjoyed no educational opportunity themselves. In some ways, antebellum school reform was like an evangelical crusade by people who shared a deep though often naive faith in the power of education to redeem individuals and to preserve and protect the existing social and political order.

Schools did not simply mirror the organization and ideology of the workplace. Although the schools provided cognitive skills and socialization that prepared children for their adult work roles, they also taught democratic and egalitarian ideas that contradicted the unequal and hierarchical aspects of the antebellum society. Schools were a contested and semiautonomous domain where different individuals and groups sought to educate and to indoctrinate the next generation with what each considered to be the proper views and values.

Most 19th-century classical economists did not devote much attention to the economic role of education. When they did discuss the subject, they stressed the importance of schools for disciplining the labor force and minimizing the tensions of industrialization. Supporters of American workers wrote of the importance of free public schooling for everyone, but they did not emphasize the value of education for enhancing economic productivity.

Horace Mann was the individual most responsible for proclaiming and publicizing the importance of education for economic productivity. His methods of analysis were biased and inadequate statistically, but he succeeded in convincing the public and many policymakers that education was a worthwhile economic investment for the individual and the society.

Most economists today continue to stress the importance of education as a form of human capital investment, but some historians have expressed serious reservations about the economic productivity of education in antebellum United States. Although the research evidence is limited, it appears that public and private schooling contributed to the economic well-being of 19th-century Americans—though in a more modest fashion than proclaimed by enthusiasts such as Mann.

These Americans also had a deep and abiding faith in the possibility and the reality of social mobility in their society. Current scholarship tends to support the notion that social mobility did exist for many Americans, but in a much more limited amount than had previously been assumed. Nevertheless, some scholars question even the possibility of any real antebellum social mobility because they view the capitalist system as merely reproducing the existing social and economic structure.

Scholars continue to disagree on the amount of such mobility and also on whether education was an important factor in fostering whatever mobility occurred. These questions cannot be resolved on the basis of the few existing studies. The weight of evidence suggests that education, especially high-school education, did contribute to the occupational advancement of individuals or their children; perhaps, however, it was not as essential then as it is today.

Finally, the rise of mass schooling and the emphasis on its role in fostering economic productivity and social mobility led to greater attention to education for the very young. When schools replaced apprenticeship as the institutions for preparing future workers, children were sent at early ages to increasingly age-graded classrooms. Moreover, as economic productivity and social mobility became more closely and narrowly identified with schooling, and as the biases against older workers grew in the second half of the 19th century, the perceived need for offering additional on-the-job training for older workers may have diminished. While the relationship between changes in schooling and the age-graded pattern of life course education remains to be thoroughly investigated, it is likely that the changes in the 19th-century schools and the economy played a key role in emphasizing the importance of formal schooling early in the life course.

This history of the development of mass public education has strategic relevance for understanding structural change more generally. It can be seen as a history of differences in the rhythms of changing individual lives and changes in social structures. Changes in educational institutions came about as interested parties from all walks of life pressed to make schools responsive to their goals. And as educational institutions changed, they mediated the relationship between changing economic and political structures, on the one hand, and the needs of people on the other. These educational changes of the 19th century have left a legacy of an age-graded educational system that today appears to lag behind changes in the life course. Educational institutions have still not caught up with the ever-changing needs of children, the growing number of capable older people eager for more education, or the need for continuous retraining to be available for people of all ages.

The 19th-century spread of mass public education thus has significance for understanding the phenomenon of structural lag as American society approaches the end of the 20th century. It is significant both because schools are important societal institutions in their own rights and because their unique product—the enhancement of people's abilities and aspirations—contributes to the continuing dynamic relationship of individual aspirations and societal opportunities.

REFERENCES

Achenbaum, W. A. (1978). *Old age in the new land: The American experience since 1790*. Baltimore, MD: Johns Hopkins University Press.

Anderson, C. A., & Bowman, M. J. (Eds.). (1965). *Education and economic development*. Chicago, IL: Aldine.

Angus, D. L. (1981). A note on the occupational backgrounds of public high schools prior to 1940. *Journal of the Midwest History of Education Society, 9,* 158–183.

Angus, D., Mirel, J., & Vinovskis, M. A. (1988). Historical development of age-stratification in schooling. *Teacher's College Record, 90,* 33–58.

Blaug, M. (Ed.). (1968). *Economics of education: Selected readings, I.* Harmondsworth, England: Penguin Books.

Blaug, M. (1986). *Economic history and the history of economics.* New York: New York University Press.

Blitz, R. C. (1968). Education in the writings of Malthus, Senior, McCulloch and John Stuart Mill. In M. J. Bowman, M. Debeauvais, V. E. Komarov, and J. Vaizey (Eds.), *Readings in the economics of education* (pp. 40–48). New York: UNESCO.

Blumin, S. (1969). Mobility and change in ante-bellum Philadelphia. In S. Thernstrom & R. Sennett (Eds.), *Nineteenth-century cities: Essays in the new urban history* (pp. 165–208). New Haven, CT: Yale University Press.

Bowles, S., & Gintis, H. (1976). *Schooling in capitalist America: Educational reform and the contradictions of economic life.* New York: Basic Books.

Carlton, F. T. (1908). *Economic influences upon educational progress in the United States, 1820–1850.* Madison, WI: University of Wisconsin Press.

Carnoy, M., & Levin, H. M. (1985). *Schooling and work in the democratic state.* Stanford, CA: Stanford University Press.

Carter, S. B., & Prus, M. (1982). The labor market and the American high school girl, 1870–1928. *Journal of Economic History, 47,* 163–171.

Cawelti, J. G. (1965). *Apostles of the self-made man.* Chicago, IL: University of Chicago Press.

Clifford, G. J. (1982). Marry, stitch, die or do worse: Educating women for work. In H. Kantor & D. B. Tyack (Eds.), *Work, youth and schooling: Historical perspectives on vocationalism in American education* (pp. 223–268). Stanford, CA: Stanford University Press.

Cohen, S. (1977). The history of education in the United States: Historians of education and their discontents. In D. A. Reeder (Ed.), *Urban education in the nineteenth-century: Proceedings of the 1976 annual conference of the history of education society of Great Britain* (pp. 115–132). London: Taylor & Francis.

Cremin, L. A. (1970). *American education: The colonial experience, 1607–1783.* New York: Harper & Row.

Cremin, L. A. (1977). *Traditions of American education.* New York: Basic Books.

Curti, M. (1965). *The social ideas of American educators* (p. 113). Paterson, NJ: Littlefield & Adams.

Field, A. (1974). *Educational reform and manufacturing development in mid-nineteenth-century Massachusetts.* Unpublished doctoral dissertation, University of California, Berkeley, CA.

Field, A. J. (1976). Educational expansion in mid-nineteenth-century Massachusetts: Human-capital formation or structural reinforcement? *Harvard Educational Review, 46,* 521–552.

Fischer, D. H. (1978). *Growing old in America* (rev. ed.). New York: Oxford University Press.

Fishlow, A. (1966). The American common school revival: Fact or fancy? In A. Gerschenkron (Ed.), *Industrialization in two systems* (pp. 40–67). New York: Wiley.

Fishlow, A. (1971). Levels of nineteenth-century American investment in education. In R. W. Fogel & S. L. Engerman (Eds.), *The reinterpretation of American economic history* (pp. 265–273). New York: Harper & Row.

Graebner, W. (1980). *A history of retirement: The meaning and function of an American institution, 1885–1978.* New Haven, CT: Yale University Press.

Graff, H. J. (1979). *The literacy myth: Literacy and social structure in the nineteenth-century city.* New York: Academic Press.

Griffen, C. (1969). Workers divided: The effect of craft and ethnic differences in Poughkeepsie, NY, 1850–1880. In S. Thernstrom & R. Sennett (Eds.), *Nineteenth-century cities: Essays in the new urban history* (pp. 49–97). New Haven, CT: Yale University Press.

Grizzell, E. D. (1923). *Origin and development of the high school in New England before 1865.* New York: Macmillan.

Haber, C. (1983). *Beyond sixty-five: The dilemma of old age in America's past.* Cambridge: Cambridge University Press.

Hornbeck, D. W., & Salmon, L. M. (Eds.). (1991). *Human capital and America's future: An economic strategy for the '90s.* Baltimore, MD: Johns Hopkins University Press.

Jensen, R. (1987). *Education and life chances in the job market.* Paper presented at the Social Science History Association Meeting, New Orleans, LA.

Johnson, E. A. (1964). The place of learning, science, vocational training, and 'art' in pre-Smithian economic thought. *Journal of Economic History, 24,* 129–144.

Kaeble, H. (1985). *Social mobility in the nineteenth- and twentieth-centuries: Europe and America in comparative perspective.* Leamington Spa, England: Berg Publishers.

Kaestle, C. F. (1976). "Between the Scylla of brutal ignorance and the Charybdis of a literary education": Elite attitudes toward mass schooling in early industrial England and America. In L. Stone (Ed.), *Schooling and society: Studies in the history of education* (pp. 177–191). Baltimore, MD: Johns Hopkins University Press.

Kaestle, C. F. (1983). *Pillars of the republic: Common schools and American society, 1780–1860.* New York: Hill & Wang.

Kaestle, C. F. (1987). The development of common school systems in the states of the old northwest. In P. H. Mattingly & E. W. Stevens, Jr. (Eds.), *". . . Schools and the means of education shall forever be encouraged": A history of education in the old northwest, 1787–1880* (pp. 31–43). Athens, OH: Ohio University Libraries.

Kaestle, C. F., & Vinovskis, M. A. (1980). *Education and social change in nineteenth-century Massachusetts.* Cambridge: Cambridge University Press.

Katz, M. B. (1976). The origins of public education: A reassessment. *History of Education Quarterly, 16,* 381–407.

Katz, M. B. (1987). *Reconstructing American education.* Cambridge, MA: Harvard University Press.

Katz, M. B., Doucet, M. J., & Stern, M. J. (1982). *The social organization of early industrial capitalism.* Cambridge, MA: Harvard University Press.

Katznelson, I., & Weir, M. (1985). *Schooling for all: Class, race, and the decline of the democratic ideal.* New York: Basic Books.

Kerber, L. K. (1980). *Women of the republic: Intellect and ideology in revolutionary America.* Chapel Hill, NC: University of North Carolina Press.

Kett, J. F. (1977). *Rites of passage: Adolescence in America, 1790 to the present*. New York: Basic Books.

Krug, E. A. (1969). *The shaping of the American high school, 1880–1920*. Madison, WI: University of Wisconsin Press.

Labaree, D. F. (1988). *The making of an American high school: The credentials market and the central high school of Philadelphia, 1838–1939*. New Haven, CT: Yale University Press.

Lockridge, K. A. (1974). *Literacy in colonial New England: An enquiry into the social context of literacy in the early modern west*. New York: Norton.

Luther, S. (1832). *An address to the working-men of New England, on the state of education, and on the condition of the producing classes in Europe and America*. Boston, MA: Seth Luther.

Mann, H. (1842). *Fifth annual report of the Board of Education together with the fifth annual report of the Secretary of the Board*. Boston, MA: Dutton & Wentworth.

Marshall, R., & Tucker, M. (1992). *Thinking for a living: Education and wealth of nations*. New York: Basic Books.

May, D., & Vinovskis, M. A. (1977). A ray of millennial light: Early education and social reform in the infant school movement in Massachusetts, 1826–1840. In T. K. Hareven (Ed.), *Family and kin in urban communities, 1700–1930* (pp. 62–99). New York: New Viewpoints.

Mayhew, I. (1850). *Popular education for the use of parents and teachers and for young persons of both sexes*. New York: Harper & Brothers.

Moran, G. F., & Vinovskis, M. A. (1985). The great care of godly parents: Early childhood in puritan New England. In A. B. Smuts & J. W. Hagen (Eds.), *History and Research in child Development: Monographs of the Society for Research in Child Development, 50, 24–37*.

North, D. C. (1971). Capital formation in the United States during the early period of industrialization: A reexamination of the issues. In R. W. Fogel & S. L. Engerman (Eds.), *The reinterpretation of American history* (p. 277). New York: Harper & Row.

Norton, M. B. (1980). *Liberty's daughters: The revolutionary experience of American women, 1750–1800*. Boston, MA: Little, Brown.

Perlmann, J. (1985). Who stayed in school? Social structure and academic achievement in determination of enrollment patterns, Providence, R.I., 1880–1925. *Journal of American History, 72*, 588–614.

Perlmann, J. (1988). *Ethnic differences: Schooling and social structure among the Irish, Italian, Jews, and Blacks in the American City, 1880–1935*. Cambridge: Cambridge University Press.

Phillips, W. (1828). *A manual of political economy with particular reference to the institutions, resources, and condition of the United States*. Boston, MA: Hilliard, Gray, Little, & Wilkins.

Psacharopoulos, G., & Woodhall, M. (1985). *Education for development: An analysis of investment choice*. New York: Oxford University Press.

Ravitch, D. (1978). *The revisionists revised: A critique of the radical attack on the schools.* New York: Basic Books.

Rorabaugh, J. (1986). *The craft apprentice: From Franklin to the machine age in America.* New York: Oxford University Press.

Schultz, T. W. (1981). *Investing in people: The economics of population quality.* Berkeley, CA: University of California Press.

Simpson, S. (1831). *The working man's manual: A new theory of political economy, on the principle of production the source of wealth.* Philadelphia, PA: Bonsal.

Sixth Census. (1841). *Secretary of State, Sixth Census or Enumeration of the Inhabitants of the United States as corrected at the Department of State in 1840.* Washington, DC: Blair & Rives.

Smith, A. (1937). *An inquiry into the nature and causes of the wealth of nations.* New York: Modern Library.

Soltow, L., & Stevens, E. (1981). *The rise of literacy and the common school in the United States: A socioeconomic analysis to 1870.* Chicago, IL: University of Chicago Press.

Thernstrom, S. (1964). *Poverty and progress: Social mobility in a nineteenth-century city.* Cambridge, MA: Harvard University Press.

Thernstrom, S. (1973). *The other Bostonians: Poverty and progress in the American metropolis, 1880–1970.* Cambridge, MA: Harvard University Press.

Ueda, R. (1987). *Avenues to adulthood: The origins of the high school and social mobility in an American suburb.* Cambridge: Cambridge University Press.

Vaizey, J. (1962). *The economics of education.* London: Faber & Faber.

Vinovskis, M. A. (1970). Horance Mann on the economic productivity of education. *New England Quarterly, 43,* 550–571.

Vinovskis, M. A. (1983). Quantification and the analysis of American ante-bellum education. *Journal of Interdisciplinary History, 13,* 761–786.

Vinovskis, M. A. (1985). *The origins of public high schools: A re-examination of the Beverly high school controversy.* Madison, WI: University of Wisconsin Press.

Vinovskis, M. A. (1988a). Have we underestimated the extent of antebellum high school attendance? *History of Education Quarterly, 28,* 551–567.

Vinovskis, M. A. (1988b). *Patterns of high school attendance in Newburyport, Massachusetts in 1860.* Paper presented at the American Historical Association Annual Meeting, New York.

Wayland, F. (1843). *The elements of political economy* (4th ed.). Boston, MA: Gould, Kendall, & Lincoln.

Wyllie, I. G. (1954). *The self-made man in America: The myth of rags to riches.* New Brunswick, NJ: Rutgers University Press.

CHAPTER 9

Old Age and Age Integration: An Anthropological Perspective

Jennie Keith

This chapter reports findings from cross-cultural research about age, especially old age, as it affects people's daily lives. Cross-cultural comparison highlights the basic distinction between influences on lives set by *physical* aging and those set by *sociocultural* attitudes and structures. Paradoxically, although members of technologically advanced societies (like the United States) have conquered many physical constraints of aging, they now confront new sociocultural obstacles to full participation in society—an instance of the "structural lag" addressed throughout this book. Research on the sociocultural aspects of age also suggests forms and mechanisms for future changes and interventions that could increase age integration and release both individual and societal potential.

The specific findings I report here come from a set of anthropological field studies called "Project AGE (Age, Generation, and

Experience)." The project was sponsored by the National Institute on Aging, and was conducted by a team of seven anthropologists between 1982 and 1990 (for details, see References). Our goal was to discover how the different meanings and uses of age, across diverse cultural settings, influence the well-being of people in later life.

In a major effort to obtain diversity in the sample, we selected seven communities in four countries (see Table 9–1):

1. The !Kung San (Bushmen) and Herero in Botswana.
2. Clifden and Blessington in Ireland.
3. A midwestern blue-collar town, Momence, Illinois, and a middle-class suburb, Swarthmore, Philadelphia, in the United States.

Table 9–1
Site Characteristics

Community	Researcher	Location	Population
Hong Kong	Charlotte Ikels	Southeastern Asia, Coastal city	5 Million +
Swarthmore	Jennie Keith	Northeastern USA, 20 minutes southwest of Philadelphia	5,950 (4,650 excluding college students)
Momence	Christine Fry	Midwestern USA, 1 hour south of Chicago	3,400 in town, 4,000 in 72 square mile region
Blessington	Jeanette Dickerson Putman	Western Europe, Ireland, County Wicklow, 18 mi. south of Dublin	1,322 in town, 678 in Townlands
Clifden	Anthony P. Glascock	Western Europe, Ireland, County Galway, 50 mi. west of Galway in the Connemara	805 in town, 851 in Townlands
Herero	Henry Harpending	Southern Africa, northwestern Botswana, northern Kalahari desert	Approximately 1,500 in region
!Kung	Patricia Draper	Southern Africa, northwestern Botswana northern Kalahari desert	780

4. Four neighborhoods of varying socioeconomic status in Hong Kong.

These seven sites were chosen to vary according to such characteristics as subsistence strategy, resource level, societal scale (size, density of population, interdependence with external systems), residential stability, complexity of role structures (as in kinship or work organization).

In each community, the research team carried out traditional ethnographic observation for at least a year; interviewed a sample of 100 to 200 adults about their work, families, participation in the community, health, and age-related perceptions and attitudes about age; and recorded detailed, verbatim life stories of a dozen older people.

Table 9–1 (*continued*)

% Older Adults	Demographic Features	Settlement Pattern	Subsistence
10% over age 60	High population mobility, outmigration of young	Urban, apartments, Housing estates	International port of trade, industry
25% over age 60 (excluding college students)	High population mobility	Suburban, single-family dwellings, few apartments	Service, professional, commuting to Philadelphia
17% over age 60	Population stability, some outmigration of young	Small town, single-family dwellings	Agribusiness, light industry, service commuting to Chicago, 19% unemployment
10% over age 65	Recent inmigration of young	Small town, single-family and council housing, small and large farms	Service, light industry, farming, community to Dublin, 7% unemployment
16% over age 65	High outmigration of young, population decline 15% since 1960	Single-family dwellings, scattered homesteads, isolated	Farming, fishing, shopkeeping, tourism (50% of workers), 19% unemployment
17% over age 60	Infertility in older cohorts, doubling of birth rate since 1960	Dispersed isolated homesteads, several villages	Cattle and small stock pastoralism, some gardening, little wage labor
13% over age 60	Older adults move to Namibia to obtain dole, young males leave to join army	Small villages near permanent water sources, each ca. 30 people, very isolated	Small-scale gardening, stock raising, foraging, herding for Herero, crafts, little wage labor

MAPPING THE MEANINGS AND USES OF AGE

As a major part of our fieldwork in each site, we attempted to map the ways in which age operates as a mechanism that links characteristics of particular sites with the quality of people's lives. Focusing on *sociocultural* influences, we expected age to operate in three major ways: cognitive, evaluative, and social. Thus if our description of each research site is visualized as a rough map of age stratification (or age structuring), then the meanings and uses of age can be visualized as borders defining the age strata, as follows:

- *Cognitive Meanings of Age.* How do people think about age; what age categories do they perceive; and how do they define, indicate, or signal these categories?
- *Evaluative Meanings of Age.* What valence is attached to different ages, age categories, or indicators or markers of age; and what consensus is there about these within the group?
- *Age as a Criterion for Social Participation.* What formal and informal interactions are patterned by age; what are the norms for interactions among people of different (or similar) ages; and what are the actual behaviors?

These meanings and uses of age are listed in Table 9–2, where they are called "Dimensions of Age Structure." Table 9–2 schematizes major findings from the research, which will be presented, and later summarized, in the following sections of this chapter.

To collect information referring to these three dimensions, we used a wide variety of ethnographic field methods (Ikels et al., 1988; Keith, 1994). For example, interactions and norms were discovered through living in the group, participating in activities, and asking for "play-by-play" explanations and comments. All the researchers were experienced fieldworkers, spoke the local language, and lived for at least a year in the research communities. Across the sites, this research required participation in a wide range of field activities: In the Kalahari, it meant driving the land rover 10 kilometers to fill the water tanks, celebrating a successful hunt with kudu cooked on the campfire, listening to the old people tell stories of their own childhood years when frail elders were abandoned in the desert because they couldn't keep moving with the group. In Swarthmore, it meant entering the time

Table 9–2
Dimensions of Age Structure

Age Sites	Cognitive*	Evaluative	Social
!Kung (Bushmen)	Age marker: Functional	Negative Age = decline	No differentiation No barriers except physical
Herero	Age marker: Functional (Person) Generation (Stage) Mean = 3.9 SD = .9	Negative = age Positive = seniority	Access to ritual roles and resources from seniority
Clifden	Age marker: Chronological Mean = 4.7 SD = 1.0	Negative (young more negative than old)	Little differentiation; no barriers except physical
Blessington	Age marker: Chronological Mean = 4.3 SD = 1.3	Negative (young more negative than old)	Increased differentiation with suburbanization
Momence	Age marker: Chronological Mean = 4.7 SD = 1.5	Negative = age Positive = seniority	Access to leadership roles in community organizations from seniority
Swarthmore	Age marker: Chronological Mean = 5.1 SD = 1.8	Negative (young more negative than old)	High differentiation Many barriers
Hong Kong	Age marker: Chronological Mean = 4.3 SD = 1.3	Negative	Spatial integration Social barriers

* Mean = mean number of stages.
SD = standard deviation.

capsule of a Women's Club meeting where "ladies" in hats and gloves listened to a program of Jeanette MacDonald/Nelson Eddy songs and then had tea from a silver service, poured in turn by members in order of seniority. In Ireland, researchers sat in pubs; in Hong Kong, they watched old people do *tai ch'i* in the parks at dawn. In Illinois, they entered the gladiolus festival (our research team's entry won a prize).

Participation in such affairs of daily life provided many insights into the ways people thought, talked, and made value judgments about age:

"Poor Mrs. K_____! She's been in the hospital, and now she can't drive and her kids are putting pressure on her to move out to Ohio."

Or "Have you seen J_____ K_____ recently? I saw her at the post office, and I hardly recognized her. Honestly, her sweater was dirty—I could see what she had for lunch on it! Her lipstick was all over her face, and she was holding up the whole line looking in her purse for an address she couldn't remember. It was so sad!"

Such comments disclosed clues to what was needed to remain a full-fledged member of the community.

COGNITIVE MEANINGS OF AGE

Among the various methods used to examine cognitive perceptions of age and the life course, we used a common card-sorting task called the "Age Game" intended to maximize cross-cultural comparability across the seven communities. The cards contained a number of vignettes about individuals with different attributes, such as reproductive status, living arrangements, and social roles. We used cards with written descriptions appropriate to each culture where participants were literate, and visual representations of different attributes where most participants were not able to read. For example, in Illinois, a card with a picture of a man whom respondents usually identified as in his early 60s read:

A man who is married, has a high school education, has at least one grandchild married, has paid the mortgage on his home, and owns his own business.

We asked respondents to sort the "people" into piles representing stages of life or age categories. Using the respondents' own scheme or terminology, we asked questions about the characteristics of the life stages and the transitions between them. For example: What are the major concerns of young people? What is the best thing/hardest thing about being young? What moves a person out of this stage into the next?

We obtained two very different kinds of results from the Age Game: (1) a straightforward response to questions about age and (2) a failure to attach any meaning to the notion of age, which posed a challenge to these questions as being culture-bound (Fry, 1990; Ikels et al., 1992).

Age-Relevant Meanings

In five of the seven sites, age was a meaningful concept. In Hong Kong, the two U.S. communities, the more suburban Irish town (Blessington), and among the Herero in Botswana, respondents were able to sort "people" into age piles, name life stages, and tell us a great deal about how they defined and evaluated different phases of the life course. While age was relevant in all these settings, its cognitive meanings varied widely.

The themes used to define the stages of life vary with the extent of social differentiation in the communities. Issues of kinship and domestic status were relevant in all five communities. In sites located in industrial societies, work status appeared as an additional basis of life-stage definition. (Freud was right: *Lieb und Arbeit* are both important.) In the stable blue-collar town in Illinois, organizational affiliation becomes an additional marker of life stage: moving from the Parent-Teacher Association to the Lions or to the bridge club are recognizable stages of maturity. So is paying off the mortgage. In the upper-middle class American suburb, people added a further calibration of life experience by achievement levels within careers, and also by personal development. (We called the latter the "psychic lost and found": Respondents identified stages of life by whether they had lost or found *themselves.*)

There was also variation within and across the sites in the numbers of life stages identified. The mean number varied from 3.9 for Herero to 5.1 for the Philadelphia suburb. For each life stage identified, respondents were asked about the age range. We were especially interested in the age at which "old" would begin, and we found that from a chronological point of view, the beginning of old age varied primarily with legal ages of eligibility for benefits, such as Social Security. On average, the earliest age at which respondents would use the label "old" for a life stage was 60 in Hong Kong, and 65 in Ireland and the United States.

These age ranges also varied with the number of different life stages perceived. As the number of stages increased, the lower boundary of the oldest stage moved up. In the Philadelphia suburb, for example, the shift was from average age 61 for people who saw 3 stages of life, to 68 for those who saw 5, to 71 for those who saw 7 or more. Subdivisions of old age began to appear when people defined 5 or more life stages: As soon as two levels of old age were named, the distinction between physical and social definition became clear. Entry into the earliest phase of old age is defined by these respondents in chronological years, usually around 60, and entry into the later stage in terms of physical status. Everyone assumed physical status would decline at some subsequent age, but the age of estimated physical decline went up as more life stages were differentiated. Many pointed out that "with luck" they might never reach the later stages at all.

Age-Irrelevant Meanings

In two of the communities we studied, by contrast, the sorting task as a way of eliciting perceptions of the life course did *not* produce results anything like as clear as those I've been describing. For several months, we thought it was not producing any results at all. Among the !Kung San in particular, neither cards nor pictures worked well. The best compromise was to ask the interviewees to tell the names they used for people of different ages. Then, using their own nonchronological vocabulary of "age categories," we could go on with the questioning. Here are some typical exchanges:

> *Interviewer:* What do you call people of different ages?
>
> *!Kung:* Oh they have all kinds of names. There's John, Sue, Jane, George . . .
>
> *Interviewer:* No, I mean, when people have different ages, how do you distinguish among them?
>
> *!Kung:* Well, that's easy. Come on over here and I'll point them out to you. See, there's Jane and Sue is over there. John isn't here now but George . . .

It was not that !Kung lack vocabulary to talk about age. They have several terms for people of different ages. The problems arose from the fact that age has low salience as a marker of individual variability.

In the Irish village of Clifden, we encountered similar difficulties. Over half the interview participants did not complete the card sort.[1] If they did manipulate the cards at all, they arranged the 15 male and the 15 female cards in a single line, until what the researcher called the "table factor" intervened. Only when there was no more room on the table did they place any cards in a pile. These respondents tried to individualize the cards and pressed us to tell them which real person in the community they were supposed to represent. People in Clifden generally were little affected by age as a barrier to participation (see the "Social" column in Table 9–2), and they were also uncomfortable responding to questions that presupposed age categories. For example, when asked about problems facing older persons, people typically responded in this fashion, "Well, some do OK, and others don't. Which ones do you mean?"

Thus in Clifden, as among the !Kung, we had to acknowledge either that our method was not working or, if it was, respondents were telling us they did not have a perception of the life course.[2] We finally considered seriously the possibility that age, age categories, and the life course were not culturally salient concepts. Asking ourselves how this conclusion fit with our other sources of information, we found it confirmed in the life stories, behavioral observations, and answers to other parts of our interview. To be sure, for the !Kung, *relative* age, indicated by birth order, has significance for etiquette. It is appropriate to be rowdy and vulgar among people very close in birth order, while behavior becomes subdued when someone relatively older appears. The !Kung are not numerate, and the abstract notion of an absolute "old age" as a socially defined time of life or as a category of "old persons" was foreign to them. For example, here's what happened when we asked a question aimed at discovering preferences about contact with people of different ages.

Interviewer: If you were at your village one day and there wasn't anyone to talk to, and you were sort of lonely, wishing for conversation, what age person would you most like/not like to have visit you?

---

[1] Those who did not complete the card sort were more likely to be male, older, and locally born than those who completed the sort.

[2] One of the major methodological lessons reinforced by this project emphasizes the importance of discovering the research questions that have significance for the people we study, rather than pressing them for answers to our own.

!Kung:
—Why would I be alone at the village? If I was alone, I wouldn't want anyone to visit me!
—Well, I would prefer that someone I knew would visit me.
—I wouldn't want a stranger to visit me.
—I don't like to be visited by a Herero.

In spite of their great willingness to help us out, they missed the age element of the question completely because for them it had no meaning.

Here, the relevant distinction among individuals is physical capability, and not chronological years. Physical vigor versus frailty is a relevant continuum in all seven communities. The !Kung, however, define *every* life transition in terms, not of age, but of physiological change.

EVALUATIVE MEANINGS OF AGE

Old age was evaluated as the least desirable time of life by the majority of people in all seven research locations. However, the fewest negative reactions to old age and the most positive reactions came in the United States and Ireland, and in particular from older people themselves. The most negative reactions came from Hong Kong and from the two African communities.

Features of Being Old

We asked specifically what was worst and best about being old, and also asked for descriptions of a real person who was having an especially good old age and one who was having particular difficulty being old (Keith et al., 1990). The problems that arose with these questions were interestingly reversed in Africa and the United States. Whereas in Africa there was difficulty talking about *good* old age, suburban Americans had trouble telling us about anyone in their community who was having a *bad* old age. In Swarthmore, for instance:

> *Interviewer:* Can you think of a person you know well who is having difficulty in this stage of life [the stage person had defined as old]?

One-half of all adults and two-thirds of those under 60 could not do this. They told us such things as:

I don't know anyone in Swarthmore finding life difficult.

I can't think of anyone in Swarthmore.

I can't think of anyone [that age] in Swarthmore doing poorly.

I think they exist . . . but they're not in my circle of friends.

In contrast, the !Kung had trouble answering about older people doing well, and about the good points of being old. Two-thirds answered in terms of physical capacity, and almost half in terms of support from children. For example:

He is not yet fully aged. He can still get around.

She can still do for herself, do firewood, water, and make fire.

He is still young and can take care of himself.

If you have a child, you have a life.

It is the children of an old person that give him life. They have strength and they work for us.

The !Kung added a substantial chorus of "there is *nothing* good about being old!" Essentially, the !Kung told us that the best way to have a good old age was not to be old, but to remain youthful and vigorous. If you were truly old—that is, not strong and not able to take care of yourself—the only possible amelioration of your inevitable dependency was to have a child to give care.

Americans described many good things about being old: more time with one's spouse, travel, and, especially freedom from responsibility—"soaring freedom" one old woman told me—freedom from convention, freedom from pressure to achieve, freedom from fixed family mealtimes, freedom to "do what you want, when you want to." All of these responses were hedged, of course, by an *if:* "If you have your health . . ."

Generational Boundaries

Some of the most striking contrasts among our study sites referred to generational relationships. Issues of dependence and independence were notable in Hong Kong, in the United States, and among the Herero. The valences, however, were reversed. For the Chinese and the Herero, being dependent on others, especially children, was one of the *best* things about old age. But for the Americans, being dependent on others (again especially children) was one of the *worst*.

Among the Herero, one "best" thing about the younger life stages of life was being able to take care of elders. In contrast, the American participants mentioned care of older parents as problematic. For example, a 39-year-old woman in Swarthmore included in her reasons for high evaluation of her own well-being, "We have no problem with an aged parent." Orientations to the life course among the Herero and middle-class Americans were diametrically opposed: The Herero respected seniority, and evaluated themselves and others in terms of treatment of older family members; Americans made these evaluations in terms of treatment of children.

Answers like these contradicted many of our original hypotheses, which had pointed generally in the direction of old age being more positively viewed in the smaller, more traditional societies than in the modern industrial urban settings. More puzzling, the negative views of old age in Africa were at odds with our own observations in the field. In the !Kung villages we saw old people living in the same house or a few yards away from relatives. They were involved in all the village activities with people of all ages, and were aided with food or chores when they were frail. Yet, although lives of the elderly looked pretty good, we heard few good words about old age from the people we interviewed. Reflecting on the !Kung comments, we heard them telling us, with some exasperation, that if an old person can still take care of himself, he is young. If a person is old, there is nothing left to ask about whether life is good or bad—"I already told you she is old, didn't I?" The message comes back again to definitions of age, or of life stages. The !Kung see the boundaries of old age marked not by years, but by physical and functional capability. It might have made sense to inquire what would make life in old age "not so bad" (having children to take care of you). To ask what makes life good in old age is not sensible. From the !Kung point of view, our question about good old age is an oxymoron.

Spatial Boundaries

In Swarthmore, it was a spatial rather than a conceptual boundary that obstructed answers to our question about people having difficulty in old age. The interview participants kept volunteering to tell us about someone they knew somewhere else, or someone who used to live in Swarthmore—someone who had to move away. At the same time, we encountered other elderly residents who had moved *into* town because they were growing older. These responses led us to a new set of questions about the sources and the consequences of residential mobility. To understand why some old people moved in and some old people moved out of this suburb, we had to consider various cultural components of the "good life" and their temporal links. How did decisions at one life stage constrain the choices to be made in a later stage? What choices in midlife left a 79-year-old widow alone in a three-story house in Swarthmore, missing her friends who had left town, worried that she ought to do the same because if she became seriously ill or frail, she'd end up in a nursing home. Where did she go wrong? Nowhere. She had simply centered her earlier life in an intense and long relationship with her husband, raised her children to be independent, and encouraged them to make the choices that would lead to the greatest personal satisfactions and achievements for them. This behavior was right for the midlife mother, but for the later-life widow it has led to problems.

If we sum up with the questions about old age that the African !Kung versus the American suburbanites see as salient, we have:

For the !Kung—Will there be someone to take care of me?

For the suburban middle-class Americans—How can I take care of myself? (usually redefined as) Shall I stay in town or move?

These enunciate clearly the continuity in lives of !Kung, who always see themselves as *interdependent,* and the threat of discontinuity in the lives of suburban Americans who, having once believed themselves to be independent, plan the rest of their lives to avoid *dependence* at almost any cost (Draper and Keith, 1992).

AGE AS A CRITERION FOR SOCIAL PARTICIPATION

In addition to overt expressions about the meanings of age, we undertook to map the formal and informal age borders traced by interaction and behavior. Here we found great variation across the study communities.

In Africa

Among the !Kung, it was difficult to find *any* situation in which people of only one age category were present. The visual image that I brought back was of people tightly connected to each other—"like a coral reef," according to my field notes. People of all ages worked, rested, played, and ate together—often touching and leaning on each other.

The view into the more economically advantaged Herero village only a few kilometers away was different. Categories of gender as well as age were more discernible, although within a few hundred yards I could see everyone. Older women in imposing turbans sat under trees, children about 8 to 12 years old were in small clumps nearby. Men were separated, tending their cattle: adults near the corral, smoking and tending animals; adolescents with animals outside village, driving them to graze or to water. When a Herero village was observed for an entire day, some social borders of age became clearer. Seniority is recognized, for example. The senior wife of the senior man tends the sacred flame kept burning for the ancestors between the house and the corral. The older women command the children, who carry wood and water, watch cook fires, shoo flies, and push the churn.

These children are often not biological children or grandchildren, but have been fostered to the older person. Any older woman can demand and receive a child from a younger relative. It is not easy to know how frequently this happens, because when we asked women about their children, they named those they fostered along with those they bore. Our estimate was that about half the children were living in the household of a foster parent. This fostering was consistent with the view of the Herero as "looking up [rather than down] the life course": There is a distinctive individual social identity for older persons as being located at the apex of a lineage, while children are in the categorical relationship of "junior" or merely "kin."[3]

In the United States

Shifting to the United States communities, age is used to define comparatively more and tighter social boundaries in both the small town

[3] The recent efforts of the Botswana government to provide education for all children have affected the lives of older people because children are now available to provide household help only on weekends.

and the suburb, but there are important differences between these two. In both towns, an ethnographer finds fine age distinctions separating people who are carrying out particular activities, and who are often shut into separate spaces for many hours a day. Schools, clubs, even movie theaters and bars are age-graded, dividing people into chronological categories.

Important differences in the social meaning of age in these two communities derive from differences in the scope of age-grading, and the consequent possibility of seniority. In the small town (Momence), there is more mixing of ages *within* organizations, so that a ladder of seniority can exist within a group (such as a festival organizing committee or a chamber of commerce). Stable residence is a critical factor here: It makes having lived more years advantageous, as a person acquires seniority along with years. In the suburb (Swarthmore), age differentiation occurs across the entire community; most organizations have memberships mainly within one age range, and there is no seniority principle either within or across organizations. In the life history interviews, older residents told us that this pattern represented a change over the course of their own lifetimes. In earlier years, there had been more mixing of ages within organizations, such as the Women's Club or the Daughters of the American Revolution. They offered two explanations for the change: (1) The tendency of corporations to transfer higher level employees to various locations made the population less stable and (2) the increasing proportion of young women going to work meant that they were not available for membership in local organizations. During our research in the 1980s, new members of community groups were often women who had recently retired. The "junior" members of the Women's Club, for example, were recently retired women in their 60s, while the "senior" members were 75 and older.

Lack of residential stability undermines social seniority as a benefit of added years. Younger people new to the community cannot know and appreciate the accumulated past of the elders; old people new to the town cannot bring their social identities with them. Seniority in a church or club elsewhere is neither "vested" nor "portable." Age peers available within age-homogeneous groups offer some of the possibilities of social satisfaction and personal identity difficult to find in the wider community. There are few mechanisms, however, such as the seniority principles or role specialization found in Momence or Herero, for linking the different age groups.

The remaining haven of mixed-age relationships is the family. Even here, the amount of time, space, and activity that is truly collective and age-heterogeneous in the middle-class suburban households is less than in the blue-collar town, and far less than in the other cultures.

MEANINGS AND USES OF AGE COMPARED

Table 9–2 provides a comparative overview of the seven sites we have been discussing. The sites are arranged from lowest to highest in societal scale and level of technological development. Sharply emerging is the disjunction between physical barriers posed by age and sociocultural (cognitive, evaluative, and social) barriers posed by the society. Both the irony and the challenge of old age for our own aging society are visible in this comparison.

As the "Cognitive" column shows, increases in scale and technological development are associated with physical versus sociocultural constraints imposed by age. In the "Evaluation" column, negative rather than positive aspects of old age are emphasized everywhere. This is less so, however, among the old themselves than among younger members of some communities. Further, there is some compensatory benefit to having lived many years where a seniority principle is recognized (as it is by the Herero and residents of Momence). The third column, which lists "Social" uses of age, illustrates our major finding: In the settings of greater scale and technological development, socioculturally defined barriers are strong, overshadowing age-related physical obstacles to social participation. The table as a whole shows that barriers to age integration are not only powerful, but also multidimensional.

REDUCING AGE BARRIERS

The final question raised by these comparisons is this: How can we reduce the sociocultural barriers to full social participation by older persons? A first important step is to recognize that these barriers *are* culturally constructed and therefore can be changed: They are powerful, but not "natural." Next, we can consider the mechanisms through which social boundaries based on age are lowered or bridged. For this purpose, I will focus on three cases: Herero, Momence, and Swarthmore. In all three, age is defined chronologically; and in all three, age is used to make socially significant distinctions. In both the Momence and Herero communities, however, people in the older categories face fewer obstacles to maintaining—*simultaneously*—personal identity, channels for social participation, and access to care. In the suburban community of Swarthmore, older persons are required to make choices among those three very basic needs.

The people and their lives are so different in the Momence and Herero communities that the two important similarities affecting the lives of the elderly stand out very clearly. In both places, *kinship* and *seniority* are principles that promote full participation by older persons. Kinship among Herero is *lineal*. Affiliations perceived as kinship are traced in a line of descent from a common ancestor, either through males or through females, sometimes both, but separately. Lineal kinship defines corporate groups, within which property is owned, authority exercised, and responsibility for members shared. All Herero have a place in such a kin group; and because of the seniority principles, older Herero have a privileged place that includes entitlement to respect and to care. Because of the corporate or categorical nature of their kinship organization, these entitlements are "vested" and "portable" from village to village.

In the Momence community, kinship is also very important but is of a different type. Like most Americans of European descent, people in Momence trace their kinship *bilaterally*. This way of reckoning kinship starts with an individual and relationships are traced outward in all directions through both the mother and father. Bilateral kinship cannot form corporate groups without the addition of some other principle (e.g., the "relatives I like" or the "relatives that live nearby"). When kin share property or responsibility, it is a matter of individual choice. Position in any ad hoc kin group like this is not transferable in the way it can be in a lineal system.

In Momence, kinship can play an important role in community life because residence in the town is very stable. Kin are available to provide care for older people, although this responsibility is viewed in more individual terms than among the Herero. Residential stability also allows seniority to serve as a basis of prestige and resource control in Momence. Since American society is not structured primarily by kinship, as among the Herero, seniority within a family is not transferable into seniority in an outside community. The advantages of additional years (e.g., accumulating information, experience, and social connections) are only relevant locally and to the same cast of characters. Because residential stability in Momence makes seniority meaningful, there is a structural basis for interconnections among residents of different ages.

The residents of Swarthmore, conversely, have many fewer kin nearby. The *lack of residential stability* undermines seniority as a principle. The most readily available groups within which personal identity and social participation can be maintained in this suburban setting are age-homogeneous. For many Swarthmore residents, access to care, either from kin or in an institutional setting, requires a move away from town. Lack of residential stability and of a seniority principle presents these older people with difficult trade-offs. Personhood is best preserved in age-homogeneous groups, but at the cost of connection to others in the community. Maintaining responsibility for oneself, a requirement for full personhood, requires planning for care. Such plans often entail moving into a new setting, which may in turn weaken personhood, unless the setting is age-homogeneous.

CHALLENGES FOR THE FUTURE

The values, social structures, and quandaries we observed in suburban Swarthmore are those we can expect to affect the lives of many Americans in the future if barriers to age separation are not reduced. As the society ages, the wastefulness of setting so many people apart seems appalling. What does the comparative study suggest we can do to intervene?

First, I believe we should be vigilant to question age separation wherever it occurs, no matter how "natural" it seems. Second, rather than inventing new solutions, we should be alert to what older people themselves are saying and doing to reduce the age barriers that now impede the innovation and flexibility of older persons. Let me give some examples.

In a literacy program for Hmong refugees recently developed in Philadelphia, the goal was to teach English reading and writing skills. The program was developed for young people, to meet instrumental needs such as shopping and employment. The program planners, however, very soon received unexpected demands from elders in the

Hmong families. They wanted to be literate as well, and to them it was appropriate that older family members should acquire the important new knowledge. They also had more expressive reasons: They wanted to learn English so they would not be cut off from their grandchildren, and so they could transmit their own culture to that generation. As a consequence, the literacy program as it now exists is intergenerational.[4] An important reminder here is that—just as we must be careful to discover, not assume, the salience and meanings of age as we form questions in fieldwork—we must also be careful to discover, not assume, the salience and meanings of age as we form social programs.

Another example from my own fieldwork concerns zoning regulations in Swarthmore. Many elderly widows in three-story homes have considered the possibility of dividing their houses in order to rent to students. To an anthropologist familiar with the positive ties between alternate generations in many parts of the world, this seems like an excellent idea. However, zoning regulations in the town are based on the principle that households should contain "families." Consequently, the ordinance says that more than four unrelated persons may not form a household and share a residence. Here the cultural definitions that impede social inventiveness by older persons are not of age, but of kinship and household. Older people in the town have tried to bring pressure on the local government to change the rules, but so far without success. Meanwhile elderly residents continue to leave town partly because they cannot alone maintain large, old houses that require standing on ladders to change lightbulbs, extensive yard work, and carrying groceries and luggage up flights of stairs. The foster children of the Herero are a strong reminder that kinship and the composition of a household are not literally based in biology. These are cultural definitions that, if reified into laws, may lag behind changes in demography and social needs. We must cull this kind of outdated cultural definition from laws and regulations.

The final and poignant example from my fieldwork points to the most pressing need for removal of barriers to age integration. Older people in our suburban site who hope, when frail, to avoid having to leave town in order to provide care for themselves have begun working with an experiment called "Life Care without Walls." However, key players in this group continue to drop out of the community in response to *memento mori* such as the death of a friend, their own

---

[4] I am grateful to Dr. Gail Weinstein-Shr for this information.

experience of an illness or injury, a nudge from concerned and distant children, or a gentle threat from the director of a life-care community about the length of the waiting list. As the "elder drain" from Swarthmore continues, the remaining older residents find it difficult to maintain the momentum to create locally based solutions to health care needs. They also begin to question their own decision to stay in town at all, wondering if it's "too risky," or "too great a gamble." The gamble these people are talking about is whether to stay in a community where they have lived for 40 or 50 years! The current organization of health care financing in this country, with its focus on institutionalized response to acute rather than chronic medical needs, has made the decision to stay in the community seem a serious risk. Policy designed to improve the physical circumstances of older persons should not be allowed to create or maintain social barriers to community participation. We must be watchful that current revisions of health care reinforce rather than threaten local and personal networks of support.

In summary, I believe this comparative study provides both warnings and visions for an aging society. We must be vigilant to keep physical and cultural boundaries of age distinct. And we must be vigilant to see that sociocultural age barriers do not replace physical age barriers to full participation in that aging society.

REFERENCES

Draper, P., & Keith, J. (1992). Cultural contexts of care: Caregiving for the elderly in Africa and the United States. *Journal of Aging Studies, 6,* 113–134.

Fry, C. (1990). The life-course in context: Implications of research. In R. Rubinstein (Ed.), *Anthropology and aging* (pp. 129–152). Boston, MA: Kluwer.

Ikels, C., Keith, J., & Fry, C. (1988). The use of qualitative methodologies in large-scale cross-cultural research. In S. Reinharz & G. Rowles (Eds.), *Qualitative gerontology* (pp. 257–264). New York: Springer.

Ikels, C., Keith, J., Fry, C., Dickerson-Putman, J., Draper, P., Glascock, A., & Harpending, H. (1992). Perceptions of the adult life-course: A cross-cultural analysis. *Ageing and Society, 12,* 49–84.

Keith, J. (1994). The quality of research is not strained: Qualitative methods in comparative research. In J. Gubrium & A. Sankar (Eds.), *Qualitative methods in aging research.* Beverly Hills, CA: Sage.

Keith, J., Fry, C., & Ikels, C. (1990). Communities as context for successful aging. In J. Sokolovsky (Ed.), *The cultural contexts of aging* (pp. 245–261). Westport, CT: Greenwood.

PART III

CURRENT INTERVENTIONS: OLDER WORKERS

CHAPTER 10

Realizing the Potential: Some Examples

William McNaught[1]

In this chapter, I explore the potential for increased productive activity from older segments of the American population. There are many reasons attention to this topic is important at the present time. I note just three: First, as is well known, members of the "Baby Boom Generation" will begin approaching retirement age early in the 21st century. When this happens, the nation's burden of older people on the middle-aged—the dependency ratio[2]—will rise rapidly. As this ratio begins its inexorable increase, it will be particularly important to ensure that all able-bodied persons, regardless of chronological age, are provided the opportunity to continue in productive activities if they so desire.

A second reason for exploring ways to increase the productive contribution of older persons is the emerging reality of the modern

---

[1] William McNaught was formerly a senior program officer at the Commonwealth Fund. Among his responsibilities was the administration of the Commonwealth Fund's Americans over 55 at Work Program. Many of the facts and quotations cited in this chapter are drawn from studies sponsored by this program. These remarks represent his personal opinions only and in no way constitute the official position of the Commonwealth Fund.

[2] Defined here as the number of persons above working age (improperly set at age 65) divided by the working age population.

workplace. The organization of business, especially manufacturing, has changed significantly from the simplistic assembly line made famous by Henry Ford in the production of the original Model T. Some management theorists argue that the United States' difficulty in competing successfully in international markets is in part due to its continued reliance on organizational structures that are largely unchanged from those that were used to manage primitive versions of this assembly line. Companies that do not adapt and fully utilize their workers soon lose their competitive advantage.

It is my own opinion that management has not yet recognized the potential for older workers to contribute within a world of team production and worker empowerment. Senior workers were once seen as liabilities when working tasks were rote procedures more suited to robots than humans and speed was the foremost attribute of a good worker, but these seniors may well be assets as forward-looking companies reorganize themselves.

A third reason for attention to this question is more important than demographics or economics. It is quite simply: Providing increased productive activities for older persons is the right thing for employers to do. When older persons themselves are asked if they would like to contribute productively, they overwhelmingly say they would. In fact, surveys suggest that persons denied this opportunity are far less happy and more pessimistic about life in general than those who perceive themselves able to choose whether or not to engage in work (paid or volunteer).[3]

This chapter is organized in three sections. First, I discuss the extent to which older persons currently undertake productive activities, and most readers may well be surprised by the volume and breadth of these activities.

Second, I examine a few "success stories," drawn primarily from my own previous research, demonstrating that older workers can make valuable contributions to their companies and communities. I also cite suggestions from the gerontological literature that these success stories are not anomalies, but are consistent with the prevailing

---

[3] Older persons who are not working, but would like to be, are five times more likely than those who are working full-time to be "not at all satisfied with life." For more information about the life satisfaction of older persons who want work but cannot find it, see Davis (1991).

conclusions of most researchers who have studied the capabilities of older persons.

Third, I discuss the potential for increasing productive involvement among older persons. I begin this section with a brief look at survey evidence showing that many older persons want to work or to make other productive contributions to society and their communities. I append to this section a few brief personal observations about the types of structural changes that will be needed before American society can truly offer possibilities for "productive aging." This part of my discussion is brief because it complements and reinforces the topics of other chapters in this volume, particularly Chapter 11.

To summarize my position in advance, I believe that much could be done to change the structures that shape the work effort of older Americans. With such changes, American society would vastly improve its use of the talents of seniors.[4] If society's attitudes and opportunities for seniors were to be fundamentally altered, at least two benefits would result: First, seniors themselves would be happier, more fulfilled, and perhaps even healthier; second, the United States would be a more productive and equitable society.

CURRENT PRODUCTIVE EFFORTS OF SENIORS

American seniors are far more productive and engaged than commonly realized. Not only is the work effort of older persons generally unrecognized, but few appreciate the time and efforts spent by seniors in related productive activities: carrying out volunteer assignments, providing care to loved ones and neighbors, and educating themselves for improved performance in their tasks.

This picture of a dedicated, vital, and contributing older population conflicts sharply with the common conception that seniors are usually retired or in the midst of planning how to retire. When retired, they are pictured as pursuing lives dedicated primarily to travel and recreation. I believe that this stereotype, which I will shortly demonstrate

---

[4] In this chapter, I use the terms "senior" and "older" interchangeably. The reader is cautioned that many of my statistics and quotations are drawn from sources that define these terms rather specifically in terms of the chronological ages of the population being studied. These definitions may not coincide from one source to the next.

is largely inaccurate, has been shaped by the continuing public debate over the financing of the Social Security system. Those involved in this debate have usually implicitly assumed that the system's payments to seniors are one of the primary reasons for the federal budget deficit, and that the "posh" life styles enjoyed by many members of this generation are made possible only through the efforts of their own sons and daughters.[5]

This chapter does not comment on the issues revolving around the size of income transfers between older and younger generations in the United States.[6] I believe the truth of the size of these transfers would surprise most readers. Recent survey evidence suggests that 1 older household in 5 contributes a significant fraction of their children's or grandchildren's household income, while only 1 older household in 20 receives a sizable part of its income from children or grandchildren.

As part of its effort to examine the employment prospects of older Americans, the Commonwealth Fund recently sponsored a survey of Americans 55 and over to examine the extent of their productive activities and the possibilities for increasing these efforts. This survey interviewed 2,999 persons ages 55 and over throughout the United States.[7] The interviews were conducted between October 1991 and January 1992.

The responses to this survey indicate a very high degree of productive engagement among Americans over the age of 55. About 38 million of these Americans—or 72% of persons in this age range—are estimated to be involved in some type of productive activity. The survey defined productive activity as work outside the home for pay, work outside the home on a volunteer basis, caring for a disabled spouse or relative, or providing substantial assistance to a friend or neighbor. When tabulated, this productive effort amounts to more than 20 million full-time equivalent workers.

---

[5] Some commentators admit that current beneficiaries made similar sacrifices to make benefits possible for their foreparents. This recognition, however is usually accompanied by a calculation of how much more this generation is receiving in benefits, given their previous contributions, than was received by earlier beneficiaries. See "The Complexity of Social Security: A Primer," *New York Times,* February 11, 1993, A1–A29.

[6] The question of the motivation for saving among families has received substantial attention from economists over the past few years. Two papers that summarize the positions of two leading figures in the debate are Modigliani (1988) and Kotlikoff (1988).

[7] The sample is not strictly representative of the older population in the United States because phone calls were not made to prisons, hospitals, and nursing homes. The sample itself and the results of its analysis are described more fully in Bass and Caro (1992).

The activities engaged in by older persons varied substantially. As shown in Table 10–1, all categories of productive activity received substantial commitments from older persons. As the table also indicates, many older persons were engaged in more than one of these activities: Surprisingly, 27% were involved in at least two.

Conventional wisdom holds that the willingness of seniors to engage in productive activity decreases with age. These same survey data show, however, that the truth about productive aging is more complex than this. To be sure, work activity outside the home for pay does decline sharply at higher ages—of those over age 75, only about 4% continue to work. However, the much cited decrease in labor force participation of seniors seems to have stopped and possibly reversed itself sometime in the mid-1980s (see Chapter 11). Also, age declines are less severe in activities such as volunteering. Of those over age 75, nearly one person in four continues to give their time toward some charitable cause. This is about the same propensity to volunteer as is observed among 50-year-olds.

One of the most intriguing facts uncovered by analysis of the actual pattern of productive activity among seniors is that men are far more likely than commonly realized to be engaged in roles, such as child care, that society traditionally associates with women. For example, men were nearly as likely as women to have spent 20 or more hours in the preceding week caring for children, either their own or their children's children.

To summarize, seniors are doing quite a bit more than popularly realized. The decades-long decline in work by seniors may now have stopped. Families, in particular, seem to benefit from these efforts because many seniors care for children while both middle-aged parents work outside the home. What is even more important, the opportunity

Table 10–1
Productive Activities of Americans over Age 55

No activity	24%
One productive activity	
Work	31
Volunteering	31
Caring for children	44
Caring for sick/disabled	31
Two or more productive activities	27
Three or more productive activities	13

to remain productively engaged seems to benefit seniors themselves as well as families and society as a whole. Those who report that they remain productively engaged, particularly those who are employed, seem to be happier with the quality of their lives than those who, though they would like to be productively engaged, cannot find a position through which to make these contributions.

EXAMPLES OF PRODUCTIVE ACTIVITY AMONG SENIORS

The existence of a supply of productive workers is important, but what matters most is whether there is also a demand for these workers. In this section, I review some evidence that the talents of seniors are needed by both society in general and the corporate world in particular. I begin with some examples of successful productive contributions of seniors.

Days Inns

One of the most instructive examples of the capability of seniors to contribute productively comes from the experiences of Days Inns of America. A significant fraction of the reservation agents used by Days Inns to staff its national reservations center are seniors. The reliance on seniors to operate this critical system is of no small consequence to the corporation. Nearly all Days Inns hotels and motels are operated as franchises. Aside from the obvious benefit to an independent motel operator of using the Days Inns name, the primary service provided by the corporation to its franchisees is access to its toll-free nationwide reservation system. If this access does not increase a franchisee's bookings, then the corporation itself has little to offer the motel operator.

The reservations agents have a difficult job. They must simultaneously talk with a prospective customer, query the reservations system to find answers to the customer's questions, relay this information to the customer, and occasionally leaf through a companion binder to answer more esoteric questions such as amenities in the area of the particular motel. There is little time to rest while on duty. Managers adjust staffing levels so that agents receive a nearly continuous stream of telephone calls. Proper staffing is critical: Having too many agents drives up costs; having too few agents increases waiting times and the likelihood the customer will stay with a competitor.

In 1986, Days Inns was faced with a serious problem. It could not find sufficient numbers of agents to staff its reservations center. At this time, it was staffing its center, then located only in Atlanta, Georgia, solely with younger agents.[8] Much of the difficulty was caused by the high turnover rate for reservations agents. An obvious solution would have been to increase the wage rates of agents. However, these wages were then less than paid by local fast-food restaurants. Days Inns determined that paying wage rates high enough to compete with these restaurants would make the operation of the center uneconomical. Instead of raising wages, Days Inns decided to change their recruiting strategy and to start hiring seniors. This decision was both innovative and risky because the job of reservations agent requires many skills—handling sophisticated technology, working quickly, and executing multiple tasks simultaneously—skills not usually associated with seniors.

One aspect of the job of a reservation agent, however, was expected to suit seniors: its sedentary nature. The physical demands of the job are modest. Furthermore, some of the job's physical requirements turned out to be easily solvable. For example, special controls were added to telephones to allow agents with hearing difficulties to adjust the volume of their conversation.

Initially, the campaign to recruit seniors was not successful. Older people did not respond to targeted advertisements because they were perceived as merely a ploy to avoid age discrimination suits. However, once Days Inns shifted its tactics to recruit directly at senior citizens centers, it found many eager and suitable applicants.

Since embarking on this experiment, Days Inns has learned the following facts about its older workers:

1. With a slight adjustment in the training course, it can train a senior to be a reservation agent in the same time it takes to train a younger worker.

---

[8] Days Inns now operates two centers. The second is in Knoxville, Tennessee. When the second center was established, Days Inns, as a result of its success with its senior reservations staff, decided to staff the new center jointly with younger and senior reservations agents.

2. The turnover rate among senior workers is lower than for younger workers. After 3 years, more than 50% of the senior reservations agents remain on the job whereas only about 10% of younger agents do.

3. Although senior agents tend to take more time handling each call, they are also more likely than younger agents to complete a call with a successful reservation.

When all aspects of these findings are combined, Days Inns data show that senior reservations agents cost virtually the same amount as younger agents (McNaught & Barth, 1992). It is important to note that these cost analyses include the cost of providing health insurance. Moreover, these findings on effectiveness remain valid even after many of the characteristics of the younger and senior workers are changed substantially.

B&Q

B&Q is England's largest chain of Do-It-Yourself (DIY) stores. It operates 280 stores staffed by 15,000 employees and receives over $1.6 billion in annual revenue. In 1988, it was experiencing significant labor problems:

1. The turnover rate exceeded 100% for sales personnel.
2. Customers rated its service poorly (which management attributed to a low level of product knowledge within its sales staff).
3. Salespersons seemed generally disinterested in assisting customers.

To overcome these problems, B&Q—influenced by the latest demographic projections—decided to encourage its managers to hire older workers.[9] However, B&Q store managers, who are allowed substantial independence in the organizational structure, were reluctant to alter their traditional hiring practices. To convince its store managers of the value of hiring older workers, B&Q opened a test store entirely staffed by senior workers in Macclesfield, a city just south of Manchester.

---

[9] It is legal in Britain for "help wanted" advertisements to specify the desired age of job applicant.

Since opening in 1989, the Macclesfield store has been very successful (Hogarth & Barth, 1991). The store has proven to be 18 times as profitable as similar stores in the B&Q chain and reached its initial profitability targets earlier than the B&Q management had projected.

Among the major factors contributing to this achievement were increased workforce stability and improved customer service. Greater stability in the sales force is due to reduced worker quit rates: Employee turnover is about six times lower at Macclesfield than at comparable stores. Absenteeism is also down: Macclesfield staff are absent about 40% less than workers at comparable stores. Furthermore, Macclesfield staff have proven to be remarkably flexible about working hours: They average about 8 hours of overtime weekly.

The most direct evidence that customer service levels have improved at the Macclesfield store comes from marketing surveys that rate its service levels as far superior to similar stores. An indirect and supporting piece of evidence is that shoplifting rates have been reduced considerably from those experienced in similar stores. Shoplifting is down, management believes, because senior workers pay more attention to customer service and, by speaking frequently to customers, have deterred shoplifters.

As was the case in the Days Inns example, physical demands turned out to be no problem for B&Q. The most obvious difficulty for older sales staff was expected to be retrieving heavy items from stockroom shelves, but B&Q's managers avoided this problem by mandating that two employees, not one, would retrieve any item from any high shelf in the stockroom.

Travelers

In the late 1970s, the Travelers Corporation, an insurance and financial services company based in Hartford, Connecticut, decided to start a customer service "hot line." They needed employees familiar with the range of the company's operations to staff it. Removing full-time employees from their regular work assignments would have disrupted the company's continuing operations. Instead, Travelers decided to re-hire recent retirees to staff the hot line on a part-time basis.[10]

---

[10] The company's pension system regulations restricted retirees to part-time work.

The hot line soon became a tremendous success and encouraged Travelers to expand the experiment. In 1981, they established a retiree job bank to facilitate placement of retirees on a part-time basis throughout the company. A central office was set up to coordinate recruitment, to determine levels of skills and wages, and to handle the placement of individuals in specific jobs.

Travelers' managers responded enthusiastically to the program. By 1985, their requests for "retiree temps" more than doubled the number of available retirees. Travelers then opened the job bank to participation by retirees from other firms within the Hartford area. This expansion also proved successful. By 1990, sufficient numbers of retired temps were available so that Travelers could fill most of its needs for temporary employees from this source, rather than using traditional temporary agencies from outside. In 1980, the scope of the "Trav-temps" program was also expanded to offer temporaries some benefits normally associated with full-time employment, such as holiday pay and health insurance. By 1993, the retiree job bank was placing about 400 temporaries within the company each week. The average age of these retired temps is 67, and about 70% are women. The average retiree works 516 hours annually.

From Travelers' point of view, the most important rationale for the program is the cost savings it generates (cf. McNaught & Barth, 1991a). The difference in cost between using temporaries from the retiree job bank and from outside agencies can be estimated by comparing what it actually cost Travelers to operate the job bank and what it would have cost to fill these same positions through traditional agency referrals. (This comparison is best made from data from 1989, since this is the last year Travelers operated its internal job bank exclusively using retirees; and in that year it still filled about half of its temporary needs using agency hires.) In 1989, Travelers spent about $2.05 million to operate its retiree job bank. This figure includes the costs of benefits, including health insurance, provided to these retirees. Had it hired these temporaries from temporary agencies instead, Travelers would have spent about $3.08 million dollars to fill the same positions. Thus, in one year, Travelers saved over a million dollars in labor costs by operating its retiree job bank.

Besides saving the company money, there is some evidence that Travelers benefits from the high productivity of the temporaries the program hires. A key piece of evidence is that Travelers' managers themselves request a retired temporary more frequently than an outside agency temporary. Similarly, studies of temporary employees have found that they are productive 90% of the time, compared with a range of 65% to 85% for permanent employees (Simonetti, Nykodym, & Sell, 1988).

Gerontological Evidence

The examples just provided are in no way unique: Researchers who have studied the productivity of older workers have generally discovered managers nearly always underestimate the capabilities of seniors. Many interesting papers are available on this topic, and a selective review of the empirical evidence shows that most employers believe that older people cannot perform well, despite evidence to the contrary.[11] Initially relevant is a conclusion from my own previous work (Barth & McNaught, 1989). In that work with Michael Barth, I summarized the opinions of other retirement experts about the attitudes of employers toward older workers. Employers were seen as stereotyping them as loyal and possessing good work habits, but inflexible and difficult to train. These opinions generally agree with the standard findings from management surveys on this same topic. Older workers themselves were seen by experts as rarely choosing to retire due to health limitations but more frequently induced to retire through pension incentives.

An even more compelling piece of evidence comes from Avolio and Waldman (1989). Avolio and Waldman performed a metaanalysis on studies investigating the productivity of older workers. They found that studies using data based on observations of managers themselves usually conclude that age negatively influences a worker's productivity. However, when contrasting studies of the influence of age on productivity are based on the impressions of co-workers, age is generally found to have a positive influence on productivity.

Probably the most damning analysis of managers' opinions of older workers was performed by Benson Rosen and Thomas Jerdee (1977). They conclude that managers hold conscious opinions that are generally favorable toward older workers but unconsciously discriminate

---

[11] Among the papers illustrating the general consensus from this literature are Sonnenfeld (1978), Doering, Rhodes, and Schuster (1983), and Sterns (1986).

against them when making practical personnel decisions. These researchers selected a representative sample of managers, divided them into two groups, and asked them to imagine themselves to be an administrator who had to deal with a troublesome personnel incident. Managers in the respective groups were presented different versions of the incident, and asked to make a recommendation. Unknown to the managers, the details presented to both groups were identical except for the age of the employee involved. Managers in each group handled the incident differently and were less inclined to attempt helpful corrective action with the older worker.

To summarize, these case studies of three current situations show that older workers are making important contributions, and at the same time are generating substantial monetary returns for their companies. Older workers are, in real situations, not limited by physical problems; and they have proven themselves adept at learning new technologies and providing high levels of customer service. I have also reviewed the scant academic studies on managerial attitudes, which generally conclude that their negative attitudes are based more on stereotypes than on workers' actual performance.

ATTITUDES OF SENIORS TOWARD INCREASED PRODUCTIVE OPPORTUNITIES

The popular wisdom holds that most older persons regard themselves as "over the hill" and want nothing more than to stop working, and to remain at home or to travel and to enjoy a life of leisure. As these "dependent elders" age, according to the stereotype, their health sooner or later fails, and most eventually need extensive daily support either in their own home or in a nursing facility. The reality is that the great majority of seniors remain capable (see Chapter 1), and many remain vitally involved. Those who are not vitally involved in work or in their communities usually wish they had the opportunity to be so. In this section, I will present some evidence that many seniors want to remain productively engaged. I shall also briefly allude to a few of the changes necessary to change our current, antithetical stance toward continued productive opportunities for seniors to a stance that comes closer to age neutrality.

The Ready and Able Population

Many seniors already want work and cannot find it. In 1989, Louis Harris and Associates asked a representative sample of Americans over age 50 whether they were capable of working and whether they would like to work. Based on answers to these queries, Michael Barth, Peter Henderson, and I estimated that nearly two million persons between the ages of 50 and 64 were "ready and able" to work (McNaught, Barth, & Henderson, 1989). A subsequent survey in 1992 increased this estimate to more than five million ready and able seniors (in this case including all persons over the age of 55).[12]

Although the arguments in the previous section might seem to suggest that this ready and able population exists because managers discriminate against senior workers and pension systems facilitate their premature exit from the labor force, my own reading of current trends is somewhat different. Rather, I suspect that the size of this ready and able population has risen markedly during the 1980s, because of demographic factors but also because of a different set of economic factors. I think it grew largely due to the continuing difficulties of American corporations. These corporations have been caught in a lengthy period of contraction that has made downsizing the norm, not the exception in the business world. This downsizing has largely been accomplished by squeezing both ends of the working age spectrum. At the low end, companies have substantially reduced their hiring of young people. At the high end, they have encouraged older employees to retire earlier than they ordinarily would have preferred. Early retirement has left many older workers frustrated; they are still capable of productive effort but are without access to new jobs.

My belief is that the desire for work among seniors can only grow in the future. The social and economic context that will exist when the Baby Boom generation reaches retirement age will differ significantly from the current context (Barth & McNaught, 1991b). The number of dependents still in the households of retiring baby boomers will be larger because they delayed the births of their children, and these children have remained dependent on their families longer. It is my own

---

[12] At that time, our estimates exceeded those published by the Bureau of Labor Statistics. Recently, the BLS has revised its methodology for estimating unemployment rates among groups such as, women and older persons.

casual observation that today's youth, beset by a problematic job market, find it more difficult to reach independence and start their own household than did their parents.

A second problem is likely to be the inadequate preparation for retirement of the Baby Boom generation. Actuaries have long urged workers to prepare diligently for retirement. This will be a more difficult task for Baby Boomers for several reasons. The major source of wealth accumulation for American families, increased home equity, has been interrupted by reduced price inflation within the national housing market. Moreover, the national growth in wages seems to have slowed, if not ceased altogether. This makes it doubly difficult for workers to set aside sufficient funds in their own personal savings to prepare for retirement. In addition, the nation has adopted an inconsistent approach toward fostering individual retirement saving, best exemplified by the nation's "on-again, off-again" policies for Individual Retirement Accounts.

A third difference from their predecessors that may induce longer working careers for baby boomers is the hoped-for increased demand for older workers, which could occur quite apart from any of the policy changes advocated in this chapter. It is likely that corporations will face a hiring crunch as the nation emerges from its extended recession. At that time, few qualified younger workers will be available due to the twin forces of poorer schooling and population declines in the "baby bust" generation. If younger workers are difficult to find, and if the arguments I have previously advanced are valid, managers will soon find it in their own self-interest to reevaluate their conscious and unconscious opinions about older workers.[13]

Structural Changes

I believe these facts point to a compelling national need to change the attitudes and behaviors of seniors toward retirement and work. As an essential step in this direction, better policies must be developed within the structures that shape seniors' decisions about work and retirement. Other chapters discuss the range of changes that might correct the structural lag to which this book is addressed, but I cannot resist the chance to add a few personal observations.

---

[13] Absent any major changes in national immigration policy.

I am in full agreement with the desirability of some further modification in Social Security's earnings test, but I also believe that many other equally useful and politically more palatable structural changes are possible within the Social Security system. It should not be difficult to design a system, like the one used in Sweden, that allows workers to receive partial rather than full Social Security benefits.[14] Because actuarial calculations would not affect individual lifetime withdrawals from the system, such a scheme need have no eventual effect on the size of the trust fund or the budget deficit. Nevertheless, this type of change should encourage much additional work effort: It would allow thousands of seniors to withdraw partially from the labor force while maintaining their standard of living through combined work and partial Social Security receipts.

Another useful change would alter current rules on paying medical costs for older employees who are already eligible for Medicare. Currently, these costs are first paid by the employee's private medical insurance and only paid by Medicare if private benefits are exhausted. Returning to historical rules in which Medicare served as first payer would probably substantially increase wages offered to older workers, and thus encourage their labor force participation. While the national budgetary climate of 1993 prohibits consideration of this type of change, likely reform of national medical care practices may foster increased productive opportunities for seniors. Many versions of the contemplated reforms feature universal coverage of some portion of the medical costs of young and old alike. Even if the medical costs of both younger and older employees are treated identically, such a change would implicitly favor hiring older workers since their medical costs on average exceed those of younger workers.

The American pension system must also become more favorable toward the work effort of seniors. Some such change is happening without policy intervention because more and more pensions are shifting to a structure based on defined contribution principles, instead of defined benefit ones. Defined contribution plans are generally neutral regarding the age of retirement, whereas the formulas used by most defined benefit plans implicitly encourage early retirement.

---

[14] As an example, seniors could be offered the chance to "retire" two years before "normal" retirement age, but receive only half their regular monthly benefit until reaching normal retirement age. Their benefit calculation under this option might then credit them with retirement only a year before normal retirement age.

It is also necessary to provide more opportunities for phased retirement and to support these opportunities with partial pensions. Some United States firms currently offer a phased retirement option to their employees (e.g., Corning, Polaroid). Despite employees' expressed desire for phased retirement opportunities, however, these programs are rarely used. I suspect that financial considerations are a major restraint for most employees who have no opportunity to combine a partial pension, partial Social Security benefits, and a partial wage to maintain their standard of living while flexibly retiring.

Realization of the potential of older workers, however, would require that the support for these programs within the corporate world go beyond simple alterations of retirement formulas. The nature of work opportunities themselves should be changed as well. New opportunities should be created for senior employees. The list of possible roles for talented, experienced senior employees is endless, especially if ways can be developed to reduce the labor costs to business for using workers in these new flexible roles. For example, mentoring is not typically used by businesses; yet for some businesses that find it difficult to hire skilled craft workers, mentoring programs that allow older employees to instruct younger workers would seem essential to their continuation as viable enterprises. Other possible roles for seniors—as consultants or part-time on-call substitutes—are well known to American businesses. Still other possible roles could be derived from the experiences of other countries. Japan, the most advanced society in creating these roles, offers such examples of assignments for older workers as placement within a supplying industry; trainer; and lateral transfer to a less stressful and responsible position within the company.

Ultimately, change is up to workers themselves, not the government or businesses. Useful change will require a fundamental revision of seniors' attitudes toward work. At a minimum, mature workers must begin to view education as a lifelong process, not a limited time for preparing for work during youth. And most basic of all, their prevailing view of retirement must itself be retired. Instead of anticipating retirement as a time of roleless leisure, people should see it as a time when they will have the luxury of choosing the type of productive activity they want to pursue.

It is in the interest of both business and government to facilitate such changes. Troubled American businesses already recognize the critical need to upgrade the skills of their workforce if they are to maintain their own competitiveness in international markets. Toward this end, expenditures on retraining courses are already among the fastest growing components of corporate budgets. Government can also help. For example, it can materially assist these changes by extending principles underlying a national youth service corps to include middle-aged and senior participants. This would allow seniors to contribute productively to their communities while fulfilling their own needs to remain active.

CONCLUDING OBSERVATIONS

America's seniors are already doing much more than is popularly appreciated, and millions of them wish to do more. Ample and mounting evidence shows that seniors are capable of continued productive effort far beyond age 65—or beyond what is usually regarded as the "normal" age for retirement. Natural forces within the economy seem destined to change today's antithetical environment toward continued productive efforts from seniors to one more favorable to these efforts. Acceleration of this trend is in everyone's interest. Many sectors of American society can assist in changing the existing attitudes. At the very least, government and business should take the first steps toward a comprehensive reform of society's Social Security laws and pension policies. Ultimately, however, seniors themselves must decide that productive engagement enriches their own lives. Reducing the *structural lag* will first benefit seniors, and then society as a whole.

REFERENCES

Avolio, B., & Waldman, D. (1989). Ratings of managerial skill requirements: Comparison of age- and job-related factors. *Psychology and Aging, 4*(4), 464–470.

Barth, M. C., & McNaught, W. (1989). *Why workers retire early*. Americans over 55 at work program (Background Paper #1). New York: The Commonwealth Fund.

Bass, S., & Caro, F. (1992). Patterns of productive activity among older Americans. *In Depth, 2,* 59–74.

Burkhauser, R., & Quinn, J. (1993). Changing policy signals: How to increase work effort at older ages. In M. W. Riley, R. Kahn, & A. Foner (Eds.), *Age and structural lag: Essays in changing work, retirement and other structures*. Washington, DC: American Association for the Advancement of Science.

Davis, K. (1991). *Life satisfaction and older adults.* Americans over 55 at work program (Background Paper #6). New York: The Commonwealth Fund.

Doering, M., Rhodes, S., & Schuster, M. (1983). *The aging worker: Research and recommendations.* Beverly Hills, CA: Sage.

Hogarth, T. C., & Barth, M. C. (1991). The costs and benefits of older workers: A case study of B&Q's use of older workers. *International Journal of Manpower, 12.*

Kotlikoff, L. (1988). Intergenerational transfers and savings. *Journal of Economic Perspectives, 2,* 41–58.

McNaught, W., & Barth, M. C. (1991a). *Using retirees to fill temporary labor needs: The Travelers' experience.* Americans over 55 at work program (Background Paper #5). New York: The Commonwealth Fund.

McNaught, W., & Barth, M. C. (1991b). The impact of demographic shifts on the employment of older workers. *Human Resource Management, 3*(1), 31–43.

McNaught, W., & Barth, M. C. (1992). Are older workers 'good buys'? A case study of Days Inns of America. *Sloan Management Review, 33,* 53–63.

McNaught, W., Barth, M. C., & Henderson, P. (1989). The human resource potential of Americans over 50. *Human Resource Management, 28*(4), 459–473.

Modigliani, F. (1988). The role of intergenerational transfers and life cycle saving in the accumulation of wealth. *Journal of Economic Perspectives, 2,* 15–40.

Rosen, B., & Jerdee, T. (1977). Too old or not too old. *Harvard Business Review, 55*(6), 97–106.

Simonetti, J. L., Nykodym, N., & Sell, L. M. (1988). Temporary employees: A permanent boon? *Personnel, 63,* 50–56.

Sonnenfeld, J. (1978). Dealing with an aging workforce. *Harvard Business Review, 56*(6), 81–92.

CHAPTER 11

Changing Policy Signals[1]

Richard V. Burkhauser and Joseph F. Quinn

Age, like beauty, is in the eye of the beholder. If by old age we mean the period of life characterized by a significant reduction in market work, then over the past half century the old among us have gotten considerably younger. Recently, however, the trend toward early retirement among men appears to have leveled off, and there is reason to believe that both men and women may work even longer in the future. This would be a reversal of a dramatic and significant postwar trend. Future labor market withdrawal decisions—when and how to leave the paid labor force—will depend on the opportunities, incentives, and constraints facing older Americans. Changes are already underway that could significantly affect the retirement process.

In this chapter, we review labor force participation trends of older workers and some of the factors that have influenced them. We argue that our current retirement system systematically encourages individuals to work full-time with a single firm until retirement age and then to switch jobs or leave the labor force altogether. Social Security reforms begun in the 1970s and aimed at reducing this antiwork bias at older ages are not likely to change work patterns dramatically unless employers also change the incentives in their retirement plans. If

---

[1] Based on a paper originally prepared for presentation at the Annual Meeting of the American Association for the Advancement of Science, Chicago, February 1992.

both employers and government change their antiwork policies, a significant minority of workers would increase their time in the labor market.

WORK AT OLDER AGES

The decline in the labor force participation rates of older American men is well known and well documented. In 1950, market work by older men was common; nearly one of every two men aged 65 and over was in the workforce. In the 1990s, work at this age is the exception, with fewer than one in six in the labor force.

Male early retirement trends can be seen in Figure 11–1, which shows participation rates from 1964 to 1992, for men aged 45 to 49 through 70+. The long-term trend is clear and is most dramatic at older ages. The percentage declines since 1964 are about 30%, 40%, and nearly 50% for men aged 60 to 64, 65 to 69, and 70+ respectively, and only 4%, 6%, and 12% for the younger three age categories. However, this long-term trend appears to have stopped. For those aged 55 and over, participation rates since 1986 have remained virtually unchanged, with the 1992 rate within 0.1 point of the rate in 1986.

Because some of the retirement incentives discussed in this chapter go into effect at particular ages, it is instructive to look at trends for one-year age categories. The Department of Labor has gathered such participation data since 1968 and Figure 11–2 shows these rates for men aged 60 through 65. The long-run trend and its cessation are seen again, as is the increasing importance of retirement at age 62, the earliest age of Social Security eligibility. In 1968, the first year in Figure 11–2, the largest single-year change in participation (the largest gap in the age lines at the left of the figure occurred at age 65, the age for full Social Security benefits. In the last year on the chart, 1990, the gap is largest at age 62. A gap at 65 remains, but much of the action has already occurred by then.

For women (Figure 11–3), the trends are very different, because two phenomena are at work. People are retiring earlier, but women, especially married women, are more likely to work than before. For the oldest female workers, those aged 60 and older, the two phenomena are offsetting, and the trends are flat. For the younger groups, the work effect dominates, and participation rates are on the rise.

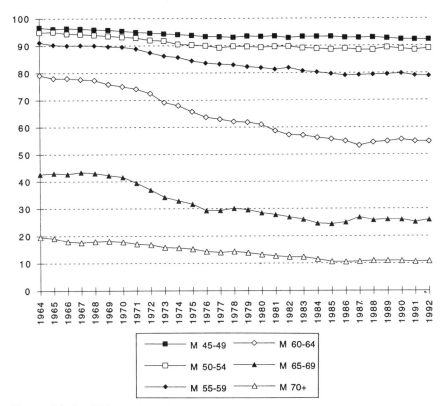

Figure 11-1   U.S. Male Labor Force Participation Rates, by Age, 1964–1992 (*Source:* U.S. Bureau of Labor Statistics [various years])

Between 1986 and 1992, the participation rates of all six female age categories increased, up about one point for the oldest (aged 70+) to nearly six points for the two youngest groups (aged 45–54).

THE DECISION TO RETIRE

As these figures show, the labor supply of older American men has declined dramatically over the past four decades. For older women, the participant rate has declined relative to that of younger women. Circumstantial and econometric evidence suggest that our retirement income programs and the economy have played an important role in this drama. Social Security and employer pensions grew significantly

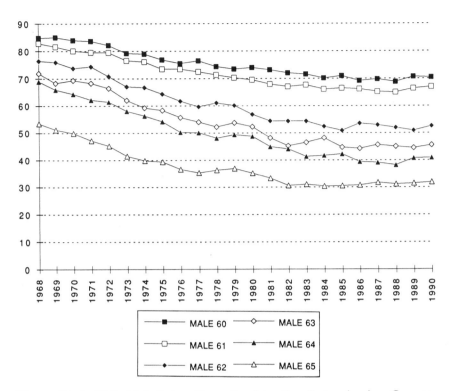

Figure 11–2   U.S. Male Labor Force Participation Rates, by Age Groups, 1968–1990 (*Source:* Unpublished data, U.S. Bureau of Labor Statistics)

over this same period, and the financial incentives embedded in these plans discourage work late in life.

Since its inception in 1935, the Social Security program has expanded coverage so that it is now nearly universal, has relaxed eligibility rules, and has provided large increases in real benefits. Grad (1990, Tables 1 and 47) estimates that by 1988, 92% of all aged couples and single persons received Social Security benefits, and that this one source provided almost 40% of their aggregate income. Between 1950 and 1990, real Social Security expenditures in 1990 dollars, excluding Medicare, grew from about $5 billion to well over $250 billion per year, from 2% to 20% of all federal spending, and from a negligible amount to almost 5% of gross national product (GNP) (USDHHS, 1991; U.S. President, 1992).

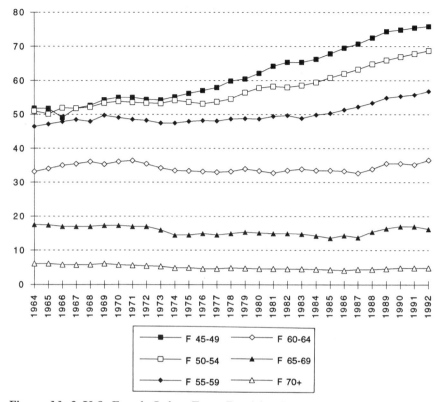

Figure 11–3 U.S. Female Labor Force Participation Rates, by Age, 1964–1992 (*Source:* U.S. Bureau of Labor Statistics [various years])

Over the postwar period, employer pensions grew as well. Kotlikoff and Smith (1983) report that the number of employer pension plans in the United States rose from 14,000 to over 600,000 between 1950 and 1980. Turner and Beller (1992, Tables 1.1 and 4.10) estimate that there were 730,000 plans in 1988, covering 42 million workers, 16 million of whom were covered by two or more plans. Pension coverage increased from a quarter to nearly half among private sector wage and salary workers, and from 60% to 90% among state and local government workers (Kotlikoff & Smith, 1983; Turner & Beller, 1992). The growth of Social Security and pension plans and the declining labor supply of the aged could be related for at least two reasons. Boskin, Kotlikoff, Puffert, and Shoven (1987) have shown that cohorts retiring up to the 1990s have received aggregate Social Security benefits

Table 11–1
U.S. Male Labor Force Participation Rates (%) by Age, 1940–1991

Year/Age	55	60	63	65	68	70
1940	90.9	82.9	78.2	66.1	54.9	43.4
1950	87.8	82.1	77.6	67.7	54.2	44.5
1960	89.9	83.2	75.7	53.6	39.4	33.2
1970	91.8	83.9	69.4	49.9	39.4	30.1
1980	84.9	74.0	52.3	35.2	24.1	21.3
1982	86.4	72.1	45.2	30.6	24.8	21.1
1983	85.7	71.5	46.5	31.0	22.7	19.2
1984	84.3	70.2	48.2	30.4	21.3	18.8
1985	83.7	71.0	44.7	30.5	20.5	15.9
1986	84.1	69.2	44.3	30.7	20.7	17.1
1987	83.9	69.8	45.6	31.7	22.9	17.1
1988	82.5	68.8	45.0	31.1	22.5	18.1
1989	83.7	70.7	44.5	31.4	22.2	17.9
1990	85.3	70.5	45.5	31.9	23.4	17.1
1991	82.5	70.6	44.6	30.6	21.2	16.9

Source: Labor force participation rates for 1940, 1950, and 1960 are based on decennial U.S. census data. Thereafter, they are from unpublished Department of Labor statistics, based on annual Consumer Population Survey labor force participation questions.

that far exceeded the value of the contributions plus interest made by them and their employers. These intergenerational transfers of wealth may have financed earlier retirement. In addition, Social Security and pension plans alter the lifetime pattern of compensation for many workers, encouraging work at some ages and penalizing it at others, as discussed later in this chapter. Our research suggests that these pension-related changes in compensation may have induced earlier retirement for many workers.

Aggregate data are consistent with the story that Social Security, employer pensions, and the economy have influenced these retirement trends. Table 11–1 shows male participation rates for selected ages since 1940. The first great reduction in work effort by older men occurred in the 1960s, as pension and Social Security coverage expanded dramatically.[2] In this one decade alone, participation rates for those aged 65, 68, and 70 dropped by 25% to 30%, while they rose for those aged 55 and 60, and changed little for those aged 63. Men aged 62 to

---

[2] According to Turner and Beller (1992, Table 4.1), the percentage of private sector wage and salary workers covered by employer pensions rose from 25% to 41% between 1950 and 1960. By 1970, it reached 45%, and has remained around that level since.

64 first became eligible for reduced Social Security benefits in 1961, and their participation rates (shown for those 63) dropped by over 8% between then and 1970. The substantial reductions during the 1970s in labor force participation at all ages between 55 and 70 were associated with a combination of economic stagnation and increasingly generous Social Security and employer pension benefits. As noted earlier, the recessionary years of the early 1980s brought additional decline, and economic growth during the second half of the decade coincided with stable participation rates.

Economic Incentives: An Asset Value Approach

There is growing evidence that the financial incentives inherent in our Social Security and employer pension plans are important determinants of work across an individual's entire life. Social Security and employer pensions not only affect work decisions at older ages but may also influence behavior at younger ages as well.

A single-year framework is inadequate for understanding lifetime retirement incentives, since Social Security and employer pensions are multiyear in nature. Contributions are made during the work life, and a stream of benefits is later repaid in retirement. Current work decisions affect future benefits. Social Security benefits depend on a person's monthly earnings averaged over 35 years of work, so their value changes with continued work. While the specific details of employer pension plans vary greatly, the majority of covered workers have defined benefit pensions, whose benefits, like Social Security are usually based on some combination of years of service and average salary. Unlike Social Security, however, the "average salary" in pensions is often based on just the last few years of work with the particular employer.

Because retirement income rights are entitlements to future income, they are best described as an asset that yields a stream of benefits, much like the dividends on a municipal bond. The value of this asset depends not only on the size of the future benefits, but also on when they are claimed, the life expectancy of the individual (and in some cases a spouse), their inflation protection, and the interest rate. When viewed this way, these rights have positive value even before the person is eligible to receive them.

Prior to pension eligibility, an additional year of work usually increases future benefits and therefore the asset value of pension rights.

This *increase* in pension wealth, called pension accrual, is really part of compensation—the reward for working another year. In this sense, pensions subsidize work by increasing compensation during much of the work life.

After eligibility, however, the situation may change. An eligible employee who is considering working another year is really choosing between two retirement income streams, one starting today, with lower annual benefits, and another beginning in a year, but with higher benefits per year. If the asset value of the delayed stream is larger, the employee gains twice by working, receiving a paycheck *plus* the wealth accrual for working that year. Total compensation exceeds traditionally defined earnings as it did prior to eligibility. If the two streams are equal, the pension is called actuarially fair, and the asset value is unaffected by the timing of receipt. But if the delayed second stream is smaller in present value (future benefit increments are worth less than the initial benefits foregone), then the worker loses retirement income wealth by working, and true compensation is less than the paycheck by the amount of the wealth loss.

Considerable research, reviewed in Quinn, Burkhauser, and Myers (1990), has established that this last scenario describes many American retirement plans, and that these incentives affect individuals' decisions. At some age, workers who stay on the job begin to lose retirement income wealth and thereby suffer a hidden pay cut. At age 65, for example, the Social Security delayed retirement credit falls from about 8% per year of delayed receipt to only 4%. The latter is less than actuarially fair, so Social Security wealth drops if the person forgoes benefits beyond 65. Relatively few people these days work beyond age 65, as we have seen.

It is more difficult to generalize about employer pensions, since there are so many of them, each with its own rules and regulations. But considerable research suggests that typical defined benefit pensions provide a strong incentive to retire at the age of normal retirement, and that most employer pensions begin to do so at the earliest age of plan eligibility. Kotlikoff and Wise (1989) document this, and estimate that the wealth loss for retiring at age 65 rather than at age 62 can equal a quarter to a third of annual earnings. Although this is only one of many factors in the retirement decision, those facing large work disincentives, other things equal, are more likely than others to leave their career jobs and often the labor force as well.

Do Older Americans Want to Work?

In the spring of 1989, under the auspices of the Commonwealth Fund, Louis Harris and Associates conducted telephone interviews concerning work and retirement preferences with over 3,500 older Americans. About half were women aged 50 to 59; the others were men aged 55 to 64. About 2,000 were still working and the other 1,500 were already out of the labor force.

McNaught, Barth, and Henderson (1991) have analyzed the responses of those who were already out of the labor force. Nearly a quarter said they wished they were working and were capable of doing so. The authors then narrowed this sample by requiring that they also pass a series of specific labor market commitment tests, and they still found a substantial minority—nearly 14% of those retired representing about 1.1 million retirees—who were willing and able to work (cf. Chapter 10).[3]

We have analyzed the plans and preferences of those still employed, and found that most expected to stop working when they wanted to (Quinn & Burkhauser, 1994). But about 10% of men and 13% of women—representing about a million people altogether—said that they expected to retire before they really would like to. Most of those individuals wanted to work a significant number of additional years, and over a third implied that they wanted to work as long as possible.

A desire to work was confirmed by responses to questions about work preferences under alternative scenarios. About one in four respondents, representing 2.4 million workers, said they would work longer if their employers' contributions to retirement benefits continued at the same level after age 65; about one in three, representing 2.9 million workers, said they would work longer if offered employment at somewhat lower pay, but with reduced hours and responsibilities; and well over a third, representing 3.5 million workers, said they would work longer if offered a job that required retraining but had different responsibilities and tasks and the same hours and salary. Half the

---

[3] Individuals had to say that they had either worked or had looked for a job in the previous year or that they were "discouraged workers" (felt that no jobs were available or that they were too old or lacked appropriate skills), that they were willing to work in currently available jobs (from a specific list of 16 such jobs), that they had realistic wage expectations, that they had a financial need for employment, that they could accomplish relevant physical tasks, and that they were willing to accept difficult work conditions (McNaught et al., 1991).

respondents said yes to at least one of these questions, implying over 5 million people would be willing to work longer than they currently planned if their financial incentives or working conditions were changed.

Other studies, based on specialized samples, further specify desired qualities of work. Jondrow, Brechling, and Marcus (1987) found that many workers would like to retire gradually. In one survey, 80% of respondents over age 55 preferred part-time work to complete retirement. In another, 60% of a sample of managers preferred phased retirement. Two-thirds of another group said they would consider a transitional step of part-time employment. Most of these would have liked part-time work with their full-time employer. Christensen (1990) reported on a large survey of union retirees, in which 40% of those under age 65 either held or said they would like to hold post-career jobs. Only 13% of those who wanted to work preferred a full-time job.

There are reasons to be skeptical of questionnaire responses. It is easier to say what one would like to do than it is to do it. Nonetheless, these surveys responses suggest that many older Americans are willing and able to work longer than they have or plan to and that they might respond favorably to terms and conditions of employment different from those they actually face.

Obstacles to Work at Older Ages

Despite these preferences, the modal (but by no means the only, as will be shown) pattern of retirement still involves an abrupt transition from full-time work to complete labor force withdrawal. Most wage and salary workers who are able to reduce hours must switch jobs to do so. Why do desires and opportunities not match? What accounts for the structural lag?

One reason is that part-time hourly pay is usually much lower than full-time compensation. According to Gustman and Steinmeier (1985), partially retired older workers suffered an hourly wage loss of 10% if they remained with their previous full-time employer (a rare event) and 30% if they did not. Herz and Rones (1989) reported that hourly wages declined by 30% to 40% when full-time workers became part-time employees. Quinn et al. (1990) report similar findings— severe wage losses associated with movement to part-time work, especially if accompanied by a change in employer.

Blank (1990) and Ehrenberg, Rosenberg, and Li (1988) have studied extensively the relative compensation on full-time and part-time jobs and find that part-time work generally pays less. The mean differential in the Ehrenberg et al. study was 18%; Blank found hourly wage decrements of about 20% for women and 30% for men.[4]

The losses are compounded when fringe benefits are considered. Blank (1990), Ehrenberg et al. (1988), and Levitan and Conway (1988), have all shown that part-timers are much less likely than those employed full-time to be covered by employers' health and pension plans.

The wage losses are largest when workers switch employers because much of the experience they gained with their previous employer does not carry over to the new job.[5] If so, then why don't workers reduce hours on their career jobs? According to Gustman and Steinmeier (1983, 1985), they do not because they cannot. Only 15% of firms responding to a 1979 survey permitted some employees to reduce hours as they approached retirement. Only 7% offered this option to all employees. A survey of individuals suggested that two-thirds to three-quarters of older wage and salary workers were unable to work fewer hours. The reasons for this inflexibility are not clear. Some analysts have mentioned the fixed costs of employment that, for instance, would make two half-time employees more expensive than one full-time worker, or a fear that the productivity of older workers does not justify their wage. The self-employed, on the other hand, with more control over their hours, are much more likely to utilize a transitional period of partial retirement.

But even if workers were permitted to work part-time on their career jobs, they would have to do so for reduced compensation. Social Security and most defined benefit plans offer declining and often negative wealth accruals to workers who stay on the job. This is especially true in those cases where future benefits depend on actual earnings of

---

[4] These estimates were based on single-equation estimates, often with part-time work as a dummy variable. With more sophisticated simultaneous equations techniques to control for individuals' choice of labor market participation and part-time employment, the results became a little clouded. Although part-time men continued to be paid less, women in some occupations appeared to be paid more than they would have earned per hour in full-time work (Blank, 1990).

[5] Shapiro and Sandell (1985) studied wage declines among older workers who were forced to look for new jobs and estimated that about 90% of the earnings decline was due to the loss of type of specific experience.

the last few years—finishing a career job on a part-time basis could actually lower future annual pension benefits, in addition to not receiving them during the part-time years, resulting in a significant loss in pension wealth.

Many older Americans, then, face unattractive alternatives as they age. Continued full-time employment on a career job eventually results in significant losses of retirement income wealth; in essence, a pay cut. Part-time work on this job is rarely available for the wage and salary population, and even if it is, may often result in reduced retirement income wealth. New part-time, and to a lesser extent, new full-time, employment means a significantly lower wage rate. Faced with these alternatives, many older Americans stop working. Is the decision voluntary? Yes, in the sense that they choose to do it under the circumstances. But no, in that the circumstances may have changed dramatically as they aged.

Work after Retirement

Most recent economic research has focused on the theoretical formulation of the retirement decision and on the specification of the explanatory variables, particularly the financial incentives. Much less attention has been paid to the left-hand side of the equation—the behavior being explained. Until recently, retirement has generally been modeled as an "either you are or you aren't" decision that was irreversible for those who retired. But recent investigation suggests that for many Americans, actual withdrawal patterns are far more varied than the traditional view would indicate (cf. Chapter 3).

Quinn et al. (1990) analyzed patterns of disengagement from career jobs, defined as full-time jobs held at least 10 years. They showed that most Americans spend considerable time on a single job. This pattern of long tenure on a "career" job is consistent with the view that defined pension plans substantially penalize those who leave a career job "too early," and thereby deter mobility. Many leave this career job and the labor force simultaneously, but many do not.

Over a quarter of the wage and salary employees in the Social Security Administration's Retirement History Study, a 10-year long study of the work behavior of men aged 58 to 63 in 1969, did not stop work when they left full-time career employment. Of those who remained employed, most began a new job quickly and stayed at it for at least two years. The new positions often represented a new line of work, lower down the socioeconomic scale, often at considerably lower pay. Many workers, were augmenting these earnings with Social Security and/or employer pension checks.

With 1989 data from the Commonwealth Fund survey and a similar definition of a career job, Ruhm (forthcoming) found even more post-career employment than in the first wave of the Retirement History Survey 20 years ago. He estimated that 30% to 40% of those aged 58 to 63 and employed in 1989 were working on postcareer bridge jobs. Although people of all types utilize these intermediate steps toward retirement, there is some evidence that those at the extreme ends of the economic scale are most likely to do so (Quinn et al., 1990). We suspect that the poor continue to work because they have to. In addition, they are less likely to face dramatic age-specific pay cuts since they are often not eligible for employee pension benefits. The wealthy work because their employment provides nonpecuniary benefits in addition to a paycheck and because their losses in retirement income wealth are likely to be dwarfed by their earnings potential.

What this suggests is that work after "retirement" is not a rare event. But it is unlikely to grow in significance unless employers show more flexibility in hours of work and unless pension plans follow Social Security's lead toward greater age neutrality.

CHANGES IN PUBLIC POLICY TOWARD RETIREMENT (1970–1990)

The institutional environment surrounding retirement is itself changing. Important legislation concerning mandatory retirement and Social Security was passed in the 1970s and 1980s, and the nature of employer pension plans continues to evolve. Most of these changes work in the direction of encouraging more work at older ages, but significant obstacles remain.

From an Antiwork Policy to Neutrality

Mandatory Retirement Rules.   In 1978, an amendment to the Age Discrimination in Employment Act outlawed mandatory retirement before age 70 for most American workers. Many states went further, and outlawed mandatory retirement at age 70 as well (Rhine, 1984). In 1986, the federal government followed suit, and mandatory retirement, with a few exceptions, was eliminated.

This legislation was enacted with the hope that it would drastically alter retirement patterns, since many workers retired at mandatory retirement age. But econometric evidence suggested otherwise. We found that mandatory retirement was closely intertwined with both Social Security and employer pension incentives (Burkhauser & Quinn, 1983). As mentioned earlier, the Social Security delayed retirement credit drops significantly at age 65, from about 8% per year of delay to 4% in 1992 (and was 3% prior to 1990 and only 1% before 1982), which is less than actuarially fair. This implies a pay cut at age 65, which was also the most common age of mandatory retirement before 1978. In addition, mandatory retirement was usually accompanied by an employer pension plan that often added work disincentives of its own. Our research suggests that at least half the difference in behavior between those with and without mandatory retirement was due to factors other than mandatory retirement and that even this unexplained residual was probably an overestimate of the mandatory retirement effect. We predicted that the mandatory retirement legislation would have only a modest effect on elderly labor supply, and this appears to be the case.

Social Security.   Concern for the financial solvency of the Social Security system and the labor market implications of earlier retirement in an aging society led President Reagan to form the Greenspan Commission to investigate policy options. Their recommendations led to the 1983 Amendments to the Social Security Act, several of which were designed to prolong the working life of older Americans (see Svahn & Ross, 1983, for details of the amendments). Two amendments currently affect older workers. The delayed retirement credit after age 65 was increased to 3.5% for those reaching age 65 in 1990, to 4.5% in 1994, and will increase by 0.5% every other year until it reaches 8% per year of delay in 2009. It will then be close to actuarially fair.

In addition, in 1990 the benefit loss associated with an additional dollar of earnings above the exempt amount dropped from 50 to 33 cents for full-benefit retirees. A third amendment is to begin after the turn of the century. The age of eligibility for full Social Security benefits is scheduled to rise from 65 to 66 by the year 2009 and to 67 by 2027. Benefits will still be available as early as age 62, but the reduced benefits will only be 70% of the full amount rather than the current 80%.

All these changes reward additional work and should help reverse the long-term trend toward earlier retirement. Most studies predict that the aggregate impact on retirement age will be modest—average delays on the order of months, not years (see Quinn et al., 1990, for a fuller discussion). But these estimates are only preliminary because they assume that the other factors of the environment—in particular, employer pensions—remain unchanged. This is the great unknown.

Employer Pensions.   The growth in employer pension coverage has ceased. According to Turner and Beller (1992, Table 4.1), the proportion of private sector workers covered has remained constant over the past two decades. They estimate that 45% of private wage and salary workers were covered in 1970, compared with 46% in 1987. When only full-time workers are considered, coverage remains steady at 52%. But over these 20 years, there have been important changes in the types of plans offered.

Most workers with pensions still have primary coverage in a *defined benefit* plan in which the worker is promised an annuity on retirement from the firm. The benefit is usually based on some combination of earnings and years of service (Schulz, 1988). There are also *defined contribution* plans, in which the firm periodically deposits funds into an account that belongs to the worker on retirement. These are basically just savings accounts with tax advantages.

According to Turner and Beller (1992, Table 4.10), fewer than 13% of the private sector workers with employer pension plans had their primary coverage in a defined contribution plan in 1975. By 1987, this had risen to 32%. Defined contribution plans are even more popular as supplementary coverage, where they are nearly universal. This is an important trend since the dramatic work disincentives (accrual patterns and pay cuts) discussed earlier come from the benefit calculation formulas of defined benefit plans. There are no such work disincentives with defined contribution plans because the employer's contribution is merely a constant wage supplement. Nearly half of all private pension coverage (and two-thirds of primary coverage) is still in defined benefit plans, so they remain very relevant to the current environment. But if the trend toward defined contribution plans continues and if the Social Security delayed retirement credit after age 65 becomes close to actuarially fair as scheduled, then the importance of these work disincentives at older ages will diminish.

From a Neutral to a Prowork Policy

Economic research suggests that retirement trends are very much influenced by public policy. The institutional environment continues to evolve. Some changes are already underway or legislated for the future; others may occur as the composition of the work force shifts; and others may require additional legislation. The following menu of policies could have a significant effect on work at older ages.

Mandatory Retirement Rules.   After 1994, mandatory retirement practices are banned in all firms including universities with the exception of a few senior executives, and a few cases where there is a specific age-related justification. A 1991 study commissioned by the National Academy of Science, however, predicts that this ban will have very little impact on the retirement patterns of university faculty, with the possible exception of a small number of prestigious research institutions (Hammond & Morgan, 1991). Most faculty retire well before 70 anywhere, and in a few states where mandatory retirement has already been eliminated for faculty, very little change was observed.

Social Security.   As previously discussed, work disincentives imposed by Social Security have declined over the past decade, but much remains to be done. Ending the earnings test would remove the last major age-specific tax on work. In 1991, the Senate voted to end the earnings test for those aged 65 to 69 but no vote was taken in the House. Since then, increasing pressure has been put on legislators to increase the earnings Social Security recipients can receive without penalty.

The Social Security Amendments of 1983 allowed the first taxation of Social Security benefits. Since 1984, single persons with "provisional income" over $25,000 and married couples with "provisional income" over $32,000 have had up to 50% of their total Social Security benefits subject to federal taxation. ("Provisional income" is adjusted gross income, plus half of Social Security benefits, plus interest on tax exempt bonds and certain foreign source income.) Beginning in 1994, up to 85% of Social Security benefits are taxable for singles with "provisional income" over $34,000 and couples over $44,000. (The 50% rule remains in effect for those above the old thresholds but below the new ones.) Since these limits are not indexed for inflation, an increasing number of older Americans are likely to be affected by these provisions over time.

Taxing Social Security benefits discourages retirement relative to work, and brings the tax treatment of Social Security benefits more into line with that of employer pensions and offset to some degree the federal budget costs of ending the earnings test. Taxation of Social Security benefits at all income levels would have little or no effect on older people whose only source of income is Social Security since they rarely have enough income to pay federal income tax.

Employer Pensions.   But even these proposed changes in mandatory retirement rules and Social Security benefits will not ensure significant increases in work at older ages. Much depends on how private employers react to these changes in their employment decisions and in their pension benefit calculations.

Recent evidence suggests that pension incentives are very important in determining individual and aggregate retirement behavior. They influence both the timing and nature of labor force withdrawal. The fact that work effort has fallen dramatically between ages 55 and 61, ages below the minimum for early Social Security retirement benefits, suggests that Social Security incentives are not the only reason for reduced work at older ages.

A key factor, about which little is known, is how employer pension plans will change in response to the new Social Security environment. Will pensions augment or offset the changes in Social Security incentives? Would additional federal government initiatives concerning pensions be nullified by other alterations in the compensation package? In general, how would the long-run general equilibrium impacts compare with the partial equilibrium changes we have suggested?

We simply do not know the answers to these questions. But we do know that the pension rules negotiated in the future will significantly affect retirement decisions. Most people do not retire because they can no longer find or perform work. Rather they retire "voluntarily," while they are still able to work and there is demand for their services.

But they might not if the rewards for work were increased or the conditions of work changed. There will always be people at the margin, and these people will change their behavior in response to changes in the choices before them.

Bureau of Labor Statistics projections (U.S. Department of Labor, 1989) show that over the next 15 years, the population aged 55 and older will increase while the population aged 16 to 34 will decline. Some foresee labor market shortages emerging from these demographic shifts, given the current labor force participation of older people. If employers share this concern, then we may see substantial changes in pension policy as firms reduce the incentives for early retirement embedded in most defined benefit plans. If not, however, employers may shift lifetime benefits even more toward those who leave at early retirement ages in order to offset the Social Security changes now underway.

There is some evidence that employers did change pension plans to offset the effect of a previous governmental policy—the delay in and then elimination of mandatory retirement. Mitchell and Luzadis (1988) found that during the 1970s, when the mandatory retirement age was increased from 65 to 70 and the movement to eliminate it altogether was gathering momentum, pensions that had required mandatory retirement below age 70 altered their benefit incentives to encourage earlier retirement.

On the other hand, there are many instances of policy compliance. One reason that most pension plans in the United States chose age 65 as their normal retirement age was that Social Security used that age. One of the original purposes of Social Security policy was to encourage older workers to leave the labor force and, until 1972, earnings above an exempt amount were taxed at 100%, while benefits postponed beyond age 65 earned no actuarial credit. With these very strong disincentives to full-time work, it is not surprising that firms developed institutions that conformed. To do otherwise would have required firms to pay workers higher wages past age 65 to offset the Social Security penalties. Likewise, the establishment of early Social Security benefits at age 62 may have encouraged firms to follow suit.

A final speculation concerns the influence of Social Security changes on the type of work that will be done by older Americans. If pension rules continue to discourage full-time work on career jobs, then we expect to see more postcareer bridge employment and more second careers. This is because the easing of Social Security work disincentives will make work more attractive relative to complete retirement, whereas employer pension rules continue to discourage work on career jobs. The result? Keep working but switch jobs to do so. But, if firms complement Social Security changes by reducing the penalty for postponing retirement, then workers should work longer by delaying departure from their career jobs.

A final and important variation on this theme is the possibility of part-time work on a career job. This has the advantage of eliminating the loss of special job skills that accompany a job change and reducing the wage loss ordinarily associated with part-time employment. Research has established that the self-employed, who rarely have pension-related work disincentives, are much more likely than wage and salary workers to move from full- to part-time work on the same job (see Quinn et al., 1990). Currently, defined benefit pension rules, especially when benefits are based on earnings in the last few years of employment, make this a costly choice for wage and salary workers who desire part-time work. What may be needed is the introduction of partial pension schemes in which workers can combine partial pension benefits, as they can now with Social Security, with part-time employment on the career job.

Toward a More Flexible Workplace

Retirement decisions are influenced by the economic incentives that workers face. We have outlined how employer pension and Social Security rules alter work incentives. But it is also true that as workers age, they may desire greater flexibility in their jobs. The most obvious reason for this is that older workers are more likely than younger workers to have a health condition affecting their ability to work. Furthermore, even if their health is fine, many older workers prefer to work at a slower pace and fewer hours than younger workers. How likely is it that employers will accommodate these preferences?

The Americans with Disabilities Act of 1990. Keeping workers with health impairments on the job is the major goal of this recent policy initiative. The Americans with Disabilities Act of 1990 (ADA) requires employers to make "reasonable" accommodations to workers with disabilities unless this would cause an "undue" hardship for the operation of business. This policy thrust follows civil rights legislation of the 1960s in extending protection from employment discrimination to people with disabilities. In July 1992, all firms with 25 or more employers were covered under this Act. In July 1994, this was extended to firms with 15 or more employees (Burkhauser, 1992; Weaver, 1991).

Despite the now familiar wheelchair as the symbol of people with handicaps and the high profile of people with sight and hearing impairments in the battle for the ADA, only a small fraction of the population with handicaps are blind or deaf, or are wheelchair users. The great majority of those currently on the disability insurance rolls suffer from one of four broad health conditions (see Table 11–2): mental disorders, circulatory diseases (predominately heart problems),

Table 11-2
Characteristics of U.S. Disability Insurance and Supplemental Security
Income Adult (age 18–64) Recipients, 1989 (Percentage Distribution)

Diagnostic Groups	All Beneficiaries[a]			Newly Enrolled[b]		
	Below 50	50–64	All	Below 50	50–64	All
Disability Insurance						
Mental disorders	40.0	17.7	27.7	34.6	9.9	20.9
Circulatory diseases	6.3	25.4	18.2	8.5	25.0	17.6
Musculoskeletal diseases	12.4	22.9	18.9	12.7	20.0	16.8
Neoplasms	2.6	3.6	3.3	9.2	16.4	13.2
All others	38.7	30.4	31.9	35.0	28.7	31.5
Total	100.0	100.0	100.0	100.0	100.0	100.0
Total (millions)	1.10	1.77	2.87	.18	.23	.41
Total (percent)	38.4	61.6	100.0	43.9	56.1	100.0
Supplemental Security Income						
Mental Disorders (other than retardation)	32.7	22.0	28.9			
Mental Retardation	33.5	8.4	24.4			
Circulatory Diseases	3.0	18.6	8.7			
Musculoskeletal Diseases	3.7	16.8	8.5			
Neoplasms	1.1	2.4	1.7			
All Others	26.0	31.8	27.8			
Total	100.0	100.0	100.0			
Total (millions)	1.26	.72	1.98			
Total (percentage)	63.6	36.4	100.0			

Source: Derived from tables in the U.S. Department of Health and Human Services (1991), Table 6.C.

[a] December 1989.
[b] 1988.

musculoskeletal diseases (predominantly arthritis), and neoplasms (cancer). They did not have these handicaps during most of their work lives. Approximately three out of five of those on the Social Security Disability Insurance rolls in December 1989 were between the ages of 50 and 64. Almost half of all older beneficiaries suffer from either a circulatory or a musculoskeletal condition. Thus, the ADA may have an important impact on work effort at older ages.

But whether the law will significantly increase accommodation, especially to older workers with handicaps, remains to be seen. The ADA's accommodation criteria are far from precise. Oi (1991) has suggested that workers with handicaps are more often constrained by their time and energy than by physical barriers with respect to job performance, since the time and energy they expend in day-to-day maintenance is greater than that of those without handicaps. Future court decisions on the reasonableness of accommodation through more flexible hours, or even permanent part-time work, are likely to be much more important in shaping the future workplace than decisions about the reasonableness of physical changes.

Regulatory Changes. More flexible work schedules may be the single greatest change that accommodation brings to the workplace. If so, it will go a long way toward restructuring the labor force for workers who are older or have handicaps and desire part-time work. Although it is possible that a broad interpretation of ADA by the courts will force this change, there are more direct ways for government to achieve it. For instance, employers who offer pension benefits to employees are required, under the federal Employment Retirement Income Security Act of 1974 (ERISA), to pay these benefits to part-time workers who fulfill a minimum requirement of service—1,000 hours per year, or 20 hours per week for a year. This discourages firms from hiring part-time workers. Changing the rules to let part-time workers receive an equivalent portion of these benefits would allow more flexible work contracts and encourage employers to accommodate workers in this way.

Using Direct Government Expenditures to Increase Work at Older Ages

Mandated accommodation is only one of many ways to integrate older workers or workers with disabilities into the workforce. If the federal government were willing to take on some financial responsibility to achieve this goal, a wide range of policy instruments are available that could target funds on older workers, especially those with low income who want to work.

Changes in the Medicare Payout Rule.   To reduce federal costs, Congress changed Medicare eligibility rules to prevent those over age 65 who were covered by an employer health plan to use Medicare until their own coverage was exhausted. While this policy change reduced Medicare expenses, it raised a major barrier to the employment of older workers, whose medical costs are a serious concern to employers. Medical insurance is the fastest growing fringe benefit expense of private employers. By denying older workers access to Medicare benefits, the government saved money at the expense of jobs.

Extending the Earned Income Tax Credit.   The most direct means of helping poor older workers is by extending to them the earned income tax credit now available to younger workers in poor families with children. This would effectively subsidize the kind of low-skill, part-time work that many older workers could perform while receiving Supplemental Security Income or Social Security benefits.

Accommodation Tax Credits.   Employers in many European countries are reimbursed for accommodating workers with handicaps. This recognizes that the economic burden of accommodation need not fall entirely on employers. If employing particular types of workers is a social goal, society as a whole should help finance its achievement (see Burkhauser & Daly, 1994).

Job Training.   The Job Partnership Training Act of 1983 replaced the Comprehensive Employment and Training Act as the principal mechanism for putting fringe workers into jobs. While the percentage of successfully placed trainees has been quite high in this program, it has been argued that the most difficult to place have been systematically excluded. Anderson, Burkhauser, and Raymond (1993) provide some evidence of "creaming" in this program and show that older people and those with handicaps are underrepresented in the trainee population. Changes in the reward structure for the councils that choose candidates for training could lead to increased use of this program.

Optioning out of Social Security. In 1993, Social Security taxes paid by employers and employees amounted to 15.3% of the first $57,600 of wage income. Another method of encouraging the employment of older workers would be to allow them to option out of the Social Security system after some age, perhaps, age 65. This prowork policy could be focused on part-time work by exempting only the first $10,000 in income from Social Security taxes past some age.

CONCLUSION

The policy options sketched in this chapter are not meant to represent a specific legislative agenda, but a sample of the kinds of creative prowork changes in government policy that would increase the likelihood of employment for older people. Some are marginal in nature, other radical. All have been ignored to date because they directly affect the government budget. Yet several of them are likely to affect low-income older workers or workers with disabilities more than the Americans with Disability Act of 1990.

Some of the policy changes that have been made in the past decade, or that we have suggested, will encourage continued work on any job while others will induce people to stay on their career jobs. The former include many of the Social Security changes enacted in the 1983 Amendment and others that have been mentioned here, such as the elimination of the earnings test or the exemption of Social Security recipients from Social Security taxes on part-time earnings. The latter relate to employer pension plans and include policies favoring defined contribution plans, age-neutral defined benefit plans, or flexible partial pension schemes.

Surveys of older workers suggest that many of them would like to retire gradually, to include a period of partial retirement in the transition from full-time work to complete labor force withdrawal. Currently, only a minority do. But this would change if the federal government acted both to remove the remaining antiwork aspects of current Social Security rules and to initiate new policies that make it less costly for firms to hire part-time workers and less costly for older workers to accept part-time employment.

In the end, fuller utilization of our older workforce will only occur when employers see that it is in their best interests to do so. The federal government can and should set the stage. Social Security changes are moving in the right direction, and other initiatives can also help at the margin. The stage also includes the state of the macroeconomy. When aggregate demand for labor is weak, firms are likely to see older workers as expendable and continue to provide financial inducements for employees to leave the firm—to give them offers they can, but are unlikely to, refuse. When labor markets tighten, either because of stronger economic growth or because of the demographic changes on the horizon, then firms will be as creative in devising ways to keep older workers on the job as they have been in moving them out.

REFERENCES

Anderson, K., Burkhauser, R. V., & Raymond, J. (1993). The effect of creaming on job placement rates under the job training partnership act. *Industrial and Labor Relations Review, 46,* 613–624.

Blank, R. M. (1990). Are part-time jobs bad jobs? In G. Burtless (Ed.), *A future of lousy jobs?* (pp. 123–155). Washington, DC: Brookings Institution.

Boskin, M. J., Kotlikoff, L. J., Puffert, D. J., & Shoven, J. B. (1987). Social security: A financial appraisal across and within generations. *National Tax Journal, 40,* 19–34.

Burkhauser, R. V. (1990). Morality on the cheap: The Americans with disability act. *Regulation, 3,* 47–56.

Burkhauser, R. V. (1992). Beyond stereotypes: Public policy and the doubly disabled. *The American Enterprise, 3,* 60–69.

Burkhauser, R. V., & Daly, M. C. (1994) The Economic Consequences of Disability: A comparison of German and American people with disabilities. *Journal of Disability Policy Studies,* 5, forthcoming.

Burkhauser, R. V., & Quinn, J. F. (1983.) Is mandatory retirement overrated? Evidence from the 1970s. *Journal of Human Resources, 18,* 337–358.

Christensen, K. (1990). Bridge over troubled waters: How older workers view the labor market. In P.B. Doeringer (Ed.), *Bridges to retirement: Older workers in a changing labor market* (pp. 175–207). Ithaca, NY: ILP.

Ehrenberg, R. G., Rosenberg, P., & Li, J. (1988). Part-time employment in the United States. In R. A. Hart (Ed.), *Employment, unemployment and labor utilization* (pp. 256–281). Boston, MA: Unwin Hyman.

Grad, S. (1990). Income of the population aged 55 or older, 1980. *Social Security Administration* (Publication No. 13-11871). Washington, DC: U.S. Government Printing Office.

Gustman, A. L., & Steinmeier, T. L. (1983). Minimum hours constraints and retirement behavior. *Contemporary Policy Issues, 3,* 77–91.

Gustman, A. L., & Steinmeier, T. L. (1985). The effects of partial retirement on wage profiles for older workers. *Industrial Relations, 24,* 257–265.

Hammond, P. B., & Morgan, E. P., (1991). *Ending mandatory retirement for tenured faculty.* Washington, DC: National Academy Press.

Herz, D. E., & Rones, P. (1989). Institutional barriers to employment of older workers. *Monthly Labor Review, 112*(4), 14–21.

Jondrow, J., Brechling, F., & Marcus, A. (1987). Older workers in the market for part-time employment. In S. H. Sandell (Ed.), *The problem isn't age: Work and older Americans* (pp. 84–99). New York: Praeger.

Kotlikoff, L. J., & Smith, D. E. (1983). *Pensions in the American economy.* Chicago, IL: University of Chicago Press.

Kotlikoff, L. J., & Wise, D. A. (1989). *The wage carrot and the pension stick.* Kalamazoo, MI: Upjohn Institute for Employment and Research.

Levitan S. A., & Conway, E. A. (1988). Part-timers: Living on half rations. *Challenge, 31,* 9–16.

McNaught, W., Barth, M. C., & Henderson, P. H. (1991). Older Americans: Willing and able to work. In A. H. Munnell (Ed.), *Retirement and public policy* (pp. 101–114). Dubuque, IA: Kendall/Hunt Publishing Company.

Mitchell, O. S., & Luzadis, R. (1988). Changes in pension incentives through time, *Industrial and Labor Relations Review, 42,* 100–108.

Oi, W. (1991). Disability and a workforce-welfare. In C. Weaver (Ed.), *Disability and work: Incentives, rights, and opportunities* (pp. 31–45). Washington, DC: American Enterprise Institute.

Quinn, J. F., & Burkhauser, R. V. (1994). Public policy and the plans and preferences of older Americans. *Journal of Aging and Social Policy, 6,* forthcoming.

Quinn, J. F., Burkhauser, R. V., & Myers, D. C. (1990). *Passing the torch: The influence of economic incentives on work and retirement.* Kalamazoo, MI: Upjohn Institute for Employment Research.

Rhine, S. H. (1984). *Managing older workers: Company policies and attitudes.* New York: The Conference Board.

Ruhm, C. (forthcoming). Secular changes in the work and retirement patterns of older men. *Journal of Human Resources.*

Schulz, J. H. (1988). *The economics of aging.* New York: Van Nostrand Reinhold.

Shapiro, D., & Sandell, S. H. (1985). Age discrimination in wages and displaced older workers. *Southern Economic Journal, 52,* 90–102.

Svahn, J. A., & Ross, M. (1983). Social Security amendments of 1983: Legislative history and summary of provisions. *Social Security Bulletin, 46,* 3–48.

Turner, J. A., & Beller, D. J. (1992). *Trends in pensions: 1992.* Washington, DC: U.S. Government Printing Office.

U.S. Department of Health and Human Services. (1991). *Annual supplement to the Social Security Bulletin.* Washington, DC: U.S. Government Printing Office.

U.S. Department of Labor. (1989). *Older worker task force: Key policy issues for the future.* Washington, DC: U.S. Government Printing Office.

U.S. President. (1992). *Economic report of the President, 1992.* Washington, DC: U.S. Government Printing Office.

U.S. Bureau of Labor Statistics (various years) Employment and Earnings. Washington DC: U.S. Government Printing Office.

Weaver, C. (1991). *Disability and work: Incentives, rights, and opportunities.* Washington, DC: American Enterprise Institute.

CHAPTER 12

Endnote:
The Reach of an Idea

Anne Foner

T he preceding chapters in this book discuss the place of age in some of the major transformations in modern society, and point to the problems and future possibilities they have created. Each chapter emphasizes changes in structures in a particular domain—work, retirement, family, education, leisure—but all are organized around a single unifying concept: structural lag. In combination, the chapters show how exploring that one conceptual issue—the lag or mismatch between people's rapidly changing lives, on the one hand, and the less rapidly changing social structures and age constraints surrounding these lives, on the other—can increase understanding of both social change and the life course from birth to death as a social and psychological, as well as a biological, phenomenon. This final chapter highlights some of the theoretical and substantive implications of the chapters[1] that precede it.

---

[1] Identified herein by the names of the contributors. Names followed by dates are listed in the References.

SOME THEORETICAL ANTECEDENTS

The concept of structural lag has a familiar ring. It resonates with variations on a theme common to numerous social theories that antedate the explorations in this book: the theme of dissonance (or mismatch) among components of society. The differences, as well as the similarities, between structural lag as defined here and such earlier theories of dissonance are instructive.

Selected Examples

Notably (as explained in Chapter 1, by Matilda and John Riley), structural lag is reminiscent of Ogburn's (1922) concept of "cultural lag," which specifies the interdependence among various elements of culture. Ogburn was concerned with the relationship between changes in the material culture—primarily technology—and changes in the nonmaterial culture—a residual category that includes customs and social organization. It was Ogburn's thesis that typically these latter elements do not change as quickly as the former, but lag behind changes in the material culture.

The notion of "structural lag" also calls to mind the Marxian concept of "contradiction," the asymmetry and anomalies inherent in the economic system in a given historical period. In the productive system in capitalist society, a major contradiction and a key source of asymmetry resides in the relationship between capitalists who own and control the means of production and wage laborers who are employed by and dependent on the capitalists. This asymmetrical relationship results in the exploitation of the workers, on the one hand, and is a source of profit to the capitalist, on the other. In the continual search for profit, intrinsic to the capitalist system, the exploitation of workers is intensified. But as workers struggle against their exploitation and alienation, the system itself is subject to change (e.g., Marx & Engels, 1848). In short, the very structure of the social relations of production tends to produce forces that transform it.[2]

---

[2] In his various writings, Marx employs the concept of contradiction to refer to several types of inconsistencies and oppositions; and, of course, his analysis is considerably more complex than the thumbnail sketch outlined here.

Schumpeter (1955) articulated another idea. In addressing the question of what historical conditions give rise to a particular class structure, he argued that every social situation takes over the culture, dispositions, and "spirit" of preceding situations as well as their social structure and concentrations of power. He pointed to one implication of this generalization that is particularly relevant for this book's exploration of social change: In each social situation, elements survive from preceding periods that are alien to the current trends.

In still another vein, Merton (1957, p. 191) calls attention to the disjunction between socially defined goals and socially approved means for achieving these goals. The resulting conflict between culturally accepted values and the socially structured difficulties in living up to these values can lead to rebellion in a substantial segment of the population, with the potential for reshaping both the social structure and its norms.

Distinctive Features of Structural Lag

Although structural lag is reminiscent of these and other earlier formulations, it is distinguished from them in several ways. First and foremost, it emphasizes the relationship between *people* and *social structures* (including the culture and values institutionalized in these structures). By contrast, many related theoretical approaches (such as those previously noted) are focused more exclusively on the disparities among elements within the social structure and its culture. Structural lag explicitly introduces the place of *people* and the processes of their growing up, growing older, dying, and replacing themselves with new cohorts (or generations) of people.

As its second distinguishing feature, structural lag emphasizes the *dynamic interplay* between these "people" processes of aging and cohort succession, on the one hand, and changing social structures, on the other. Thus structural changes both influence and are influenced by the "people" processes of aging and cohort succession.[3]

A third distinguishing feature of structural lag follows: the unique dynamic of structural change it implies. This dynamic arises from the very different rhythms and patterns[4] that characterize changes in lives

---

[3] For further details of these two "dynamisms," see Chapter 1.
[4] Described by the Rileys as "asynchrony" and "external" sources of change.

and changes in social structures and the resulting pressures for structural change when structures lag behind changing lives.

To be sure, many earlier theories include people and the reciprocal influences of people's behaviors and attitudes and societal structures as key elements in their analyses. For example, Marx[5] deals explicitly with the inherently conflictual relations between classes of people in the productive sphere and points to the resulting pressures for revolutionary change. However, the focal point of structural lag is not limited to the productive sphere. And, while pressure for structural change often ensues as a result of structural lag, organized conflict is but one mechanism that can come into play to reduce the lag. Thus the dynamic of change inherent in the concept of structural lag—the interplay between aging processes and social structures—is more inclusive than Marx's and other related theories. Aging over the life course from birth to death and alterations in life course patterns from one cohort to the next are universal, ongoing, recurrent "biopsychosocial" processes that continually intersect with economic, political, and other social forces. Structural lag occurs when the changes in people's lives are not accommodated by the various institutional structures of the society, even when these structures are themselves in flux. Efforts to reduce the lag lead to further structural change.

ELEMENTS OF STRUCTURAL LAG

However influenced by earlier works on structure and its changes (note especially Blau, 1975; Coser, 1975), numerous special treatments by the authors included in this book help to specify and clarify key aspects of the emerging understanding of structural lag. These relate to changing lives, changing social structures, and the intersection between age and other bases of social structure.

Changing Lives

What is it about changing lives that appears to have created structural lag by overwhelming social institutions in recent decades? The most dramatic instance noted by several authors is the marked increase in

---

[5] Similar parallelism could be drawn from the work of Merton and others.

life expectancy,[6] together with the increases in the numbers and proportions of old and very old people, especially in advanced societies.
But it is not only changes in the *numbers* of older people that have
confronted unprepared societal institutions. There has also been a
change in the *kinds* of older people in society, that is, in their abilities
and capacities, and therefore in their needs and goals. As Kahn (Chapter 2) notes, today's older people are healthier than those of previous
cohorts and they have the capacity to participate in and to contribute
to important societal affairs. On the whole, however, ways have not
been found for social institutions to make use of this increasing and
underutilized pool of qualified members of the society.

Furthermore, it is not only the way people grow *old* that has
changed; the way people *grow up and mature* is also subject to alter-
ation. As Hareven (Chapter 6) notes, the timing of transitions over
the whole life course has varied historically. Especially noteworthy is
the rise in age of first marriage. With regard to the life course patterns
of women's lives, Moen (Chapter 7) and Hareven show how these patterns today differ from those in the earlier part of this century. Most
significant is the fact that women have entered and remained in the
paid labor force throughout their childbearing, child-rearing, and
adult years.

Similarly (although less emphasized in this volume), there have
been numerous changes over the past century in the lives of children
and adolescents. For example, there has been variation in the years
devoted to formal education, and in the extent to which schooling and
paid work are combined. And there have been notable changes in the
family environment in which infants, children, and adolescents have
been growing up, as in the dramatically rising proportion of single-
parent families.

Whatever ages are involved, then, the process of growing up and
growing older appears to be out of step with patterns of earlier times.
Children are said to be learning too little, but growing up too quickly,
while young adults are slow to assume the full responsibilities of family roles. Those in the long middle years of work and parenthood are

---

[6] While the unprecedented increases in life expectancy, both at birth and at the later ages, impinge directly on changes in the life course, it is the long-term declines in fertility that are
primarily responsible for the changing age composition of the population—the increasing
proportions of the old, and the decreasing proportions of the young.

overburdened with multiple roles, while older people face long years with too few major responsibilities. Lives have changed; but social structures have not caught up.

Changing Age Structures

As the Rileys point out, age structures—roles open or closed to people of different ages, norms about appropriate age-related activities, and the values that underlie those roles and norms—do change, but often the pace of change is not synchronized with changes in people's lives. Moreover, as several contributors to this volume emphasize, in some life domains there is a *lack* of appropriate institutional change, or countertendencies rather than mere slowness of change. Burkhauser and Quinn (Chapter 11), and Kohli (Chapter 4), for example, discuss the paradox of the increasing numbers of capable older people, on the one hand, and the trend toward earlier and earlier retirement, on the other—in part, a failure in the economic structures to utilize or appreciate older workers. In the meantime, given patterns of early retirement, Henretta (Chapter 3) points to a gap in medical insurance for those no longer covered by employers and too young for Medicare. And Moen and Hareven show how the social organization of work has not fully adapted to the entry of mothers with young children.

Structural lag is not confined to the economic sphere; other institutional areas have also been affected. Again it is Moen and Hareven who show how both family and community structures have lagged behind the changes in women's lives. For example, because the norms of the division of labor in the household have remained largely unchanged, young and middle-aged women now have the double burden of work inside and outside the home. Nor have adaptations in community and public institutions emerged to provide adequate child-care facilities. Keith (Chapter 9) also speaks to problems in community institutions; she notes, for example, that municipal housing regulations and the way community associations are organized lag behind the needs of older people and hinder making provisions for them. Such incongruencies can be experienced as stress or strain by the people involved, and they may often result in pressures for structural change (as by evoking a sense of unfairness or even resentment of those who are seen as less overworked, less burdened, or less constrained).

The Intersection of Age with Gender, Ethnicity, and Class

Structural lag, with its components of changing lives and changing age structures, emphasizes age as a primary basis of social structure and social change. As several of the authors indicate, the age system— the configuration of people of different ages in relation to the structure of age-related roles and norms—is also affected by and affects other forms of social differentiation and stratification that rest on race, ethnicity, gender, class, or other bases.

Henretta provides an important example, showing that the impact of changing life course patterns of employment varies with gender and ethnicity. These life course patterns are increasingly affected by the division of workers between those in the "internal" market (with lifetime careers and pension benefits) and those in "contingent" jobs (jobs of short duration and with few benefits). The increase in contingent jobs has meant less security and earlier-than-desired job exit for certain types of workers. Since women and racial and ethnic minorities are disproportionately employed in contingent jobs, they have different work life patterns and different pathways out of the paid labor force than their counterpart white males. Thus, even people who are at similar stages of the life course can be dissimilar in response to other structural constraints, and the rhythm and pattern of their changing lives can differ markedly.

The connection between the age and gender systems is a theme that crops up in a number of chapters. Kohli provides one dramatic instance in the outcome of the collapse of the East German labor market following economic union with the West. Working-age women, more than their male counterparts, were hard-hit by the large-scale unemployment that ensued. Moen, looking to the future as well as the past, suggests that creating greater flexibility in working hours and work-life patterns would benefit not only working women but would be of help to older people also. To be sure, caution about such predictions is in order; new opportunities may bring new competitors. Kohli's discussion of the future recognizes that labor market opportunities that seem to open up for older people might instead be taken by women and immigrants.

Nor is the intersection between class and age overlooked. Plakans (Chapter 5), for example, notes how, in earlier periods of Western history, the availability of unstructured time was class related, the privilege of nobility. In France in the modern era, Plakans suggests, the working class is more likely than other classes to experience their free time in retirement as "empty," and less convertible to meaningful leisure. It seems likely, however, that there are class differences in the forms of leisure that are considered "meaningful," as well as obvious differences in the use of leisure time and in the resources to enjoy it.

Such examples of the intersection of age and aging processes with gender, race, or class point to a broader principle: These other divisions of the societal structure, although external to the age system, nevertheless impinge upon it. Changes in these other systems, therefore, can affect aging processes and age structures, just as changes in the age system can, in turn, influence patterns based on gender, race, ethnicity, and class (Foner, 1979). In the continuing future explorations of the implications of structural lag, such reciprocal influences must be more fully investigated.

REDUCING STRUCTURAL LAG

Contributors to this book not only analyze various manifestations of structural lag and the consequent need for change; they also discuss both general and specific ideas about reducing the lag. They touch on mechanisms through which structural changes occur and the obstacles to change; and they include some proposals for deliberate interventions, noting the dangers of unintended consequences.

Mechanisms of Change

How is it that changes occur that might reduce, or fail to reduce, structural lag? Many changes arise quite apart from deliberate intent, through fluctuations in broad societal trends, or through the intersection of structures based on age with those resting on gender and other bases. Certain changes, however, result from deliberate interventions (cf. Riley & Riley, 1989). Still other changes are traceable to alterations in the lives of people, as the continuing interplay between lives and structures presses for revisions in age constraints. Among the mechanisms selected for discussion in this book, some are already at work and others are potential activators of change.

Policymakers' Initiatives.   One obvious mechanism of deliberate change is for policymakers to institute action: enact laws, issue executive orders, and allocate resources. In the normal course of political dialogue, experts and interested parties alert policymakers to problems and suggest remedies.

For example, Burkhauser and Quinn offer a number of specific, apparently feasible, policy proposals to increase work opportunities for older workers. Among these are altering federal pension regulations to encourage firms to hire part-time older workers, extending the earned-income tax credit to older workers, making room for older people in job-training programs, and bringing tax treatment of Social Security benefits more nearly into line with that of employer pensions. Kahn proposes two possible mechanisms: (1) giving recognition for unpaid as well as paid productive work, by including unpaid work in federal statistics as an identifiable component of gross national product[7] and (2) accepting the reality of part-time employment, by using a 4-hour module as the standard accounting unit for paid work. In another social arena, the policymakers of the early 1990s had already made partial response to the problems faced by working parents by enacting family leave legislation—albeit unpaid.

Admittedly, there are many difficulties of bringing about policy changes (the initial family leave legislation took a long time in coming, for example). Moreover, once enacted, policies do not always have their intended effect. As Burkhauser and Quinn note, the elimination of mandatory retirement did not result in an appreciable increase in retirement age, nor did taxing part of Social Security benefits bring about dramatic increases in paid work at older ages.

Cohort Norm Formation.   A very different mechanism of change arises from alterations in people's lives. One such pressure, formulated by Matilda White Riley (1978) is dubbed "cohort norm formation." This occurs when large numbers of individuals, reacting independently but in a similar fashion to societal changes, produce new patterns of behavior and norms that spread from one cohort to the next to recognize and reinforce these new patterns.

---

[7] At the time of her overall editing of this book, Karin Mack noted just such a recommendation put forth in a proposed piece of legislation by Congresswoman Barbara-Rose Collins (*New York Times*, August 1993).

One such new norm that may be in the making concerns the timing of retirement. As a result of a number of considerations touched on in earlier chapters—job loss, financial pressures, the desire to keep busy, recognition of the extreme length of retirement today—the long-term trend toward increasingly early retirement appears to have somewhat abated; in the early 1990s, many individuals between the ages of 58 and 63 were still working at career jobs, or at postretirement jobs. These tendencies could be the first signs of new norms about the appropriate age of retirement. Another straw in the wind noted by both McNaught (Chapter 10) and Burkhauser and Quinn comes from national surveys of older Americans indicating that substantial numbers would continue to work longer if conditions of employment were different from those they actually face. Postretirement, contingent employment seems to be a poor substitute for the flexibility, greater responsibility, and utilization of skills they would like to see designed into their jobs.

There are examples of cohort norm formation in other social arenas as well. The century-long trend[8] toward increased labor force participation in successive cohorts of women was triggered by the independent actions of millions of women and their employers (cf. Riley, Johnson, & Foner, 1972). And with the current extensive labor force participation of mothers of young children, individual women have independently devised a variety of informal child-care arrangements in the absence of government support for such care. For example, many women—a considerable number themselves mothers of young children—have undertaken to care for a small number of preschool children of working mothers. These arrangements have engendered problems, as accounts in the mass media occasionally remind us; but they indicate how women themselves have taken action to fill a gap in social institutions.

Still other examples of cohort norm formation come from actions of people at terminal stages of the life course, as they press for new norms of dying through such arrangements as hospice care, living wills, informed consent, medical ethics committees, and a wide variety of structural changes proposed by the "right to die" movement (Riley, 1991).

---

[8] Though this trend is often attributed to World War II, it actually began much earlier (cf. Riley, 1993).

Age Conflicts and Social Movements. One source of structural change, whether through their impact on policymakers or on many millions of discrete individuals, lies either in reactions to conflicts in the society or to social movements that press for particular policies or practices.

In the past, age-based conflicts have emerged at the societal level only infrequently (Foner, 1974). Whether they will erupt over "intergenerational equity" or other issues discussed in this volume is uncertain. For example, it may be that younger workers would like to ease the burden of taxes they contribute toward financing Social Security, but it is questionable whether they will challenge older people to remain in the workforce for longer periods. Younger workers have benefited from Social Security policies that provide incentives for older workers to retire, thereby opening up jobs and promotions for themselves. More likely, younger workers might support, even if older people oppose, policies that would reduce or tax older people's benefits; and such policies might operate indirectly to keep more older workers in the labor force. At least in the past, however, two built-in factors have encouraged the young to resist proposals to reduce older people's entitlements: (1) Existing policies free younger people from the financial burdens of caring for older members of their own families and (2) paying now helps guarantee their own financial security in old age. In the future, to be sure, if the financial squeeze on the working-age population increases markedly, young and old might indeed clash on the Social Security benefit structure or related issues.

At the same time, age-related social movements or organized pressure groups may direct efforts toward structural change by policymakers, and other agents of change; but these organized efforts do not necessarily generate conflict across age groupings. For example, Vinovskis (Chapter 8) shows how, in the 19th century, groups representing different segments of the society—workers, religious leaders, some industrialists—engaged in efforts to reform and expand educational institutions for children and young people to conform with changed economic and political conditions. In our own times, there are numerous examples: The American Association of Retired Persons, while promoting programs to benefit older people, has also backed policies to meet the needs of children. On its part, the Children's Defense Fund and its supporters do not seem to be acting in conflict with other age groups, except perhaps in the general sense that resources are always scarce. At the oldest end of the age spectrum, the heroic treatment of late-stage terminal illness has generated a number of organized efforts to put such final decisions in the hands of patients and their families, rather than subject them to the judgment of medical staff (or the courts) alone. Such "right-to-die" efforts on the part of older people do not seem to be in conflict with the interests of other age groups.

At this historical juncture, major conflicts between age groups (over such issues as early retirement or child care) seem unlikely to arise or to be reinforced by age-based social movements. But there will undoubtedly be new policy proposals for change and new norms taking form around other issues discussed in this book. Whether the new policies are easily implemented and have the hoped-for effects and whether the norms spread widely are open questions. The obstacles to change are numerous and imposing.

Obstacles to Structural Change

As Schumpeter reminds us, even revolutionary change does not completely do away with old patterns of behavior and hence with old structures. While the Rileys' "ideal type" of a fully age-integrated society may indeed be regarded as revolutionary, the specific proposals for reducing structural lag discussed throughout this volume are more modest. Yet even proposals with limited aims typically meet with certain resistance, especially if costs are involved and are unequally distributed. Economic obstacles are powerful, but so is the hold of ideology and values entrenched in earlier times.

The Economy.   Consider proposals to extend the work life of older workers. A major obstacle to such proposals has been unemployment, which in some countries has persisted at high levels for more than a decade. As Kohli remarks, early exit of older workers from the labor force has been one of the bloodless ways of coping with unemployment. If "recovery" occurs—but without appreciable increases in employment, if (as in the United States) jobs continue to be exported to cheaper wage areas, and if corporations continue "downsizing" their workforce, there is little promise that the demand for older workers will rise.

Costs of Changes. The real and perceived costs entailed present a further obstacle to implementing various proposals to reduce structural lag. Thus major deterrents to institutionalizing sabbatical leaves or of retraining older workers are the estimated cost of financing such programs and the low payoff perceived. Even the relatively moderate Family Leave legislation adopted in the United States—involving leaves for workers with family-related needs, but without pay—was resisted by some businesses as too costly. Similarly, the readiness to employ older workers on a part-time basis is affected by the fact that the costs of many fringe benefits tend to accumulate on a per capita basis, rather than in proportion to hours of work. There are remedies for this disincentive (e.g., the financing of medical care so that it is independent of work status), but each remedy brings with it its own proponents and opponents.

Institutional Resistance. Such considerations raise the question of institutional inertia, the nearly universal resistance to change itself. Consider Kahn's two imaginative and reasonable proposals: for government data collection agencies to treat unpaid work like paid employment in terms of hours, type, location, and market value; and to move to a 4-hour module as a standard unit of accounting labor time. Quite apart from the possible increased costs of adding people to the employment rolls, nonfinancial objections are likely to reflect the preference for familiar over new ways of thinking and acting. Or consider the resistance to changed zoning regulations in the Philadelphia suburb studied by Keith. While sheer resistance to change may be a factor here, the proposed rezoning may also be perceived as clashing with the vested interests of certain homeowners.

The Influence of Values. Paramount among obstacles to structural change are persistent values that may have been consistent with previous social arrangements but are now outdated. The concern here is not with the classical argument: values *versus* social structure, but with values *built into* social structure. Basic values—broadly accepted ideas about what is good and true, and about the nature of society and relationships among its members; and specific ideas about how people of particular ages *should* act and think—do influence people's behavior and attitudes and hence the forms of social organization. Even

Marx, who emphasized the primacy of social structural influences on people's ideas ("consciousness"), spoke of the potency of the ideas of the dominant classes in blocking the development of a "class conscious" working class. In our own time, Katona (1951) reversed the Marxian priorities with a convincing array of data for what he called "the psychological foundations of economic behavior." The sensitivity of the economy to consumer confidence, now measured at frequent intervals, seems scarcely less important than the sensitivity of consumer confidence to the state of the economy.

Several contributors to this volume show how persistent values serve as obstacles to structural change. Some examples concern the societal roles of men and women in society and the structural implications for family and work. Moen laments the "rigidity of ideological traditions," such as the doctrine of two spheres that relegates to wives and mothers the home as their province. She criticizes the laissez-faire orientation of our society, which serves to delay the inclusion of family goals in the political agenda. Hareven makes the more controversial argument that enshrining privacy as a central value governing contemporary family life serves to increase the separation of the nuclear family from extended kin, and thereby renders the family less able to handle crises. To Hareven, cultural stereotypes upholding narrow concepts of the ideal family and of women's roles are obstacles to meeting the needs of a changed family, as well as changes in women's roles and in the whole life course.

The Rileys, in postulating elements of age integration as a possible means of reducing structural lag, recognize the need for value adaptation as the most formidable obstacle of all (see also Riley, 1993). The ideal types of age-flexible structures of work, education, and retirement fly in the face of accepted values that stress economic competition, comparative achievement, and consumption. Moreover, in the interplay between changing structures and changing lives, to make age less relevant as a structural marker for career change and choice challenges deeply rooted customs and norms defining the appropriate way to move through the life course.

That there are various ideological obstacles to reducing structural lag does not mean that values cannot change. A mere glance back to the 1950s and 1960s in the United States suffices to demonstrate numerous rapid changes in norms and life styles among successive cohorts of college students. Meanings of retirement too have changed.

Whereas early in this century retirement was considered appropriate only for those physically unable to work, by the 1970s it had become a reward for a lifetime of work, a well-earned rest (Foner & Schwab, 1981). And although ideas about women's roles still lag behind the realities of their lives, there have been marked changes in popular views about women working outside the home and about working mothers.

Obstacles notwithstanding, change does take place. It occurs when the perceived costs of change are outweighed by the benefits, when the structure of the economy turns favorable, and when the interests of those pushing for change become more salient than the forces of resistance. Since not even basic values are permanent, when they are altered, the floodgates to structural change are opened.

Unintended Consequences of Structural Changes

Change occurs but, even in its most effective mode, tends to bring with it unanticipated consequences. Since, in this volume, some of the possible changes and specific proposals to reduce structural lag have centered on extending work life, we focus on some possible difficulties if these changes were implemented.

First, older workers today who take new positions after the conventional age of retirement generally receive lower pay and prestige than in their former lifetime jobs. With older workers added to the pool of younger workers (for the most part, women and minorities) available and competing for jobs primarily at the low end of the socioeconomic scale, there is little incentive to improve working conditions for young or old. According to Kohli, jobs that do open up might not go to older workers at all, but be allocated to women and immigrants. In short, if conditions of chronic job scarcity continue, the decision by large numbers of older workers to remain in the labor market rather than to retire might increase competition among old and young, male and female, white and nonwhite. The unintended effect would be to heighten the divisiveness in society along lines of age, gender, and ethnicity.

Second, new norms that applaud a longer work life might have the unintended effect of stigmatizing retirement. If that were to occur, the entitlement to retirement would be undermined, thereby discrediting those unable to work or those who have worked at onerous jobs and who see retirement as an earned rest after 30 or 40 years of arduous toil. In this regard, it is well to bring historical perspectives to the problems of unstructured time among today's retirees. History does not let us forget either the hardships of older workers in former times, who continued to work despite physical and health limitations, or the poverty of those for whom no work was available.

Third, if present patterns persist, there may be an increasing contrast between two population segments: large numbers of older workers with inadequate pensions or in low-level, low-paying jobs, on the one hand; and, on the other hand, a different set of older people able either to continue in well-paid career jobs or to retire with generous retirement benefits. The consequence would be sharpened class divisions within the older population. And such divisions among older people could block consensus and concerted action to work for policies that would benefit the elderly as a whole.

In other social arenas, the unintended consequences of actions to reduce structural lag bring caveats through lessons from the past. For example, all ages *were* integrated into productive activities in earlier times; but there was also a great deal of exploitation of the very young and the very old, as the Rileys indicate. Furthermore, a downside can be imagined to the malleable families of the past who took in kin in times of need. Surely there were conflicts ensuing from the close encounters of kin within the household (Foner, 1978). And when the collective good of the family took precedence over the needs of individual members, such priorities undoubtedly took a toll on offspring (often daughters remaining home to care for elderly parents) and prevented them from pursuing their own interests. Such difficulties in past times are not likely to be repeated exactly, but they remind us of the complexities generated by new social arrangements.

STRUCTURAL LAG AND THEORIES OF CHANGE

This final chapter began by reinvoking the organizing concept of structural lag and remarking on some of its theoretical antecedents. It will end by boldly suggesting some ways that this volume's exploration of structural lag may contribute to current dialogues on theoretical and pragmatic issues related to social change.

The discussions here about the reciprocities between changing structures and the changing lives of people have relevance for theoretical exchanges concerning the relative emphasis on actors versus social structures (for a recent discussion, see Sewell, 1992). They recall earlier controversies about the relative importance of heredity versus environment. Our approach to such issues is similar to that of the geneticist Dobzhansky (1962): Because the two elements are intertwined, trying to assess which element is key is meaningless. With regard to people and structures, we see these as interacting and eschew efforts to assign priority. Nevertheless, we do wish to emphasize the role of people—and their dynamic processes of aging and cohort succession, simply because that element has often been played down in analyses of social change.

As for theories concerning the motive power of social change, we recognize the importance of values (including ideas and ideologies) as sources of change; but we do not enter the debate over whether value changes or structural changes come first. What we do stress is that values influence both people's behavior and social arrangements, just as social structures in their turn shape values. Moreover, while new values can promote social change, old values can retard needed changes. Several contributors to this volume stress this latter point, as they show how holding to traditional views of gender or family can stand in the way of needed social policies implicating age.

Finally, this book points to a dynamic of change rarely discussed in the literature of the social sciences: the pressure for change arising from "asynchrony"—from the differing rhythms and patterns of people growing up, growing old, and replacing each other, on the one hand, and the shifts and transformations in social structures, on the other.

The contributors to this book share the conviction that further recognition of this dynamic linkage between life course and social institutions, and thus between people's lives and societal trends, can enlarge the theoretical grasp of the social and behavioral sciences. Perhaps even more hopeful, they share the belief that, as we look to the future, discussions within this framework can improve the quality of policy deliberations, research methods[9] to test the feasibility of policy changes, and the wisdom of choice.

---

[9] As in the field experiments recommended by Kahn.

REFERENCES

Blau, P. (Ed.). (1975). *Approaches to the study of social structure.* New York: Free Press.

Coser, L. (Ed.). (1975). *The idea of social structure: Essays in honor of Robert K. Merton.* New York: Harcourt Brace Jovanovich.

Dobzhansky, T. (1962). *Mankind evolving: The evolution of the human species.* New Haven and London: Yale University Press.

Foner, A. (1974). Age stratification and age conflict in political life. *American Sociological Review, 39,* 187–196.

Foner, A. (1978). Age stratification and the changing family. In J. Demos & S. S. Boocock (Eds.), *Turning points: Historical and sociological essays on the family* (pp. 340–365). Chicago, IL: University of Chicago Press.

Foner, A. (1979). Ascribed and achieved bases of stratification. *Annual Review of Sociology, 5,* 219–242.

Foner, A., & Schwab, K. (1981). *Aging and retirement.* Monterey, CA: Brooks/Cole.

Katona, G. (1951). *Psychological analysis of economic behavior.* New York: McGraw-Hill.

Marx, K., & Engels, F. (1848/1978). Manifesto of the communist party. In R. Tucker (Ed.), *The Marx-Engels reader* (2nd ed., pp. 473–500). New York: Norton.

Merton, R. (1957). *Social theory and social structure.* Glencoe, IL: Free Press.

Ogburn, W. (1922/1950). *Social change with respect to culture and original nature* (rev. ed.). New York: Viking.

Riley, J. W., Jr. (1991). Death and dying. In E. Borgatta & M. Borgatta (Eds.), *The encyclopedia of sociology.* New York: Macmillan.

Riley, M. W. (1978). Aging, social change, and the power of ideas. *Daedalus, 107,* 39–52.

Riley, M. W. (1993). The coming revolution in age structure. First annual Pepper lecture on aging and public policy, Florida State University, Tallahassee, Florida.

Riley, M. W., Johnson, M., & Foner, A. (1972). *Aging and society: Vol. III. A sociology of age stratification.* New York: Russell Sage.

Riley, M. W., & Riley, J. W., Jr. (Eds.). (1989). *The quality of aging: Strategies for interventions* (Special issue of *The Annals*). Newbury Park, CA: Sage.

Schumpeter, J. (1955). *Imperialism and social classes.* New York: Meridian.

Sewell, W., Jr. (1992). A theory of structure: Duality, agency and transformation. *American Journal of Sociology, 98,* 1–29.

Author Index

281

Subject Index